F. A. Hayek and the Modern Economy

Jepson Studies in Leadership

Series Editors: George R. Goethals, Terry L. Price, and J. Thomas Wren

Managing Editor: Tammy Tripp

Jepson Studies in Leadership is dedicated to the interdisciplinary pursuit of important questions related to leadership. In its approach, the series reflects the broad-based commitment to the liberal arts of the University of Richmond's Jepson School of Leadership Studies. The series thus aims to publish the best work on leadership not only from management and organizational studies but also from such fields as economics, English, history, philosophy, political science, psychology, and religion. In addition to monographs and edited collections on leadership, included in the series are volumes from the Jepson Colloquium, which bring together influential scholars from multiple disciplines to think collectively about distinctive leadership themes in politics, science, civil society, and corporate life. The books in the series should be of interest to humanists and social scientists, as well as to organizational theorists and instructors teaching in business, leadership, and professional programs.

Books Appearing in This Series:

The Values of Presidential Leadership
edited by Terry L. Price and J. Thomas Wren
Leadership and the Liberal Arts: Achieving the Promise of a Liberal Education
edited by J. Thomas Wren, Ronald E. Riggio and Michael A. Genovese
Leadership and Discovery
edited by George R. Goethals and J. Thomas Wren
Lincoln's Legacy of Leadership
edited by George R. Goethals and Gary L. McDowell
For the Greater Good of All: Perspectives on Individualism, Society, and Leadership
edited by Donelson R. Forsyth and Crystal L. Hoyt
Executive Power in Theory and Practice
edited by Hugh Liebert, Gary McDowell, and Terry L. Price
Leadership and Global Justice
edited by Douglas Hicks and Thad Williamson
On Effective Leadership: Across Domains, Cultures, and Eras
G. Donald Chandler III and John W. Chandler
F.A. Hayek and the Modern Economy: Economic Organization and Activity
edited by Sandra J. Peart and David M. Levy

F. A. Hayek and the Modern Economy

Economic Organization and Activity

Edited by

Sandra J. Peart
and
David M. Levy

palgrave
macmillan

F. A. HAYEK AND THE MODERN ECONOMY

First published in 2013 by
PALGRAVE MACMILLAN®
in the United States—a division of St. Martin's Press LLC,
175 Fifth Avenue, New York, NY 10010.

Where this book is distributed in the UK, Europe and the rest of the world, this is by Palgrave Macmillan, a division of Macmillan Publishers Limited, registered in England, company number 785998, of Houndmills, Basingstoke, Hampshire RG21 6XS.

Palgrave Macmillan is the global academic imprint of the above companies and has companies and representatives throughout the world.

Palgrave® and Macmillan® are registered trademarks in the United States, the United Kingdom, Europe and other countries.

ISBN: 978–1–137–35958–2

Library of Congress Cataloging-in-Publication Data is available from the Library of Congress.

A catalogue record of the book is available from the British Library.

Design by Newgen Knowledge Works (P) Ltd., Chennai, India.

First edition: December 2013

10 9 8 7 6 5 4 3 2 1

To our friend and mentor James M. Buchanan, 1919–2013,
the "Relatively Absolute Absolute"

CONTENTS

FIGURES AND TABLES

Figures

Tables

PREFACE

F. A. Hayek: Social Theorist and Philosopher of Liberty

BRUCE CALDWELL

Friedrich A. Hayek was born in 1899 in fin de siècle Vienna, the capital of the Austro-Hungarian Empire. He grew up in the city of Sigmund Freud and Ludwig Wittgenstein (the latter a cousin of Hayek), of Gustav Klimt and Gustav Mahler, of Ernst Mach and Stefan Zweig. Hayek saw military service in the First World War, and entered the University of Vienna when hostilities ended.

Social turmoil wracked Europe following the war. The fighting decimated an entire generation, and a worldwide influenza epidemic killed even more people in the winter of 1918–1919. As the war's aftermath, ancient empires collapsed, and new states formed as boundaries were redrawn. In the most dramatic transformation, a violent revolution changed the Russian empire into a Soviet communist state. The "Carthaginian Peace" that emerged from Versailles soon enough bore its own fruits, as first hyperinflation and then reactionary street gang thuggery swept central Europe. Fascists gained political influence in Italy, Germany, and on the Iberian peninsula. The collapse of the Austro-Hungarian Empire brought still other proposals for reorganizing society. While the countryside remained conservative, socialism took hold in the capital city of Austria, earning it the epithet of "Red Vienna."

Hayek finished his first degree in 1921, and soon thereafter began working in a government office responsible for settling international debt claims. Like many progressive young intellectuals of his day he was sympathetic to socialism, though he rejected the doctrinaire Marxism he had encountered in the streets of Vienna. His views on the merits of socialism gradually began to change after he read a book penned by one of the directors in the government office, the economist Ludwig von Mises.

In his book, Mises challenged the economic feasibility of socialism. In its purest form, socialism calls for the total abolition of private firms, which are replaced by state ownership of the means of production. If the state owns the means of production, there are no markets in which factors of production are bought and sold, and consequently there are no prices attached to them. Mises pointed out that the absence of market prices means that factory managers have no information about which resources are relatively scarce, and which are relatively plentiful. Socialist managers then have no way of telling, when choosing among a huge array of technologically feasible input combinations, which are economically feasible. Mises concluded that socialist economies would be much less efficient in using resources than free-market economies. Market prices inform market participants about the relative scarcity of goods, and by bidding for them, market participants help ensure that resources flow toward their highest valued uses.

Mises, who quickly became Hayek's mentor, was also a monetary theorist, and Hayek soon followed his lead. Money helps to facilitate trade and serves as both a unit of account and a store of value, but its presence in an advanced economy can also contribute to the business cycle. Financial crises in the late nineteenth century had led to the creation of agencies like the Federal Reserve system in the United States to help avoid panics. But much about the workings of an advanced monetary economy remained unknown. What policies would best enhance the positive effects of money while forestalling its potential for disruption? Building on earlier theories, Hayek developed his own variant, and in early 1931 was invited to give some lectures on the subject at the London School of Economics. They were such a success that he was appointed the next fall to a visiting position there, and a year later to a named chair. He was only 32 years of age.

Soon after arriving in London, Hayek became embroiled in a heated debate about monetary theory with a prominent British economist, John Maynard Keynes. (Keynes would become even more famous with the publication of *The General Theory of Employment, Interest and Money* in 1936.[1]) While the details of their theoretical dispute need not detain us, the two positions they staked out—Keynes believing that only with substantial government intervention could a free-market system survive, Hayek believing that with the proper institutions much less government intervention is necessary for a market system to provide an effective mechanism for coordinating the actions of millions of individual market participants—would set the grounds for a debate about the proper role of government in the economy for the rest of the twentieth century. As noted in the Public Broadcasting Service (PBS) video documentary series *Commanding Heights: The Battle for the World Economy*, Keynes was widely viewed as the victor for much of the period, but by the end of the century, Hayek's vision had become dominant. During the recent financial crisis, Keynesian and Hayekian explanations of both the causes of the downturn and the appropriate policy response to it have been on offer.

Britain's recovery from the First World War had been slow and painful. During the 1920s, the unemployment rate never fell below 10 percent, and labor unrest was sufficiently virulent to cause a General Strike in 1926. By the time that Hayek began his teaching duties in the fall of 1931, England had abandoned the gold standard, the Labour government had fallen, and the Great Depression was well underway. The latter was taken by many as evidence that the old liberal economic order—one based on free markets, democratic government, and individual self-determination—was at an end. The only question was: What would replace it? There were indeed fascists and communists in England, but middle opinion favored socialism. Socialist planning was viewed as a middle way between a failed market order and totalitarianism of the communist or fascist varieties. Hayek, who disagreed with both the diagnosis and the proposed cure, decided to introduce his British readers to the insights he had gained about the limitations of socialism the decade before.

Hayek's contributions built upon, but also went beyond, those made by Ludwig von Mises. Mises had demonstrated that market prices provide essential information about relative scarcities. To this Hayek added the idea that a market system helps to solve "the knowledge problem," the coordination of human action in a world in which knowledge is dispersed. In a market system, millions of agents make consumption and production decisions every day. Their decisions are based in part on the vast array of prices that they confront in the market, prices that give them information about relative scarcities. But in addition, agents have access to particular bits of knowledge, knowledge that is specific to time and place, and this also shapes the decisions that they make. Their market activity reflects local knowledge, and such knowledge becomes embedded in the array of market prices. In short, market activity is both price-determined (prices shape what people do) and price-determining (what people do, based on local knowledge, determines what prices are). In this way, market prices coordinate the specific knowledge of time and place possessed by millions of market agents. Freely adjusting market prices act as a giant communication network. Socialist schemes that involve price fixing, as many of the proposals did, would keep the communication system from working. Hayek began having these insights in the 1930s, but perhaps his clearest statement is found in his seminal 1945 article, "The Use of Knowledge in Society," one that is still quoted today by economists working in the economics of information.

Although Hayek felt that he had launched a telling attack against socialism, few among the intelligentsia in the late 1930s were persuaded by his economic reasoning. Hayek began to realize that the attractiveness of socialism went far beyond economics. Socialists promised a society that was not only more efficient than capitalism, but also one that was more just, where individuals have more self-determination and greater political freedom, and in which scientific reasoning would be used to improve upon a host of outdated social institutions. If he were to successfully challenge these utopian visions, economic arguments were not enough. Hayek would need to develop political, historical, and ethical arguments against them as well.

During the Second World War he began doing just that, in a massive piece of work that he called The Abuse of Reason Project. Although the project as a whole was never finished, sections of it were. By far the most widely known part was what would become Hayek's most famous book, *The Road to Serfdom.*

As noted earlier, many of its advocates had promised that socialism would bring with it greater political freedom. In *The Road to Serfdom,* Hayek countered that planning of the economy would soon lead to increasing political control as well. One of the virtues of a market economy is that it allows people with very different tastes to express them, and (for those with the means) to get them satisfied, through the market. In a planned economy, socialist managers must decide which goods, and how much of them, get produced. Invariably some people will not like the decisions that are made, and will protest. A change in the mix will cause others to protest. If any progress is to be made, even democratically elected socialist regimes will at some point be forced simply to make the decisions for the people. This is much easier to do if political dissension is suppressed. Hayek's claim was that, to run a fully socialized planned economy successfully, its socialist managers ultimately must secure control of the political process as well.

Although famous as a critic of socialism, Hayek also made a number of positive contributions to social theory. In such books as *The Constitution of Liberty*[2] and *Law, Legislation and Liberty*,[3] he made the case for a return to a liberal market order. Hayek was no Pollyanna about laissez-faire: He believed that a market system by itself holds few guarantees, that only if it is embedded in a set of other social institutions—a democratic polity, with strong constitutional protection of a private sphere of individual activity, operating under the rule of law, with well-defined, enforced, and transferable property rights—would it have a chance of working. In these mature works Hayek expounds his philosophy of liberty, describing and defending the complex of institutions, norms, and beliefs that he felt would best promote the discovery, transmission, and use of knowledge, so that individuals are able to use that knowledge to succeed in the pursuit of their own chosen goals.

This preface has only touched on some of Hayek's contributions. His critique of socialism and his foundational work on the informational role of prices are now considered seminal insights within economics. His rehabilitation of the classical liberal approach within political philosophy has helped to reshape the nature of the debate in that field. But in addition, his work on complex adaptive "spontaneous orders" has piqued the interest of those exploring the relevance of complexity theory, neural network models, and agent-based computational models for economic and social analysis. Furthermore, philosophers of mind, evolutionary biologists, and neuroscientists have been attracted to his "connectionist" approach for understanding the development and functioning of the brain, as revealed in his remarkable book on the foundations of psychology, *The Sensory Order*.[4] Most remembered as a philosopher of liberty, F. A. Hayek was also a polymath social theorist. Fascinating in itself, his intellectual journey also helps us better to comprehend the contours of the development of twentieth-century social thought.

Notes

1. John Maynard Keynes, *The General Theory of Employment, Interest and Money* (London: Macmillan, 1936).
2. Friedrich A. Hayek, *The Constitution of Liberty* (Chicago, IL: University of Chicago, 1960).
3. Friedrich A. Hayek, *Law, Legislation and Liberty* (Chicago, IL: University of Chicago, 1973, 1976, 1979), 3 vols.
4. Friedrich A. Hayek, *The Sensory Order: An Inquiry into the Foundations of Theoretical Psychology* (Chicago, IL: University of Chicago, 1952).

ACKNOWLEDGMENTS

Many friends and colleagues have contributed to this work, and the editors wish to acknowledge and thank them for their help and encouragement along the way. Perhaps most importantly, though his name seldom appears on the pages that follow, this collection would not have been possible were it not for the ideas and insights of our late mentor and friend, James M. Buchanan. For the past 13 years, Jim has opened the Summer Institute for the Preservation of the History of Economic Thought with papers that stimulated our participants and gave us much to think about. Jim not only told us the story of Hayek and the Mont Pèlerin Society, recounted in chapter 2, he also helped us come to realize how important Friedrich Hayek was as a leader. We return to that thought in the conclusion.

We are grateful to Bruce Caldwell, first for his willingness to take a chance on a Mill scholar to edit a Hayek volume in the *Collected Works of F. A. Hayek*, second for his patience and encouragement along the way in that project, and third for his participation in the *Hayek and the Modern World* conference at the University of Richmond in April 2013, as well as for his contribution, the preface to this book.

That conference formed the backbone of this book and we are grateful to all the participants for the lively discussions that ensued on that occasion as well as the chapters that are included in this volume. Many of the conferees traveled under difficult personal and professional circumstances and we appreciate their dedication. We thank them for submitting essays to us at a busy time of the academic year and appreciate their willingness to revise their essays in light of our editorial comments. Andrew Farrant and Nicola Tynan, who did not attend the conference, were nonetheless kind enough to submit their fine piece for consideration.

The conference was one of a series of Hayek-related events sponsored this year by the John Marshall International Center for the Study of Statesmanship and the Adam Smith Program, both under the auspices of the Jepson School of Leadership Studies. We are grateful to the Thomas W. Smith Foundation for its support of the John Marshall Center; and to private individuals, including James Buchanan, for their support of the Adam Smith Program. Without their generosity, neither the conference nor the keynote address by the esteemed Václav Klaus, former president of the Czech Republic, would have been possible.

We were extremely fortunate that President Klaus agreed to speak at the University of Richmond. Our colleague Dalibor Roháč proved helpful as we first thought about this, and Deputy Director Jiří Brodský and Karolína Králová were most helpful in making the arrangements during and then after the political season. We are grateful to Ambassador Petr Gandalovič, for escorting President Klaus to campus. Both Ambassador Gandolvič and President Klaus attended the majority of sessions at the conference. At the Jepson School, Shannon Best graciously and skillfully handled all arrangements for this complicated set of events, an academic conference followed by a public keynote address.

We thank the Jepson Studies in Leadership series editors, George R. Goethals, Terry L. Price, and J. Thomas Wren, for their suport and encouragement as we prepared the proposal for *F. A. Hayek and the Modern Economy: Economic Organization and Activity.* The series managing editor, Tammy Tripp, has responded to our many queries with good humor and sense. It was she who prepared the volume for submission to Palgrave Macmillan and we thank her for doing so. Before the submission, Jane Perry handled many editorial tasks at George Mason University. We are also grateful to our editor at Palgrave Macmillan, Charlotte Maiorana, and to editorial assistant Leila Campoli for their enthusiastic support and assistance.

Each book takes a good deal of energy and time that cannot be recouped or spent elsewhere. Sandra Peart thanks her boys, Nathan and Matthew Heinicke-Peart, and Craig Heinicke, for their forbearance during the past months.

Introduction

Sandra J. Peart and David M. Levy

In April 2013, the University of Richmond's Jepson School of Leadership Studies hosted a conference on Friedrich A. Hayek to examine his thought in the context of social, philosophical, and economic concerns that have become more pressing over the past five years. We note at the outset the following perhaps idiosyncratic set of reasons for why it is appropriate to consider Hayek in the context of leadership and statesmanship in 2013.

First, in 2006—so, notably, well before the financial crisis—we were invited to the Italian economists' conference in Lecce, Italy,[1] and Sandra Peart gave the plenary talk. As she was at that point beginning a project for the general editor of the Hayek works, Bruce Caldwell, a republication of Hayek's 1951 book, *John Stuart Mill and Harriet Taylor: Their Friendship and Subsequent Marriage*,[2] she wrote a talk provocatively entitled "Did Mill Ruin Classical Liberalism?"[3] The audience and discussion were lively. But the most telling comment came from her then eight-year-old son, Matthew, who listened to the session and, at the end, proclaimed that Mill was wrong and Hayek was right. This was an early wake-up call—to redouble our efforts to appreciate Hayek!

Then, more than four years ago, Russ Roberts stopped us at the Allied Social Sciences Association annual conference in January and showed us—hot off the presses—the now famous first Keynes–Hayek rap video.[4] In April 2013, that video had obtained about 4.2 million views. In 2012, Peart designed and taught a course at the Jepson School of Leadership Studies entitled Economic Policy and Leadership using the Keynes–Hayek debates as the backdrop. One student in the class reported that while he was watching the video in the library a female student approached him and asked what he was watching. He reportedly replied "Only the coolest rap video ever made!" In 2009, Peart spent a week at Duke University lecturing for a National Endowment for the Humanities program alongside Bruce Caldwell. Caldwell's republication of Hayek's 1944 *The Road to Serfdom*[5]—the original of which our Jepson School colleague Gary McDowell reminded us earlier this spring influenced the late Margaret Thatcher[6]—reached number one on Amazon that week. For a scholarly publication to achieve such heights suggests the economics of F. A. Hayek warrants renewed and vigorous attention.

Taken together, the foregoing is evidence of a renaissance of interest in Hayek scholarship. Importantly, this has included a reexamination from the left as well as the right: Hayek's challenge to socialism has recently been explored by market socialists such as Theodore Burczak.[7] Our hope for this book is that it will further our understanding of Hayek as a leader in the dimension of ideas and in policy space. Many know of the Nobel laureate's influence through his *Constitution of Liberty* or *Law, Legislation and Liberty*. Experimental economists and psychologists have explored insights from both his thoughts on the "division of knowledge" culminating in the 1945 "Use of Knowledge in Society"—about which Václav Klaus writes so dramatically later—and *The Sensory Order*. The chapters included in this book examine the foundational influences on Hayek, his insights for economic, political, and social organization and activity, and his legacy in terms of policy making. We benefited greatly from the lively discussions in April, discussion that not surprisingly yielded common themes across essays.

Perhaps most importantly, this book focuses on Hayek's views on the role of human agency. As an economic and political theorist first and foremost, Hayek explored this question in two ways. First, what role does any one individual have in determining one's economic and social well-being? Kenneth Minogue's contribution explores Hayek's trenchant views on the conditions of individual freedom. Perhaps not surprisingly, however, Minogue quickly turns up the collectivity, what Minogue views as Hayek's denial of the plausibility of socialism on factual and logical grounds. Peter McNamara points out that, notwithstanding his great admiration for Adam Smith, Hayek does not emphasize the sympathetic process that Smith elaborates in his *Theory of Moral Sentiments*.

So, second, the question arises as to how we make decisions when we are connected, as Hayek emphasized, to others in groups of varying importance to the self, groups that range from the tight-knit family to the polity and the extended order of the marketplace. From this follows the additional question of what agency policy makers, those who might be thought of as leaders, possess in determining overall well-being of those in the polity. This is the focal point for Minogue and also for Bruce Caldwell, in the preface to this volume. The question ultimately leads to a consideration of Hayek's views as they relate to socialism and to planning. As is well known, Hayek maintained that prices and outcomes that emerge from the marketplace convey important information to producers and consumers, information that no one central planner (leader) can obtain. Consequently, he argued that planning invariably leads to the imposition of the desires and best guesses of the planners upon the rest of the group, the polity.

This book explores the question of agency, first from a foundational level, as a number of authors—McNamara, Sandra Peart, and David Levy—examine Hayek's relationship to liberalism of the nineteenth century and more recent sort. Hayek drew a line between the work of Scottish moral philosophers such as Adam Smith and the later work of those "false" individualists, including John Stuart Mill. Peart, Levy, and McNamara consider whether that line is well placed and, perhaps more importantly, whether and how the distinction between true and false individualism informs the analysis of economic policy today.

Peart and Levy demonstrate how Hayek distanced himself from a second sort of (self-identified) "individualist," in the mid-twentieth century. Hayek, prompted by the Mont Pèlerin Society elders such as Knight's follower, James Buchanan, even allowed his manuscript to be given over for editing. More than this, he distanced himself from the individualists such as William F. Buckley Jr., at a time when these intellectuals enjoyed enormous influence as public intellectuals.

We attempt in what follows thus also to situate Hayek's writing as it relates to economic organization and activity, in particular to assess what role Hayek assigns to leaders in creating and sustaining economic progress. We ask, what is the scope for policy makers to lead the economy through crises and the inevitable ups and downs that accompany economic expansion? How much agency should policy makers assume and when are unusual mechanisms called for? Second, what leadership role do economists legitimately play in the development and implementation of new economic policy? Hayek held that economists should take center stage in terms of advocating economic policy but his was a quite different sort of advocacy. He disagreed with some of his contemporaries on what economic policies were best suited to promote economic expansion and stability. The book explores the nature of these disagreements.

An overriding theme in what follows is Hayek's challenge concerning knowledge and the difficulty of accumulating information about aggregates of the economic system. For Hayek, economic aggregation is fraught with methodological difficulties and hence no scientist or policy maker has the wherewithal to direct market transactions. The contributions by Bruce Caldwell and Emily Skarbek examine these questions. Gerald Gaus explores the related question of rules versus discretion that follows on Hayek's distinction between law and legislation. Focusing on a Hayekian-inspired account of social evolution, Gaus establishes conditions under which facts about cultural adaptation inform us about how well we are doing morally.

The evolutionary argument in Gaus's elegant reformulation focuses on the traditional optimization problem posed when there are multiple local optima. The powerful insight he offers takes advantage of the result in the theoretical literature that a number of less competent agents can outperform a single more competent agent, assuming as he does that solutions can be shared. The sharing of solutions requires language, often missing from the economic models put forward in the optimizing tradition. Solutions by trial and error that are then passed on to others in "rules" or "institutions" are difficult to describe. Approaches like Hayek's that stress the importance of evolved "rules" are sometimes seen to be at odds with the economists' more typical optimizing approaches because evolved rules do not carry with them their own proof of efficiency or optimality. Emily Skarbek traces the role that F. B. Kaye's celebrated edition of Bernard Mandeville's *Fable of the Bees*[8] played in Hayek's account of social evolution as a foundation for constitutional thinking.

Christopher S. Martin explores the question of evolved institutions and the self in the polity using a rather extraordinary lens. Martin suggests that Hayek employed the political history of ancient Athens to illustrate his claims about democracy and liberty. He examines the Athenian features of Hayek's model constitution, including one rationale for the constitution, the control of factional politics. He demonstrates that Hayek's institutional proposals might have been improved had he not underrated the record of Athenian democracy. The ancient practice of citizen selection by lot for law review duties appears to avoid criticisms of Hayek's constitution while still furthering his goal of a more impartial politics.

Election by lot is an example of an evolved institution because there was no one with the statistical insight to design such a thing along probabilistic principles in ancient Athens. The Athenians seemed to have had a rough and ready appreciation of the lot's workings but they did not fully understand its properties. One challenge for those in the Hayekian tradition is thus to examine and perhaps improve our understanding of evolved institutions. Hayek's views have also had a direct and lasting impact on policy. Several of the chapters in this book provide telling evidence of this impact. We begin the section on "Political Economy and Policy Making" with a contribution that examines Hayek's influence in Britain in the first half of the twentieth century. Using a great deal of primary evidence drawn from the time, Andrew Farrant and Nicola Tynan argue that Hayek's arguments were taken up by those who were eager to lambast Clement Attlee's postwar Labour Government. So, for example, they show that the Conservative Parliamentarian Sir Waldron Smithers frequently invoked *The Road to Serfdom* during parliamentary debates in the 1940s and 1950s and urged Winston Churchill to heed Hayek's message "to arrest the race down the road to the totalitarian State." Ekkehard Köhler and Stefan Kolev argue that Hayek connects the work of Henry Simons in Chicago with that of Walter Eucken in Freiberg. It was through Hayek and the Mont Pèlerin Society that Milton Friedman met Eucken and learned about totalitarianism from the inside.[9]

Moving forward in time and without attributing direct influence to Hayek, Jason Clemens and Niels Veldhuis review recent fiscal experience in Canada in the light of Hayekian themes. They demonstrate that the late 1980s and the entirety of the 1990s were a profound period of change and reform in Canada with reforms toward a smaller fiscal imprint for the federal government. This period of retrenchment coincided with an extraordinarily prosperous time in Canada with balanced budgets, declining debt, and tax relief coupled with a robust economy, strong job creation, and plentiful opportunities. Furthermore, Clemens and Veldhuis examine how many of the reforms enacted during this period contained a Hayekian dimension in terms of decentralizing authority and responsibility for service provision.

A third example of Hayek's influence on policy making follows, given by Václav Klaus, former president of the Czech Republic. The chapters conclude with a transcription of President Klaus's remarks, the culminating presentation at the conference. President Klaus begins with an account of how, behind the Iron Curtain, Hayek's "The Use of Knowledge in Society" became read, and widely so. It escaped the censors' prohibition because it appeared originally in the *American Economic Review*, which was too technical for them to appreciate or contraband. At about the same time, copies of *The Road to Serfdom* were published illegally and, one senses, eagerly read in what was then Czechoslovakia. Klaus next recounts how, immediately following the Velvet Revolution, policy makers began to dismantle the institutions of communism and he, as minister of finance, oversaw the rapid and significant transformation of the Czech economy by allowing privately held companies, liberalizing, deregulating, privatizing, and desubsidizing.

We have, of course, the perfect natural experiment with which to consider policy questions and the disagreement over whether to intervene, or not to intervene: since 2008, the United States and many European nations have experienced severe contractions and sluggish recoveries. What would Hayek say about the last five years and the road to recovery? These questions, too, underscore many of the chapters in this book. Our hope is that the book as a whole and the chapters individually shed light on very practical as well as more esoteric matters.

Notes

1. The Associazione Italiana per la Storia dell'Economia Politica (STOREP) conference in 2006; see the program http://www.storep.org/lecce2006/ProgrammaConvegnoStorep2006.pdf (accessed May 3, 2013).
2. Friedrich A. Hayek, *John Stuart Mill and Harriet Taylor: Their Friendship and Subsequent Marriage* (Chicago, IL: University of Chicago, 1951).
3. Sandra J. Peart, "Did Mill Ruin Classical Liberalism" (lecture, STOREP conference, Lecce, June 2006). The lecture formed the starting point for the Editor's introduction to *Hayek on Mill: The Mill-Taylor Friendship and Related Writings*, ed. Sandra J. Peart, vol. 16 of *The Collected Works of F. A. Hayek* (Chicago, IL: University of Chicago Press, 2014).
4. "Fear the Boom and Bust" A Hayek vs. Keynes Rap Anthem, http://www.youtube.com/watch?v=d0nERTFo-Sk (accessed May 3, 2013).
5. Bruce Caldwell, ed., *The Road to Serfdom: Text and Documents—The Definitive Edition*, vol. 2 of *The Collected Works of F. A. Hayek* (Chicago, IL: University of Chicago Press, 2007).
6. See the full text of the Bishop of London's remarks from Lady Thatcher's funeral service, "The Bishop of London's Address at Margaret Thatcher's Funeral," *The Guardian*, April 13, 2013, http://www.guardian.co.uk/politics/2013/apr/17/bishop-address-thatcher-funeral-text (accessed May 3, 2013).
7. Theodore A. Burczak, *Socialism after Hayek* (Ann Arbor, MI: University of Michigan Press, 2006).
8. Bernard Mandeville, *The Fable of the Bees or Private Vices, Public Benefits*, ed. F. B. Kaye (Oxford: Clarendon Press, 1924), 2 vols.
9. Milton and Rose Friedman, *Two Lucky People: Memories* (Chicago, IL: University of Chicago Press, 1998), 160: "One participant who made an especially strong

impression on me was Walter Eucken of Germany. I shall never forget his pleasure at eating the first orange he had seen in seven or eight years. More important, he made vivid what it was like to live in a totalitarian country, as well as in a country devastated by war and by the rigidities imposed by the occupying authorities. His courage in resisting the Nazis became legendary. He was a teacher of Ludwig Erhard, and helped inspire Erhard's currency reform in 1948, which initiated what came to be called the German economic miracle. More generally, his theory laid the groundwork for West Germany's 'social market economy'."

PART I

Foundations

CHAPTER ONE

On Hayek's Unsentimental Liberalism

PETER MCNAMARA

This chapter has two goals. First, and most importantly, I wish to make clear one of the most distinctive features of Hayek's thought—his unsentimental liberalism. To bring out this feature of Hayek's thought I compare his account of human nature with the eighteenth-century science of human nature as it was elaborated by Adam Smith. What is strikingly absent from Hayek's deep debt to that eighteenth-century science is a "theory of the moral sentiments." I will draw out some of the implications of this significant absence in Hayek's thought. The second but related goal is more speculative, and that is to use Hayek to reflect on the status of liberalism in the post–Cold War world. Let me begin there.

Hayek began his intellectual life during a world crisis. The First World War shook Europe in a way that had not been experienced since the French Revolution and the Napoleonic Wars. The human toll was just one aspect of the crisis. The war's social, political, economic, and intellectual impact was just as fundamental. Keynes argued, in *The Economic Consequences of the Peace*, that the war shattered the "delicate, complicated organization" of European civilization. He put the change this way: "In continental Europe the earth heaves and no one but is aware of the rumblings. There it is not just a matter of extravagance or "labour troubles"; but of life and death, of starvation and existence, and of the fearful convulsions of a dying civilization."[1] Hayek experienced the crisis firsthand when he returned from the Italian front to find his home, the enlightened, cosmopolitan, and imperial city of Vienna, in a desperate state. Austria and Europe's convulsions were, of course, only in their early stages. Keynes's sense of foreboding was vindicated. The questions about the future of capitalism and the broader fate of Western civilization that Keynes would reckon with in the years following the Versailles Treaty were very similar to those that would engage Hayek, especially after his move from economics to political philosophy. What was the explanation for the extraordinary events that followed the Great War? Hayek broke ranks with many liberals and all socialists by pointing to the common roots of communism, Fascism, and Nazism. Rather than seeing Nazism as somehow a reaction against communism and as an outgrowth of capitalism, Hayek famously argued in *The Road to Serfdom* that left-wing and right-wing totalitarianism had the same roots in the move toward greater state control of society that emerged in late-nineteenth-century Europe.[2]

Hayek died in 1992 soon after the collapse of Soviet communism and did not leave us with any analysis of that momentous fin de siècle event. It is not hard to guess the basic outlines of what would have been Hayek's analysis of the economic failures of the Soviet Bloc. But what of his broader reflections on the future prospects for liberalism? What might they have been? Hayek is still often portrayed as a free market ideologue, a starry-eyed optimist, and a rationalist. To the numerous errors of this caricature that scholars have already pointed out, I would like to suggest another.[3] Hayek certainly did see the Cold War as a battle of ideas, of competing political philosophies.[4] And, it is true that, broadly speaking, Hayek's ideas won the day. But Hayek was too cautious a thinker to believe that even a momentous victory was an "end of history"–type moment that signaled liberalism's inevitable global victory. Hayek's caution, one might say, his conservatism, is evident in his understanding of the foundation of liberal societies and, in particular, in his account of human nature, which makes clear the "complicated" and "delicate," to use Keynes's words, foundations of a liberal political order.

Hayek and the Eighteenth-Century Science of Human Nature

Hayek's admiration for and debt to the classical liberalism of the eighteenth century is well known and much explored. Indeed, it is no exaggeration to say that Hayek engaged in an attempt to revive the eighteenth-century science of human nature that underwrote classical liberalism. The goal of Hayek's restatement of classical liberalism was to provide a clear and appealing picture of the foundations and the benefits of a "free civilization." Most prominently, Hayek drew much of his notion of spontaneous or unintended orders from the work of Bernard Mandeville, David Hume, Adam Ferguson, and Adam Smith. The concept threads through Hayek's work in economics, politics, and morality. Closely related to the idea of spontaneity in the economic realm was Hayek's emphasis on the inescapable role of self-interest in providing the motivation for socially beneficial economic activity. He did not, however, endorse the idea of *homo economicus* as either theoretically useful or practically true. Most importantly, Hayek deliberately left open the question of the ultimate ends that individuals pursue when they engage in economic activity. Hayek's thought as a whole is also certainly deeply affected by Hume's skeptical turn, especially insofar as it highlighted the limits of human reason. Thus, spontaneous order, the invisible hand, self-interest, and the limits of human knowledge comprise Hayek's chief debts to the eighteenth century.

Yet, there is an interesting and consequential omission in Hayek's borrowings from the eighteenth-century science of human nature. Hayek generally neglects the notion of sympathy and the related theory of the moral sentiments that Hume and especially Smith elaborate at such great length, and that comprised such a large part of that science of human nature. In terms of Smith's published work, *The Theory of Moral Sentiments* comprised fully one half.[5] The "theory of the moral sentiments" was an essential component of Smith's attempt to extend Hume's project of elaborating a science of man.[6] *The Theory of Moral Sentiments* is particularly interesting because it is in that work that Smith pushes, what Hayek considered, the anti-rationalistic turn of the eighteenth century to its greatest extent in the area of morality. Smith in *The Theory of Moral Sentiments* attempts to remove, to the extent possible, the last elements of rationalism from Hume's account of the origins of morality. The key step was his grounding of morality even deeper in human nature by exploring what he saw as the natural human faculty of sympathy.

Smith and the Eighteenth-Century Science of Human Nature

For present purposes, four features of the eighteenth-century science of human nature warrant our attention: its belief in a universal human nature; its thick moral unity; its connecting of morality and progress; and its confidence. Together they form a powerful theoretical outlook that is capable of underwriting a great deal of confidence in the future of liberal societies. Of the four, I will focus on the first two: universalism and thick moral unity. My summary is made with an eye to the comparison with Hayek.

Universalism

Hume, and even more so Smith, believed in an underlying universal human nature. They rejected the argument that so-called physical causes—climate especially—played a significant role shaping human behavior. Hume and Smith focus on "moral causes"—what we would call culture or education—as the force that in conjunction with human nature shapes human behavior.[7] Smith and Hume tell the history of mankind as the gradual unfolding of human capacities for cooperation, production, and for morality brought about by changing economic circumstances, specifically different levels of economic development. It was Smith who famously described the four stages of economic development (hunting, shepherding, agriculture, and commerce) each accompanied by particular forms of government and society. The final stage of commercial society coincided with what Smith also calls "civilization" and which he contrasts with noncommercial or "barbarous" societies. This pattern of development repeats itself across the globe subject, of course, to contingencies of time and place that may disrupt the natural course of things.

Smith's assumption of a universal human nature shows itself as well in his treatment of apparent anomalies in this story of progress. In what I think to be the most embarrassed part of *The Theory of the Moral Sentiments*, Smith confronts the problem of seeming extreme departures from ordinary moral norms. "Can there," he asked, "be a greater barbarity . . . than to hurt a child?" Yet, Smith must acknowledge that the practice has been widespread even in the Western world. Smith had to explain such departures in terms of the effect of what he called "custom." For example, in the case of the "polite and civilized Athenians," infanticide was once *thought* necessary because of the conditions of extreme poverty. Smith does not seem to think that it was or is ever necessary. He explained its continuance, though it was clearly no longer necessary, in the civilized nations of the ancient world as the effect of "uninterrupted custom."[8] The power of custom was such that even the enlightened of the time did not register an objection: "Aristotle talks of it as what the magistrate on many occasions ought to encourage. The humane Plato is of the same opinion, and, with all that love of mankind that seems to animate his writings, nowhere marks this practice with disapprobation."[9]

Smith, throughout his writings, crucially assumes that with the advance of civilization, an advance that is fueled by the spread of commerce and science, there is an accompanying advance in moral sensibilities. In particular, the harshness of earlier stages of human existence gives way to a more humane moral sensibility. Smith explained departures, such as infanticide, from this general tendency in terms of what he called "particular usages," by which he meant isolated exceptions that do not affect his general argument. And to take just one example from David Hume, when he comes to speak of Sparta in his paradigmatic essay "Of Commerce," he remarks as follows: "Were the testimony of history less positive and circumstantial, such a government would appear a mere philosophical whim or fiction, and impossible ever to be reduced to practice."[10] In other words, Sparta is so strange that we do not really need to consider it as an objection to our theory. Hume wrote this in full knowledge of the fact that it was Sparta—the closed society—that defeated Athens—the open society of its day—in the Peloponnesian War.

Thick Moral Unity

According to Smith, both our capacity for moral judgment and the norms that constitute morality grow out of a process of continued interaction with and learning from others. Smith explains that we first experience moral judgment through our judgments of others. Such judgments are made possible by our ability to enter into the passions of the actor. Approval takes place when we are able to enter into, in the sense of feeling the same or, more precisely, an analogous passion in ourselves. Disapproval is signified by our inability to experience such a commonality of feeling. It is our imagination, specifically, our capacity for what Smith calls sympathy that makes possible such experiences. Although the product of the imagination, Smith understands such experiences to be powerful and natural and, therefore, as a fixed "principle" of our nature.

Smith's account of sympathy is one of two key contributions to moral theory—the other being his account of the impartial spectator. Sympathy is the imaginative mechanism that allows us to enter into the situations of others. We find joy in their joy and pain in their pain. Smith's claim is that we can fully sympathize only with moral behavior—not with the joy of a successful criminal or with the pain of that criminal later undergoing fair punishment. Hence, for Smith it is sympathy that gives rise to the *moral* sentiments. As noted, we arrive at our understanding of what is moral by modulating our behavior in accord with what others can sympathize with. We are moved to do this by our desire for approval, what Smith calls mutual sympathy, by which he means a genuine harmony or concord of feeling among human beings. From mutual sympathy we derive a genuine pleasure that is unrelated to our desire for any external reward. Contrary to the view of Hobbes, human beings take real pleasure in each other's company. We really are social animals. When someone laughs at your joke, you feel pleasure not simply because your vanity has been gratified or because you have attained a certain amount of power and status, but because you really enjoy the company of your friends.

Now Smith is aware that sympathy does not always lead to *moral* sentiments but in these cases he contends that the wisdom of nature, a favorite concept of Smith, is such that these anomalies are beneficial to society and even to morality. We sympathize with the rich and the great even though they do not always display good character. Smith argues that this helps social stability. Smith claims that when weighing behavior we tend to focus on results. A well-intentioned action that fails through absolutely no fault of the doer is not praised as much as one that succeeds. This anomaly has the good tendency of steering us away from futile acts of benevolence. One last example: We feel more for those we know and who are near us than those we do not know and who are far away even though all are human beings and all entitled to respect and concern. This moral anomaly has the good effect of focusing our attention on those whom we can truly and efficiently help rather than those we cannot. Human beings in their glories and in their apparent failings are truly "fitted by nature" for society, according to Smith.

As noted, our awareness that we judge others is soon followed by the awareness that our own actions are the subject of frank judgments by others. We seek their approval, Smith says, because it is pleasurable to us and because their disapproval is both unpleasant and threatening to us. Smith does not, however, reduce morality to the mere search for the approval of others. Rather, as he famously explains, we are not satisfied with approval that is undeserved, nor are we simply satisfied with the approval of the actual observers, the spectators, of our conduct. Beyond what Smith sees as the uncertain and variable and, therefore, unsatisfying praise of actual spectators, Smith argues that we seek the surer and, therefore, more satisfying praise of the impartial spectator. We hypothesize an impartial and informed observer of our conduct and seek through our actions the approval of this construct of our intellect and imagination. It is the impartial spectator that helps us make the tough calls and hard decisions. The impartial spectator is in effect his interpretation or understanding of the phenomenon of conscience. Smith develops it without the aid of revealed religion and with only the most limited, one might even say perfunctory, theological basis in rational deistic religion. Smith also elaborates his moral theory without recourse to the ideas that had made problematic earlier moral theories, such as innate ideas, a specific faculty of the moral sense, a rationally knowable natural law, or a divine law.

Thus, Smith has much in common with contemporary theories and research that locate the foundation of morality in our emotions, in our doing rather than our thinking—a natural basis that is the product of our evolutionary history. The striking parallels between Smith's theory and contemporary research in biology, neuroscience, and evolutionary psychology is a point to which we will return.[11] Smith argues that the socialization process that gives rise to morality is not merely conventional. Morality is, he argues, grounded in nature, especially in our desire for mutual approbation,[12] our desire to be praiseworthy and not just praised,[13] and, perhaps most fundamentally, in our natural resentment at injustice.[14] For present purposes, Smith's discussion of the natural roots of our sense of justice is most important. Justice for Smith is, as it was for Hayek, the essential social virtue. Furthermore, Smith's definition of justice is, as we will see, essentially the same as Hayek's.

> In the race for wealth, and honours, and preferments, he may run as hard as he can, and strain every nerve and muscle, in order to outstrip all his competitors. But if he should justle, or throw down any of them, the indulgence of the spectators is at an end. It is a violation of fair play, which they cannot admit of.[15]

Justice conceived of as a set of fixed rules applicable to all is common to both Smith and Hayek.

There are four critical components to Smith's account that stand in striking contrast to Hayek's account of the same. First, Smith believes that, as a sort of self-defense mechanism, we harbor a natural and strong resentment at injustices. This resentment prompts us not only to defend ourselves but to punish ("to retaliate"[16] against, as Smith puts it) an offender. Second, Smith believes that we naturally experience a sympathetic resentment at the sight of injustices done to others. Third, according to Smith, nature has planted in us a sense of remorse that fills us with the dread of retribution. Fourth, Smith believes that violations of justice are more keenly felt than violations of other virtues such as personal slights or acts of ingratitude. These might be condemned but that cannot be enforced except by social condemnation. Thus, nature supports the virtue essential to the establishment and preservation of society. It does so without needing to call on the aid of any calculations of interest. Smith allows that our notions of justice will change with the development of society but the underlying natural support for justice in human nature does not change.

Progress and Confidence

The final two elements of the eighteenth-century science of human nature—progress and confidence—may be dealt with more briefly. Human nature, society, and morality are tightly linked together in Smith's account of the rise of civilization. Progress, powered by commercial progress, leads in Smith's account to a more humane society. Progress allows the gentler, humane side of human nature to emerge fully and to guide individuals and societies. Something is lost in terms of the decline of the sterner virtues but the gains of a civilized society are real, substantial, and lasting. The confidence of a Hume or a Smith grows out of the belief in the naturalness of commercial society and the implied lack of naturalness or incomplete naturalness of *earlier* societies.

Hayek on Human Nature

Let us now turn to Hayek and consider his account of human nature in light of the four characteristics of the eighteenth-century science of human nature. I will deal with the first two characteristics in this section and the last two in my conclusion. Throughout, our main focus will be to highlight and ponder Hayek's omission of a "theory of moral sentiments." It is true that during much of Hayek's life Smith's *The Theory of Moral Sentiments* and the kinds of arguments it advanced were neglected. The book itself was difficult to come by and, more importantly, sentiment-based arguments concerning morality took a back seat to arguments drawing on positivism and rationalism, not to mention relativism. Yet, this context does not explain much. Hayek was engaged in a deliberate project of reviving forgotten classical liberal ideas. Why did he overlook Smith's sentimental theory? The question grows in significance when we take into account that Hayek did not neglect Smith's *book, The Theory of Moral Sentiments.* He quotes from it approvingly on numerous occasions. What he does not enter into is the main substance of the book. As we have seen, Smith attempted to extend Hume's reasoning so as to establish a coherent and plausible system of morality. One might think that this should have held great appeal for Hayek because it pushed the anti-rationalistic insight of Hume and the Scottish Enlightenment generally an important step further and in a way that was very supportive of classical liberal ideals. Smith's other main goal in *The Theory of Moral Sentiments*, one that begins with the opening sentence of the work, was to refute Mandeville's (and Hobbes's) account of morality as being based ultimately and completely in self-love. Hayek instead focuses on what he saw Mandeville and Smith as having in common, namely, an understanding of spontaneous orders.[17] In his appreciation of Mandeville's accomplishment, Hayek does exactly this. He brackets the issue of Mandeville as a moralist and focuses on his contribution to the twin ideas of evolution and spontaneous order. Interestingly, he does take time to praise Mandeville as a psychologist and student of human nature. The point here is not to call into question Hayek's grasp of intellectual history, it is to emphasize what Hayek thought important or not important about Smith and Mandeville.

Universalism

Hayek never denies that there is a universal human nature but it is striking that his starting point is almost always "Western civilization" or "our civilization." Consider the language of Hayek's "Introduction" to *The Constitution of Liberty*:

> It has been a long time since that ideal of freedom which inspired *modern western civilization* and whose partial realization made possible the achievements of *that civilization* was effectively restated. In fact, for almost a century the basic principles on which *this civilization* was built have been falling into increasing disregard. Men have sought for alternative social orders more often than they have tried to improve their understanding or use of the underlying principles of *our civilization.* It is only since we have been confronted with an altogether different system that we have discovered that

> we have lost any clear conception of *our aims* and possess no firm principles which we can hold up against the dogmatic ideology of *our antagonists*.[18]

In other words, Hayek begins with Western Civilization and the liberty that it has achieved. While Hayek was an internationalist rather than a nationalist, he was also what we might call a *civilizationist*. Hayek asserts liberty as a value or *the* value in that it is the essential value and without which other values cannot be realized. He does not, however, attempt to ground his explanation and defense of liberty in a full account of human nature or, for that matter, any other kind of foundationalist argument. Hayek wrote as a political and economic philosopher rather than as a moral philosopher. It is tempting to say that Hayek asserts liberty as the most important value knowing that it is one of many values but that it is the one that has made the West what it is not only in terms of liberty but also in terms of wealth, power, and dynamism. But let me turn to matters that are less speculative and closer to the theme of this chapter.

Moral Unity

On the subject of moral unity the differences with Hume and especially Smith are very clear and worth exploring at length. The differences are most visible in Hayek's vigorous attack on Edward O. Wilson's "sociobiology" (usually known as "evolutionary psychology" today). Sociobiology attempts to apply the methods and conclusions of biology, broadly understood, to human behavior and to the workings of society. Hayek's critique, most conspicuously in the "Epilogue" to *Law, Legislation and Liberty* and in his last book *The Fatal Conceit: The Errors of Socialism*,[19] is well known but commentary on it has tended to focus on the issues it raises as regards the mechanics of cultural evolution versus those of biological evolution (individual versus group selection especially) and on the potentially problematic consequences of relying on cultural evolution alone (especially its seeming relativism). Less commented upon is the way in which Hayek's attack on sociobiology and his accompanying account of cultural evolution amounts to a substantial departure from Hume and especially Smith.[20]

Before turning to Hayek's attack on sociobiology per se it is important to observe that Hayek had raised significant objections to the biological approach *prior* to the advent of sociobiology. Indeed, in the Epilogue to *Law, Legislation and Liberty*, he mentions that he had been following closely this general line of research for some 50 years.[21] What the advent of sociobiology did was to crystallize for Hayek the serious difficulties in the overall research program. In *The Constitution of Liberty* he raised two criticisms of the biological approach. The first criticism comes up when Hayek contrasts what he terms the British and Scottish (and his own) anti-rationalistic evolutionary approach, which acknowledged the importance of undesigned orders for the growth of civilization, and the French rationalist and constructivist approach that insisted on designing society on the basis of a theoretical plan. Hayek is at pains here to point out two things. First, he maintains that the evolutionary approach makes no rosy assumptions about either human nature or the existence of a natural harmony of interests among human beings. The evolutionary approach recognizes that the fundamental social problem is to manage self-love and that this requires traditional institutions, law, and morals. "The Scottish theorists," he explained, "were very much aware how delicate this artificial structure was which rested on man's more primitive and ferocious instincts being tamed and checked by institutions that he neither had designed nor could control."[22] Hayek went on to say that the evolutionary approach has in common with the "Christian tradition" a belief in the "fallibility and sinfulness of man." Typically, Hayek leaves things at this and does not go on to outline his own view of human nature in any detail. Hayek observes that one characteristic of the French/rationalist/constructivist approach was that it believed it had a firm understanding of human nature and (he quotes d'Holbach) "could easily find the morals which suited it."[23] Now the *philosophes*, like d'Holbach and Helvétius, who championed this view, emphatically rejected the idea of any sort of innate moral sentiments but what they do have in common with Smith and with today's evolutionary psychologists is a belief that they have grasped the complex inner workings of human nature. The *philosophe* who did embrace the notion of the moral sentiments was, of course, Rousseau to whom Hayek attributed not only the sin of constructivism but also the origins of the false and dangerous ideas of the general will and, most closely related to his understanding of the moral sentiments, social justice.

Hayek emphasizes in *The Constitution of Liberty* that his idea of social or cultural evolution is emphatically different from the idea of biological evolution. In fact, he makes the case both that the idea of cultural evolution is historically prior to the idea of biological evolution and, more importantly, that cultural evolution is the method proper to the social sciences. With regard to the latter, Hayek laments the importation of the idea of biological evolution into the social sciences. He notes that ideas such as "natural selection," "the survival of the fittest," and the "struggle for existence" had both confused and damaged the cause of classical liberalism. The critical difference between biological and social evolution is that in social evolution "the decisive factor is not the selection of the physical and inheritable properties of the individuals but the selection by imitation of successful institutions and habits."[24] As we will see, this clear distinction between culture and biology is critical for Hayek's theory of the morality of a free society.

A second point made by Hayek in *The Constitution of Liberty* is relevant to the issue of biology and worth mentioning. Hayek points to the centuries-old trend of intellectual thought toward deterministic explanations of human behavior that have called into question human freedom and with it human responsibility. Some of these developments have focused on the external causes of human behavior while others have focused on the internal causes. Biological determinism—a close maybe inseparable companion to evolutionary psychology—is one such example. The determinist tries to eliminate the "self" or the "I" by reducing it to nothing more than "heredity and experience."[25] This general trend has seriously undermined the notion of moral responsibility among intellectuals and to some extent the public.[26] Hayek does not defend a mystical, religious, or metaphysical idea of free will. He defends free will on the basis of whether individuals are capable of responding to laws and their associated punishments. The paradox of the determinist position is that it removes any obstacle, a metaphysical "I," for example, which might be able to resist the rewards and punishments offered by society and by the law.

As noted, Hayek's clearest and most elaborate statement about sociobiology comes in the 1979 "Epilogue" to *Law, Legislation and Liberty*. E. O. Wilson's landmark *Sociobiology: A New Synthesis* had appeared just a few years before in 1975. The subtitle to the "Epilogue" is "The Three Sources of Human Values," which Hayek identifies as reason, nature or instinct, and culture. The first two have their champions; Hayek will champion culture. The emergence of sociobiology had crystallized the issue for Hayek by its seemingly binary opposition between reason and instinct. "There is surely," Hayek says, "as much justification to speak of the wisdom of culture as of the wisdom of nature."[27] This is certainly an understatement for Hayek speaks almost exclusively of the wisdom of culture. Furthermore, the harshness of Hayek's critique should not be underestimated. Sociobiology is explained as another erroneous scientistic product of Cartesian rationalism. It is lumped together with Marx and Freud, two villains in Hayek's story. And, finally, the Epilogue begins with a quotation from Goethe invoking the specter of religious fanaticism and ends with Hayek's prediction that the twentieth century will be known as an age of superstition.[28]

As mentioned, Hayek explains that it was the Cartesian rationalist outlook that resulted in the exclusive emphasis on reason and instinct. It saw culture as something "changeable at will, arbitrary, superficial, or dispensable." As a result it failed to see that "civilization has largely been made possible by subjugating the innate animal instincts to the non-rational customs which made possible the formation of larger orderly groups of gradually increasing size."[29] The Epilogue brings to a conclusion an argument that Hayek has developed over the three volumes of *Law, Legislation and Liberty*. Hayek accepts Darwinian-style biological evolution as a fact. (In the postscript to *The Constitution of Liberty* Hayek chastises conservatives for rejecting evolution.[30]) Hayek's problem with sociobiology is that human biology evolved over a vast period of time whereas human societies on any scale that is recognizably modern or human in any meaningful sense are comparatively speaking very, very recent. Furthermore, our natural moral sentiments, real and formidable as they remain, Hayek argues, are not suited to the needs of any kind of large, free, modern society—what Hayek sometimes terms the "Great Society." In *Law, Legislation and Liberty* Hayek contrasts repeatedly and at length the opposition between life in the Great Society and life in what he terms "tribal society."

Life in tribal societies has been the characteristic way of human life for the longest time. Only in the last few thousand years has there been a marked departure. The Great Society is even more recent. Its existence has been but the blink of an eye in terms of the overall span of human existence. Tribal society is characterized by life in small groups where kinship bonds are strong. The members of tribal societies also have closely shared ideals and interests. In the most primitive of societies, no distinction at all is drawn between interests and ideals, between facts and values. Tribal societies have shared rules, customs, and traditions that are usually unspoken and that have evolved as adaptations to circumstances. Peace prevails in the group because of the identity of interests among members and because of the limited informational requirements needed for the smooth functioning of society. In face-to-face societies everyone knows everyone else, everyone knows everyone else's problems, and everyone knows, more or less, the available means for solving these problems. Under such conditions it is quite plausible to believe that one's efforts on behalf of the common good might be both recognized and have their intended consequences.

Hayek explains that with the enlargement of the circle of society, stemming from the obligation to treat others as equals, there also comes a corresponding contraction in the extent of enforceable obligations to others. More fundamentally still, the Great Society brings about a moral revolution in our relationship to others. Not only are deliberate efforts to help others less likely to be successful, they are likely to be less successful than the beneficial indirect effects of the pursuit of our own purposes, self-interest, or, to use the theological term, "calling."[31] Lastly, instead of loyalty to a group united for a visible purpose, members of the Great Society must feel obliged to abstract rules. The Great Society, Hayek observes, comes at the "price" of sacrificing many deeply felt emotions, desires, and sentiments.[32]

> The kind of abstract order on which man has learnt to rely and which has enabled him peacefully to coordinate the efforts of millions, unfortunately cannot be based on such feelings as love which constituted the highest virtue in the small group. Love is a sentiment which only the concrete evokes, and the Great Society has become possible through the individual's efforts being guided not by the aim of helping particular other persons, but the confinement of the pursuit of their purposes by abstract rules.[33]

The shift to the Great Society "leaves an emotional void by depriving men both of satisfying tasks and the assurance of support in the case of need."[34]

Hayek illustrated the folly of relying on nature with reference to the pivotal cases of Marx and Freud. They illustrate two different reactions to the development of civilization in opposition to our natural sentiments. Socialism represents the attempt to revive "primordial instincts" under the circumstances of modern society.[35] This is in a fundamental sense impossible. The result is an attempt to create "new morals" to satisfy the old yearnings. The idea of "social justice" is one such attempt. Freud took another way: "undoing the culturally acquired repressions and freeing the natural desires."[36] Freud, Hayek believed, was the greatest destroyer of culture of his time.

Conclusion: Hayek's Unsentimental Liberalism

It might seem unfair to lump Smith's theory of moral sentiments with sociobiology (let alone with Marx and Freud) and, as well to neglect the advances in evolutionary psychology since Hayek's time. Yet,

Hayek invites us to do so. He studiously, I would say, neglects the moral sentiments component, strictly speaking, of Smith's thought. We are invited to do also because of the many recent and impressive attempts to establish a biological basis for the social science that Smith founded simply on the basis of observation and the study of history. Granting this, one still might respond to the interpretation of Hayek given here in a number of ways other than what I will suggest later. One might reject Hayek on the grounds that he is simply in error about sociobiology and evolutionary psychology in that these sciences truly chart the course toward a unification of natural and social science. Alternatively, one might seek out a more ecumenical approach that seeks to blend reason, nature, and culture. Nevertheless, at the very least, Hayek's arguments ought to sound a note of caution before going down either of these roads.

Hayek's treatment of human nature is striking. He does not deny that there is a universal human nature. Just the same, he does not attempt to give a *complete* account of that nature or use it as a comprehensive guide for his political principles. Most fundamentally, this is because he sees civilization as an ongoing process of discovery. A full account of human nature is simply not available to us. Furthermore, Hayek's denies the thick moral unity of human nature that Smith believed he had discovered. Human beings are instead divided creatures and this is especially true in a free society. Both these conclusions on Hayek's part have implications for the last two issues to be discussed: progress and confidence. In these regards, reading Hayek's unsentimental liberalism is a sobering experience. While he is, perhaps, even more optimistic about the beneficent workings of a free market than were Hume and Smith, Hayek makes clear the grave challenges faced by those who wish to preserve and extend freedom in the modern world. Many of these challenges stem from powerful elements within human nature itself. Hayek believes that any serious attempt to satisfy the yearnings born in tribal society will result in some form of totalitarianism. Indeed, according to Hayek, "Most people are unwilling to face the most alarming lesson of modern history: that the greatest crimes of our time have been committed by governments that had the enthusiastic support of millions of people who were guided by moral impulses."[37]

One way to look at Hayek's career is to see it as a response to the extraordinary upheavals, reverses, and surprises of twentieth-century politics. Hayek's unsentimental liberalism, which combines an account of the strengths and benefits of a free society along with a sense of the profound fragility of a free society, is surely an important perspective from which to consider the end of the Cold War and the prospects for the preservation and spread of liberal ideas. [38]

Notes

1. John Maynard Keynes, *Economic Consequences of the Peace* (New York: Harcourt, Brace, [1919] 1920), 4.
2. See Friedrich A. Hayek, *The Road to Serfdom* (Chicago, IL: University of Chicago Press, [1944] 2007), Ch. 12.
3. See Bruce Caldwell, *Hayek's Challenge: An Intellectual Biography of F. A. Hayek* (Chicago, IL: University of Chicago Press, 2004), 348 and, at length, Daniel Klein, "The Ways of John Gray: A Libertarian Commentary," *Independent Review* 4, no. 1 (Summer, 1999): 63–84.
4. Friedrich A. Hayek, *The Constitution of Liberty* (Chicago, IL: University of Chicago Press, 1960), 2.
5. Adam Smith, *The Theory of Moral Sentiments*, ed. D. D. Raphael and A. L. Macfie (Indianapolis: Liberty Fund, [1759] 1982). Leonidas Montes raises the issue of Smith's neglect of the *Theory of Moral Sentiments.* He deals with it briefly and attributes it to the general neglect of the work during Hayek's life, especially because of its seeming theological underpinnings. See his "Is Friedrich Hayek Rowing Adam Smith's Boat?" in Adrew Farrant, *Hayek, Mill and the Liberal Tradition* (London: Routledge, 2011), 28–29. I am going to offer a more substantive reason.
6. Excellent overviews of Smith's project may be found in Craig Smith, *Adam Smith's Political Philosophy: The Invisible Hand and Spontaneous Order* (London: Routledge, 2005) and Nicholas Phillipson, *Adam Smith: An Enlightened Life* (New Haven, CT: Yale University Press, 2012).
7. Smith is more thoroughgoing than Hume. The key Humean text is his essay "Of National Characters," which rejects Montesquieu's emphasis on physical causes. The problematic part of this essay with regard to the question of human nature is Hume's notorious remark about the apparent inferiority of Africans.
8. Smith, *Theory of Moral Sentiments*, V.2.15.
9. Ibid.
10. David Hume, *Essays: Moral, Political, and Literary*, ed. Eugene Miller (Indianapolis: Liberty Fund, 1985), 259.
11. James Otteson summarizes the research in *Adam Smith* (London: Continuum, 2011), 157–60.
12. Smith, *Theory of Moral Sentiments*, I.i.2.
13. Ibid., III.2.
14. Ibid., II.ii.
15. Ibid., II.ii.2.1.
16. Ibid., II.ii.1.4.
17. Friedrich A. Hayek, "Dr. Bernard Mandeville," in *New Studies in Philosophy, Politics, Economics, and the History of Ideas* (Chicago, IL: University of Chicago Press, [1966] 1978), 250–51.

18. Hayek, *Constitution of Liberty*, 1–2, emphasis added.
19. Friedrich A. Hayek, *The Fatal Conceit: The Errors of Socialism* (Chicago, IL: University of Chicago Press, 1989).
20. At least two interesting lines of argument run counter to that presented here. Larry Arnhart, "Friedrich Hayek's Darwinian Conservatism," in *Liberalism, Conservatism, and Hayek's Idea of Spontaneous Order*, ed. Louis Hunt and Peter McNamara (London: Palgrave Macmillan, 2007), Ch. 7, laments Hayek's rejection of nature (and reason) in favor of culture and argues that Hayek should have embraced nature as understood by evolutionary psychology, along with culture and reason as guides. The result of this triad of sources of values, he argues, would have been a form of Hayekian–Darwinian conservatism. My argument tries to make clear why Hayek did not take that step. It is also worth noting that a Hayekian–Darwinian liberal position might not be out of the question depending on one's philosophical assumptions and how one reads the current state of the scientific evidence .Vernon L. Smith [see "The Two Faces of Adam Smith," *Southern Economic Journal* 65, no. 1 (July 1998): 1–19 and "Human Nature: An Economic Perspective," *Daedalus* 133, no. 4 (Fall, 2004): 67–76, initiated a significant line of inquiry by distinguishing between personal exchange and impersonal exchange (i.e., exchanges between strangers) and arguing that *The Theory of Moral Sentiments* deals with the former and *The Wealth of Nations* deals with the latter. Smith also argues that it was Hayek who grasped the significance of the tension between the two "orders" of exchange. Smith quotes from the *The Fatal Conceit* (p. 18) to the effect that "we must constantly adjust our lives, our thoughts and our emotions, in order to live simultaneously within different kinds of orders according to different rules." While this argument has many interesting and important dimensions to it, I am not sure that *The Theory of Moral Sentiments* is about "personal exchange." To cite just one reason, most of the book is about our sympathetic interactions with people we do not know. Following up on Vernon Smith's questions, Maria Paganelli, "The Same Face of the Two Smiths: Adam Smith and Vernon Smith," *Journal of Economic Behavior and Organization* 78, no. 3 (May 2011): 246–55, has provided a very useful argument about how one might use Smithian moral concepts to make the move from personal to impersonal exchange.
21. Friedrich A. Hayek, *Law, Legislation and Liberty*, vol. 3, *The Political Order of a Free People* (Chicago, IL: University of Chicago Press, 1979), 153.
22. Hayek, *Constitution of Liberty*, 60.
23. Ibid., 65. The d'Holbach text is *Système Social, Ou Principes naturels de la morale et de la politique* Part I, ch. v,
24. Ibid., 59.
25. Ibid., 74.
26. See also Friedrich A. Hayek, "The Moral Element in Free Enterprise," in *Studies in Philosophy, Politics and Economics* (Chicago, IL: University of Chicago Press, 1967), 232–33.
27. Hayek, *Political Order*, 155.

28. In an interesting contrast, Hayek displays much less antipathy and even some significant sympathy in *Law, Legislation and Liberty* to John Rawls's *A Theory of Justice*, another paradigm-shifting work, which had appeared just a few years earlier. See especially, Friedrich A. Hayek, *Law, Legislation and Liberty*, vol. 2, *The Mirage of Social Justice* (Chicago, IL: University of Chicago Press, 1976), 100. I think the contrast is revealing in terms of, first, the general intellectual framework in which Hayek is working, and, second, in terms of what Hayek believed was the gravest threat to misunderstanding the workings of a free society.
29. Hayek, *Political Order,* 155.
30. Hayek, *Constitution of Liberty*, 405.
31. Hayek, *Social Justice*, 145.
32. Ibid., 147.
33. Ibid., 150.
34. Ibid., 146.
35. Hayek, *Political Order,* 169.
36. Ibid., 174.
37. Hayek, *Social Justice*, 134.
38. Without implicating them in the final product, I would like to thank the participants, Bruce Caldwell and Gerry Gaus in particular, at the University of Richmond conference that is the basis of this volume for their comments on the draft of this essay.

CHAPTER TWO

F. A. Hayek and the "Individualists"

SANDRA J. PEART AND DAVID M. LEVY

F. A. Hayek famously distinguished between "true" and "false" individualism.[1] In that dichotomy, "true" individualists were comfortable with evolved institutions and rule following without fully understanding the origin or consequences of those rules. "False" individualists, by contrast, believed themselves capable of constructing the rules themselves and, as such, they imposed rules or institutions on others. For Hayek, as is well known, "false" individualists included those in the nineteenth century such as Auguste Comte and Saint Simon who advocated for the reorganization of society.[2]

Hayek, perhaps somewhat harshly, placed John Stuart Mill in a long line of rationalist thinkers, "false individualists" as he put it in the 1945 lecture, "Individualism: True and False." There, Hayek made the case that "true" individualism traced its roots from Smith to Hume, Burke, Tocqueville, and Lord Acton, in contrast with the continental rationalists, in whose ranks he included Mill. True individualists trace "the combined effects of individual actions" in order to "discover that many of the institutions on which human achievements rest have arisen and are functioning without a designing and directing mind."[3] In contrast, in Hayek's telling rationalists held that "social processes can be made to serve human ends only if they are subjected to the control of individual human reason."[4] Here, rules and institutions are designed by rational human action, a methodology that "always tends to develop into the opposite of individualism, namely, socialism or collectivism."[5]

Although Hayek's famous distinction has been much studied, his relationship with twentieth-century intellectuals who self-identified as "individualists" is obscure. Our interest in what follows is Hayek's relatively unexplored relationship with these "individualists" including in the first instance Merwin K. Hart and Rose Wilder Lane. Hart and Lane advocated free-market ideology and opposed the sort of progressive economics program advocated by Lorie Tarshis in his textbook, *The Elements of Economics*.[6] Given his strong support for what he termed "true" individualism, one might predict that Hayek would align himself with Hart and Lane. This was not the case. On the contrary, Hayek thoroughly distanced himself from Hart's circle of free-market economists even as he was putting the Mont Pèlerin Society (MPS) together in the late 1940s.

Early in his career, Hayek encountered a second group of American individualists whose work might be broadly construed as social Darwinism. First among these was President Herbert Hoover. As is now well known, Hoover subscribed to a doctrine of racial hierarchy, a "fact" that needed to be taken into account to achieve efficient social organization. Not surprisingly, Hoover's views on racial hierarchy have been discussed extensively.[7] In contrast, Hayek's detailed notes taken after his encounter with Hoover have passed entirely unremarked. We begin our discussion of Hayek and the social Darwinists with an examination of Hayek's reactions to meeting President Hoover. Following this, we discuss the racial views of perhaps the most important intellectual in the Hoover circle of individualists, Thomas Nixon Carver. Although Carver's reputation has now fallen into obscurity, perhaps because Hayek's opposition to his views helped push him out of the limelight of economics, he was a significant force in economic circles well into the twentieth century.

With the help of an unpublished manuscript on the relationship between the individual and groups written by Hayek immediately before *The Fatal Conceit* was edited, we also examine how Hayek's argument compares to the avowed social Darwinism put forward by Carver. For Hayek, innate tendencies lead to equality of outcomes in small groups, while the morals of honesty, fair dealing, and reciprocity emerge in large groups with nonunitary goals. This position put Hayek in opposition to those who argued for a hierarchy of groups based on (purported) biologically determined characteristics.

Merwin K. Hart's Circle of Individualism

Hayek interacted with, and ultimately rejected, the circle of American free-market ideology that surrounded Merwin K. Hart. Even though some of these individualists are famous, the circle itself has now fallen into obscurity, perhaps as a result of the flamboyant anti-Semitism of its central figure.[8] Hart became central to the individualists' movement in large measure because he controlled the resources that supported their publications. After a rather brazen attempt to control the historical record of the Pearl Harbor attack, the Congressional majority provided no staff resources to help the minority conduct an independent analysis of the 84 volumes of testimony. Hart provided US$25,000 to finance the staff work of the Congressional minority.[9] As will become clear later, such beneficence came with strings attached.

In a world in which one side of a contest is denied resources through standard channels, we ought not to be surprised that nonstandard channels will appear and persist. We have known for a long time that both Ludwig von Mises and Hayek himself were supported in American universities by private funds.[10] Given their stature in the academic world, this fate seems strange. What should seem even stranger is that private funds were solicited to finance the work of a Congressional committee itself.

Were we to judge by recent accounts, Hart was an eccentric figure whose anti-Semitism served to separate him from the larger individualist movement.[11] But this separation occurred only after the MPS came to dominate and to replace Hart's "individualism" with variations on liberalism.[12] One of Hart's vehicles—his National Economic Council's *Review of Books*—changed the direction of post–Second World War economics education. Lane's review of Tarshis's *The Elements of Economics* in the *Review of Books*, combined with Hart's effective campaign to purge the book from classrooms, gave Paul Samuelson's *Economics* a de facto monopoly of textbooks explicating economic theory.[13] Lane's review criticized Tarshis's Keynesian view of the government as providing a necessary stability to a capitalist economy as well as his democratic presuppositions.

Lane's review formed the basis of the chapter on economics textbooks in William F. Buckley, Jr.'s *God and Man at Yale*. Buckley quotes Lane's review of Tarshis's *Elements* in a footnote, and in the endnotes, he offers a covering citation to the Hart vehicle.[14] In the early days of Buckley's career as a public intellectual, Buckley was Hart's protégé.[15] Buckley's publisher (Henry Regnery) wrote to Hart (October 4, 1951) about the National Economic Council's plan for a dinner to celebrate *God and Man at Yale* with those likely to be supportive and he suggested that a copy be sent to all college presidents (1,800 by his count). Regnery sent copies of circulars for the book that Hart might use to include with his mailing. Hart wrote to Buckley (October 11, 1951):

Dear Billie,

> Thank you for the inscribed copy of your book which has just been received. I have read this with great interest in manuscript form and look forward to rereading it at early date.
>
> We expect to have a pretty good crowd at the dinner of the University Club the night of October 22nd. We have ordered 60 copies of your book sent to me at the University Club. If you could come in the Club early enough on October 22nd to autograph each of these, we will give them to the guests and I think it will add a great deal to the occasion.

Hart attempted to get Buckley on the program of the National Association of Manufacturers (November 1). He failed to do so but only (it seems from correspondence) because the program had already been set. He then exchanged letters and articles with Will Buckley (WFB, Jr.'s father) and sent a note to the National Economic Council mailing list offering *God and Man at Yale* for sale in the event that local bookstores might pretend they could not obtain copies. Hart asserted that "left wing influence" had been working against conservative books for 30 years.

On April 5, 1954, Hart wrote to thank Buckley for the inscribed copy of his coauthored *McCarthy and His Enemies*.[16] Hart seems not to have seen this in manuscript as he apologized for taking so long to acknowledge the gift, saying that it "took me several days to finish reading the book." He informed Buckley that a notice went out with the "last Council Letter and we have nearly 100 orders already."

Buckley responded to Hart's note:

Dear Mr. Hart,

> How terribly gratifying to learn that you have again been so kind as to promote the circulation of my book. It is especially heartening to know that you yourselves think highly of it. I wasn't a bit surprised by the reviews, evasive and dishonest though they have been.
>
> Again, my heartiest thanks for volunteering to distribute the book. I so wish we could have gotten it out cheaper. As it is, it was due to sell for $6.50 until Brent [Bozell] and I sacrificed our royalties on the first 6,000 copies in order to bring the price down.
>
> Again, I hope to see you Tuesday.
>
> Sincerely,
> Bill

In a September 21, 1959, note, Hart thanked Buckley for the autographed copy of *Up from Liberalism* and congratulated him on the meeting at Carnegie Hall, explaining that illness forced him to leave early.[17] In his final letter (March 21, 1961) to Buckley, Hart reported the rumor that the *National Review* (*NR*) was planning to attack the John Birch Society. Hart expressed his hope that the rumor was false and then pleaded that the *NR* hold off on the attack for the good of the movement. He added a handwritten note to the letter testifying to the patriotism of Robert Welch, then head of the John Birch Society.

The *National Review* response to the John Birch Society seems to have ended the relationship between Buckley and Hart. As far as we know, Buckley never discussed his early relationship with Hart. Natural occasions arose, such as the celebratory editions of *God and Man at Yale*, at which Buckley might have mentioned a word or two about Hart, either as the head of the National Economic Council or as an old friend of his father's. There is nothing about Hart in Buckley's "Introduction" to the twenty-fifth anniversary edition.[18] This silence is worthy of note because Buckley had no difficulty in confronting other aspects of the Hart circle. Late in his life, prompted by a *National Review* contributor's anti-Semitism, Buckley discussed his father's anti-Semitism candidly.[19] The adult son had no anti-Semitism of his own to disown.

Turning to Hayek's relationship with Hart, we find that Hayek first encountered the "individualists" when Albert Jay Nock, the initial editor of the *Review of Books*, reviewed *The Road to Serfdom* for Hart's *Economic Council*. Nock opened the review by placing *The Road to Serfdom* in a Spencerian context.[20]

> We will take up below in some detail the conception of biological hierarchy that prevailed amongst the "individualists" at this time. For now it is sufficient to remark that while Spencer was concerned with biological evolution, the *Road to Serfdom* focused on the evolution of institutions, a theme that Hayek would develop extensively.

Nock spends a paragraph giving the reader an idea of the drift of Hayek's argument and then focuses on a point about which Hayek "is not explicit enough," whether natural laws determine politics and economics:

> His chapter on "Why the Worst Get on Top" opens a most interesting subject, though as he says, it does not exhaust it. We all

> know the truth of Paine's saying, that the trade of government has always been a monopoly of the most vicious of all the most ignorant and the most vicious of mankind. We accept this as a fact, but seldom, probably, are we led to wonder just precisely why it should be a fact. In our history, for example, why should the Washington, Adamses, Jeffersons, Hamiltons, have been so promptly followed by the Pickerings, Wolcotts, McHenrys, etc.? Why should Henry Adams say that the successive Presidents from Washington to Grant (and what he would say now!) is almost enough in itself to upset the whole Darwinian theory? Politically, society is a mixture of oil and water which you may shake together till the cows come home, but it always settles with the oil on top. Mr. Hayek says much that is valuable about this phenomenon, but he is not quite explicit enough. He appears not to see that he has here before him the operation of certain natural laws which work as invariably and inexorably in the realm of economics and politics as Newton's law works in the realm of physics.[21]

As far as we know, Nock's review of *The Road to Serfdom* has not been discussed in recent scholarship; so we have no basis to judge its impact. Nock's successor, Rose Wilder Lane, however, had a significant impact on the landscape of economics textbooks. Her review of Lorie Tarshis, which was then featured in Buckley's *God and Man at Yale*, brought the political orientation of economics textbooks to the forefront and had the effect of removing the progressive textbook by Tarshis from the landscape of American economics textbooks.

Hayek was invited to provide a "blurb" for Buckley's book and declined to do so.[22] Hayek's letter makes it clear that he disagreed with Buckley:

> I am afraid anything friendly I could say about Buckley's book would have to be hedged about by so many qualifications that it would be useless for your purposes. I wish I could, as I almost wanted when I read it, make it the occasion for some discussion of academic freedom, but again, their [sic] are more urgent priorities.[23]

Academic freedom was not a distant concept for Hayek but was instead something of real, practical significance.[24] Hayek's conduct in support of free speech in the early days of the Keynesian revolution was remarkable enough that it was remembered decades later by those with whom he disagreed. Tarshis's friend and co-revolutionary, Robert

Bryce, referred to Hayek's conduct in testimony about the early days of Keynesian economics before *The General Theory* was published:

> Hayek at the London School was very kind to me and he let me have four consecutive weeks of his seminar to try to explain these ideas to them. The students were very interested.[25]

But Hayek would have disagreed with Buckley's *God and Man at Yale* over more than the suppression of academic freedom, significant as that was. One of Buckley's targets was central to Hayek's hopes for economic reform after the war. Consider that Hayek's 1944 *The Road to Serfdom* called attention to Simons's *Positive Program for Laissez Faire.*[26] We know now that Simons was supposed to write an American version of *The Road to Serfdom.* At the opening of the MPS in 1947 Hayek said this about Simons:

> I have many times already in the course of this outline felt tempted to refer you to the writings of the late Henry Simons, but I want now especially to draw your attention to his "Reflections of Syndicalism," which states this problem with rare courage and lucidity.[27]

While Hayek would not provide a blurb for *God and Man at Yale*, he did write this for Simons's *Economic Policy for a Free Society:*

> The source of a stream of thought to which we shall owe the preservation of a free society... the only coherent and competent picture of a society worth striving for.[28]

As we noted at the outset, it was for Hayek critically important to identify and rescue German economists who might help reconstruct a nontotalitarian Germany, a new and relatively liberal economic order in Germany. Through Wilhelm Röpke, Hayek learned in London about Walter Eucken. Eucken was the one German national who attended the initial meeting of the MPS.[29] Simons's work fit well into the line of argument that Walter Eucken had developed before the War.

Buckley by contrast singled out Simons's *Positive Program* for criticism in *God and Man.* We quote to demonstrate that Buckley opposed Simons's "statism":[30]

> One item from the reading prospectus is omitted from the foregoing list: a 37-page pamphlet by the late Professor Henry C. Simons,

> of the University of Chicago, entitled *A Positive Program for Laissez Faire,* which is introduced by Mr. Lindblom as presenting the "only intelligent conservative position."

Lindblom might, it should be noted, be reading from Hayek's blurb on the dust jacket of *Economics of a Free Society*! Now, back to Buckley:

> Mr. Simons indicts the state as bearing heavy responsibility for the evils that led to the great depression (the pamphlet was written in 1934, probably in a fit of pique), but promptly outlines a program which would give to the state unprecedented power. He equates freedom with free enterprise, and proceeds to outline a sure program for the destruction of the free economy. Mr. Simons's specific proposals include (1) reduction of inequality by heavy taxation, (2) nationalization of all railroads and utilities and "other industries in which it is impossible to maintain effectively competitive conditions," (3) abolition of private deposit banking on the basis of fractional reserves, (4) legal limitations to advertising and selling activities, (5) limitation upon the total amount of property which any single corporation may own (suggested: no more than 5% of the total output of that product), (6) enactment of laws to prohibit any person's serving as an officer in any two corporations engaged in the same line of business, (7) outright federal ownership of the Federal Reserve Banks, (8) elimination of all special tax treatment for capital gains, and (9) increased government welfarism.
>
> This, we are led to believe, is the conservative alternative to even greater statism and socialization.[31]

A footnote informs the reader that as of 1950–1951, the pamphlet was being used in the basic economics course.

Given that the students were assigned to read Simons's *Positive Program*, it is appropriate to consider the charge of biased education that Buckley pressed in *God and Man at Yale.* We quote the careful statement in John Chamberlain's "Foreword":

> But where are the countervailing quotations from Röpke, von Mises, Hayek, Frank Knight, the Walter Lippmann of the *Good Society* and other believers in free consumer choice? Mr. Buckley says they can't be produced in any volume from the texts used at Yale.[32]

The use of Simons's text provides some counterbalance to Buckley's claim. Hayek, as noted earlier, had offered the same judgment as Buckley's teacher as to Simons's importance. Simons was perhaps the greatest speaker at that time for Frank Knight's views. The commonality of Simons's views with ordo-liberalism, to which Röpke is close, is well known. Teachers can only assign so much material. Is there a better statement of classical liberal economics than Simons's? *The Road to Serfdom* was too British-centric for first-year American students, which of course is why Simons was asked to write an American version.

It seems fair, then, to distinguish between the liberalism that Hayek was reviving and promoting and American "individualism" on the basis of their willingness to consider—perhaps to embrace—reforms that would enlarge the sphere for the state after the Second World War, a vision that allowed for potential reform versus one that held out for the status quo. Buckley situated Simons's positive program somewhere between statism and socialism. Lane's letter to Jasper Crane puts Hayek in the same camp as Simons. As one of the major funders of the MPS, Crane writes to Lane about Hayek's appeal for funds.[33] Lane's response to Crane characteristically claimed that Hayek "both opposes and advocates Bismarck's Sozialpolitik."[34] This is perhaps simply an unkind way to describe the reformism that Hayek himself advocated as distinguished from Simons's views that Hayek wished at least to see considered.

The Hoover Circle of "Individualists"

In July 1946, Hayek met with then former President Herbert Hoover. We can guess at the reason Hayek would wish to talk with Hoover. We know from what he wrote as the European war was still raging that Hayek worried about how to bring Germany back into the international order. German liberalism had to be recovered from within. It could not, Hayek wrote, be imposed from outside.[35] Hoover's tireless service following an earlier European war on behalf of humanitarianism and for a reintegration of Europe had been singled out by J. M. Keynes in his *Economic Consequences of the Peace.*[36] Those in authority at the Paris Peace Conference failed to follow Hoover's lead and, in Keynes's account, thereby missed the opportunity to attain "the Good Peace."[37]

Something in his conversation with Hoover must have struck Hayek as worth remembering; his two-page memo was carefully preserved and separated from his general manuscript collection that was donated to the Hoover Institution. In this memo, Hayek recounts Hoover's report of how Stalin's betrayal of the agreement at the Tehran Conference "contributed to" Roosevelt's early death.[38]

It is not hard to guess why Hoover would wish to speak to Hayek. With the celebrity of *The Road to Serfdom*, Hayek was *the* new force in classical economic liberalism. In line with his philosophy of "American individualism," Hoover opposed New Deal "collectivism."[39]

Hoover himself subscribed to the doctrine of racial hierarchy. When one considers the efficiency of mining, he argued that the "lower races" need to be taken into account.

> In mining work the lower races require a greatly increased amount of direction and this excess of supervisors consists of men not in themselves directly productive... the lower intelligence reacts in many ways in lack of coordination and inability to take initiative.[40]

If one conceptualizes society in efficiency terms and adds a hierarchy of types to its composition then presumably its "racial" composition will be important. And if one can alter the "racial" composition then there is no end to what efficiency gains might be forthcoming. Not surprisingly, Hoover's views on racial hierarchy have been discussed extensively.[41] Less attention has been paid to the racial views of the most important economist in the Hoover circle of individualists, Thomas Nixon Carver.[42]

Carver has now been largely forgotten. His name appears in footnotes and casual asides in accounts based on the oral tradition of American free-market economics.[43] He is perhaps most often remembered as the economist who introduced the writings of Frederick Bastiat to Leonard Read.[44] Carver himself took credit for suggesting that Read start what became the Foundation for Economic Education.[45] Read's 1945 *Pattern for Revolt* in which he tells the charming story of von Mises's reaction to the hypothetical question of what he would do upon being made dictator—"I would abdicate!"—has a foreword by Carver.[46]

Published in 1944, Richard Hofstadter's *Social Darwinism in American Thought* demonstrates the pervasiveness of thinking about biological hierarchy in American intellectual thought early in the century, and makes the case that social Darwinism was an important part of free-market thinking at this time.[47] However, the essays on the postwar period in the Philip Mirowski and Dieter Plehwe 2009 collection no longer see social Darwinism as a key element of the free-market discussion.[48] Somehow the phenomenon that Hofstadter had thought important became so obscured that scholars today fail to see its significance. Carver's student, Orval Watts, is mentioned briefly in the 2009 collection, although without context.[49]

Carver was an imposing figure early in the twentieth century. He was a past president of the American Economic Association and a former chairman of the economics department at Harvard. His technical views were important enough to be targeted by Eugen von Böhm-Bawerk.[50] Politically influential, he was an overnight visitor at the Hoover White House[51] and although he was not of that religion he was a featured speaker of the official convocation of the Church of Jesus Christ of Latter-Day Saints.[52] In active retirement in Los Angeles and having published an article on monetary theory in the 1934 *Economic Journal*,[53] his one-year appointment at the University of California, Los Angeles (UCLA) was extended when Henry Schultz was killed in an automobile accident.[54] Two of his books were published in the 1940s by the Ward Ritchie Press, the center of the Los Angeles fine press movement.[55] Decades later, Armen Alchian asked Hayek about Carver on the basis of the impression Carver made on him at UCLA.[56]

A search for "moron" and "extermination" in Google books yields several of Carver's publications while at Harvard. We find, first, mention of the dangers associated with the "multiplication of the feeble-minded":

> As to the extermination of the germ plasm of the least fit, the masses, if intelligent, would favor that. The multiplication of the feeble-minded is a menace to the mass of laborers.[57]

Not surprisingly, for Carver, survival is the key to efficiency:

> Wherever the primordial struggle for existence is found, either in the human or the sub-human world, the only unpardonable sin is weakness. Neither pity nor the sense of justice will preserve the weak from extermination or exploitation. The only virtue is strength. Nature cherishes her darling, the strong, and whips the weak to death. But how can a sovereign human group, i. e., a nation, strengthen itself for this inevitable and unmitigated struggle? That is the question which transcends all others in importance. The nation which listens to other advice, and allows other questions to divert its attention from this supreme one, will pay the penalty with its life.[58]

Carver, like Thomas Carlyle, claims popular ideas and majority voting fail to carry much weight.[59] So, "popular will" is useless as a means by which planning is to occur.[60] One of the characteristics of the individualist movement in America is its opposition to democratic decision making, in particular an opposition to the principle of majority rule. This opposition led the individualists into conflict with classical liberals with whom they agreed on economic matters.[61]

Carver's Harvard scholarship also contains a lengthy discussion of the moral agency of vice as a "fool-killer." Carver begins with the public regulation of "vice." Here he makes the case that although vice acts as a "fool-killer," its results are overly imprecise:

> One of the strongest arguments against the public regulation of vice or injurious forms of consumption is that vice acts as a fool-killer and helps to rid the world of those undesirable persons who are unable to withstand temptation. There is some merit in this argument... If it were true that the individual who succumbs to vice never injured anybody else but himself, it might be argued with a good deal of reason that the best way to get rid of him would be to allow him to destroy himself as rapidly as possible,—that by so doing we should in the course of time build up a strong race of people, who could live in the presence of temptation without injury.[62]

Carver endorses public regulations to improve the accuracy of the fool-killing tendency.[63] He provides a chart to explain the issue.[64] The cancel marks are in the original. As Carver explains the chart, a laissez-faire society (column I) has an average quality of humans equal to 5.5. He suggests that when an "inaccurate and ineffective fool-killer is at work" in column II, "the average is raised only from 5.5 to 6.6"—a "pretty heavy price to pay for so slight an improvement" (Figure 2.1). By contrast, the accurate fool-killer raises the average to 7, a result entailing "less slaughter" and "higher improvement."[65]

Carver in Los Angeles

Carver's first Los Angeles publication seems to have been the 1935 pamphlet "What we must do to save our economic system."[66] Here, his Proposition 1, "The American economic system is economic voluntarism,"[67] forwarded this positive claim and then continued with the negative claims: "It is not," Carver wrote, "the competitive system";[68]

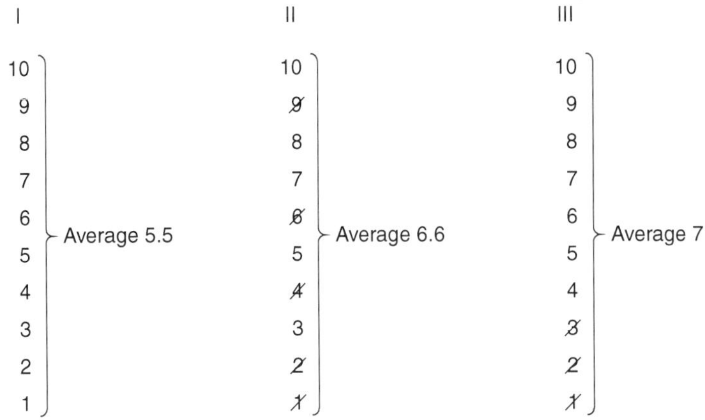

Figure 2.1 Killing fools, vice or policy.

"it is not the system of laissez faire";[69] "it is not the capitalist system";[70] "it is not the market economy";[71] "it is not the profit system."[72] Carver then pointed to the tension between laissez-faire and eugenics and he argued that lack of planning in the area of population control has been "most dangerous":

> In all this welter of discussion of economic planning, scarcely a word has been uttered by any planner on the important subject of population planning. Yet the population problem is fundamental, and *the most dangerous form of laissez faire is that which leaves the quantity and quality of our population to blind biological forces which are cruder and more dangerous than the so-called blind economic forces.* Such a let-alone policy would leave our population to be recruited from those regions where the standard of living is lowest and from the least intelligent strata of every population, our own included.[73]

After discussing the possibility of seizing Africa[74] and dismissing the possibility of communism,[75] Carver considered what might realistically be done to improve "the conditions of our people" with a given amount of land. His first solution was a proposal to "exclude immigrant labor in order to reduce the number of workers looking for jobs." Carver turned second to segregation or sterilization:

> Another is to segregate or sterilize the congenital defectives. This is one of the few rational things which have come out of

> Hitlerism. Another may be that Hitler is preparing his people to stand at Armageddon as the first line of defense against the inevitable Bolshevik invasion.[76]

Carver continued, discussing at some length knowledge of birth control and popular education to increase the productivity of working people.[77]

The pamphlet made a stir. We quote from a remarkably helpful account in the May 1, 1936, *Baltimore Sun* titled "New High in Brains":

> The theory that liberty is the *pièce de résistance* in the Republican program seems to have sustained a fearful blow from Prof. Thomas Nixon Carver, of Harvard, who is the reputed author of a little pamphlet on "What We Must Do to Save Our Economic System." In this pamphlet, according to Mr. Barkley in *The Evening Sun,* Professor Carver suggests "population planning" as a first necessity. He wants to sterilize the "palpably unfit," limit marriage to those who can afford an automobile and exclude all immigration. He suggests that Hitler and Mussolini may have the right idea, because "the hungry hordes of Russia, gazing covetously at countries blessed with capitalistic plenty, will someday invade Europe."
>
> One must conclude that Brain Truster Carver does not seem just the man to assist the Republican party in liberating us from regimentation. It is bad enough to be forced to submit to the intrusions of income tax auditors, crop control snoopers and so on, but if bureaucrats are to tell us that we may not marry unless we can afford an automobile along with a wife, then the situation, will be parlous, indeed. In view of the fact that most of these half-baked "population planning" ideas lie at the basis of Hitler's racial philosophy... Knowing the Republican leadership, we freely predict that the political geniuses will be more shocked by the anti-tariff record of Brain Trusters Tucker, Bradford and Carpenter than by Dr. Carver's extraordinary program for "population planning." Sterilization of the whole population and abolition of marriage altogether would seem less heinous in G. O. P. circles than objections to the Smoot-Hawley tariff.[78]

This was precisely the problem Hayek faced. Supposing he wanted to preserve classical liberalism, the influence of Carver and his admirers needed to be reduced entirely.

The Los Angeles Chamber of Commerce

Given Carver's impact in Los Angeles, it is not surprising that when he first appeared in the *Los Angeles Times*, at the meeting of the Los Angeles Chamber of Commerce, Leonard E. Read quoted Carver.[79] Read was taken by Carver's call for "voluntarism."[80] A notice in the *Times* tells us that Read would become "General Manager" of the Chamber as of January 23, 1939.[81] The timing is uncertain but we know from a *Times* report of July 7, 1941, that Carver was by then a director of the Chamber.[82] One suspects that General Managers report to the Board of Directors. On April 27, 1945, the *Times* announced Read's resignation of "yesterday" to become vice president of the National Industrial Conference Board.[83] In April 1945, the Chamber of Commerce published Carver's "How can there be full employment after the war?"[84] The pamphlet contained a foreword by one of Carver's "fellow members of the Board of Directors," President of the Chamber, LeRoy M. Edwards. Carver's views might explain the otherwise bizarre charge that Read was publishing "Nazi-type" material.[85]

Leading up to *The Fatal Conceit*

To make the case that Germany was fit to be reconnected with the liberal democracies, whatever allowed totalitarianism to take hold in Germany needed to be reversible. It is perhaps then no surprise that Hayek opposed any sort of racial explanation for the totalitarian experience in Germany since race is presumably irreversible.[86] But other formative figures in the MPS focused on eugenics and social Darwinism as the central aspect of the road away from liberalism. Hayek's "fellow combatant and age mate,"[87] Wilhelm Röpke, pointed to the role of social Darwinism in the founding ideology of the Hitler era. Social Darwinism in the "science" of eugenics degraded people to the level of cattle. "Stud farming" catches the horror exactly.[88]

Hayek's problem is this. He was attracted to evolutionary thinking. When his friend Jacob Viner reviewed *The Constitution of Liberty* he wondered whether Hayek's argument about institutional survival escaped the social Darwinism that he had explicitly argued against earlier.[89] James Buchanan offered the opinion that, without denigrating Hayek's contributions to economic theory, his greatest importance was as leader in the revival of liberalism. He recounted how the draft of Hayek's manuscript, *The Fatal Conceit*, was seen by the elders of the MPS as tinged with social Darwinism. Hayek agreed to have it edited and so to remove the dangerous material.[90] Many of the elders—Friedman, Stigler, Buchanan—had studied with Frank Knight.[91] The MPS, assembled by Hayek with Knight and von Mises as its intellectual leaders, was the guardian of classical liberalism against the predations of social Darwinism.[92] Famously, Hayek accepted their judgment and Popper's associate William Bartley edited *The Fatal Conceit* before its publication.[93]

In recent years, scholarly reflections on Hayek's contributions have split on the basis of the extent of evolutionary influences on Hayek. The complicated history of Hayek's most evolutionary book, *The Fatal Conceit*,[94] is often cited as a good reason not to take this as the definitive statement of Hayek's life's work;[95] indeed perhaps not to rely on it for anything of substance.[96] The question also relates to the difficulty of coming to grips with Hayek's position on evolutionary thinkers in the nineteenth and twentieth century who post-dated the thinkers of the Scottish enlightenment. John Gray has written about Hayek's relationship with Herbert Spencer[97] and Erik Angner about Hayek and A. M. Carr-Saunders.[98] Before any of this was published, Viner had expressed his concerns.[99]

A manuscript we believe to have been last in the possession of Hayek's secretary, Charlotte Cubitt, sheds light on some of these issues. This is represented as a lecture given in 1981. In the lecture, Hayek explicitly states that his argument against socialism presupposes a world comprised of small groups with unitary goals.[100] How do people find themselves with shared goals? The manuscript clarifies that Hayek's answer is genetic: Connections of altruism and sympathy among individuals in small groups are the result of our innate morality.

Now, we come to the crux of the matter. Unlike Hoover or Carver, who would enhance what is given biologically to pursue efficiency, Hayek resisted the turn to eugenics. For Hayek the morals of honesty, fairness, and reciprocity, which all conflict with our innate tendencies, emerged in larger groups with disparate goals. This put Hayek in opposition to arguments based on biologically determined (purported) hierarchy, whether the group is a race or an extended family. As Hayek saw things, because people learn to resist their innate moral instincts to equalize income, a division of labor emerges. In Hayek's telling, this had the unintended consequence of allowing more people to be born and to live. What is perhaps a surprise is how the argument ties in to population growth:

> That the selection of rules of conduct by those rules coming to prevail which lead to the most rapid increase of the number of

> those practicing them, is not a popular and is a somewhat complex story, but one which seems to me to provide a crucial key to the understanding of the growth and spread of civilizations. The first question I must try to settle briefly is why the replacement of an intuitive ethics of altruism and solidarity by a taught tradition of several property and honesty should have enabled men to maintain ever increasing numbers. The answer is contained in Adam Smith's famous dictum that "the division of labour is limited by the extent of the market." An increased density will make greater division of labour possible. Not only does specialisation or the division of labour increase productivity per head, and thereby enable human beings to maintain larger numbers, but the increase of numbers in turn increases the opportunities for division of labour and thus turns the whole into a self-accerating [sic] process.
>
> There exists today so much concern about an apprehended excessive increase of population, as well as a false belief that an increase of population normally brings about impoverishment, that the true fact, of it being really not only the regular effect but also an important cause of the growth of wealth is now rarely understood. But the greater the number of individuals in different positions who can use their distinctive knowledge and skills to serve others whom, and probably of whose existence, they do not know, by means of the assistance they receive from still others whom they also do not know, is the cause of the infinitely greater productivity of the extended and necessarily more numerous society.[101]

Hayek's argument is that increasing returns to scale brings about a higher level of productivity and consequently a larger population. The population linkage, which Hayek fails to clarify, might be the classical economists' hypothesis that higher wages in new countries where the demand for labor outstrips the supply of labor leads to early marriage.

The increasing returns argument depends upon and extends Hayek's earlier discussion of the division of knowledge.[102] As the number of people increase, and the number of connections among individuals, one way of thinking about the possible gains from exchanging knowledge, increases in a large number setting with the square of the population size (Metcalfe's Law).[103] Hayek did not believe "perfect competition" to be a useful model so he would have no difficulty integrating an increasing returns formulation in his teaching.[104]

Some passages in the published *The Fatal Conceit* seem to have been drawn from this lecture but they are altered beyond recognition.[105] One can only speculate about whether this represents Hayek's rethinking between the time of the lecture and the composition of *The Fatal Conceit*. In the book, the lecture's (Smithian) division of knowledge/increasing returns argument has been replaced with a (Ricardian) homogeneous labor input.[106]

Conclusion

In "Individualism: True and False" Hayek argued that "false" individualists were insufficiently attentive to small groups in which individuals naturally find themselves: "false" individualists were all too willing to trade the well-being of a small group for that of a larger. The debate over the abolition of slavery is one in which the question of concern for the near versus concern for the distant was most dramatically raised in the nineteenth century. Charles Dickens's criticism of "telescopic philanthropy" reflects a deep unhappiness with those like Mill who were concerned with distant people.[107]

In Hayek's 1981 lecture, he offered a genetic explanation for why we are connected in small groups and argued that these connections are attenuated when we move to large groups where universal norms of reciprocity and fairness emerge instead. Would John Stuart Mill, who offered the Sermon on the Mount as the exemplar of utilitarian ethics in *Utilitarianism*, ask for anything more? It is most pleasing to find this old disagreement between those from whom we have learned so much settled amicably.

We stress in conclusion the significance of Hayek's achievement described in the foregoing sections. In the nineteenth century "scientists" outside of political economy, in anthropology, biology, and literature, injected notions of "race," as they defined it, and hierarchy into social science theorizing. Political economists such as John Stuart Mill opposed this thinking. He worked tirelessly alongside the British evangelicals to resist explanations of social and economic outcomes based on innate tendencies that purportedly caused poverty in Ireland and elsewhere. Notwithstanding the opposition of mid-nineteenth-century political economists, hierarchical thinking entered into social science by the turn of the century. Thus, many social scientists came to accept a theoretical outlook that held some races or groups of people to be naturally less suited to making rational decisions than others.

The narrative above strongly suggests that a renewed effort to inject "race" or "nature" into explanations of economic outcomes transpired during the middle of the twentieth century. More than this, the positions put forward by Hart, Buckley, Hoover, and Carver had an added feature that might make their overall positions attractive to economists who placed their hopes in markets: Each of the intellectuals we have considered earlier also emphasized the case for limited government intervention. Again, however, the political economists in our view emerge as the "good guys," who served to rid economics of "biological" explanations of choice or poverty. Hayek, prompted by the MPS elders such as Knight's follower, James Buchanan, even allowed his manuscript to be given over for editing. More than this, he distanced himself from Buckley, from Hart, and from Carver at a time when these intellectuals enjoyed enormous influence as public intellectuals. We can only speculate about what would have happened had he not done so.

The tension between those who wish to limit the influence of government and yet who would at the same time have the government control key decisions made by some among us (those deemed to be "inferior") has mostly been eradicated from economics. It nonetheless still exists in the political arena.

Notes

1. Friedrich A. Hayek, "Individualism: True and False," in *Individualism and Economic Order* (Chicago, IL: University of Chicago Press, [1945] 1948), 1–32; Friedrich A. Hayek, "The Use of Knowledge in Society," in *Individualism and Economic Order* (Chicago, IL: University of Chicago Press, [1945] 1948), 77–91. For a more extensive discussion, see Sandra J. Peart, "Editor's Introduction," in *Collected Works of F. A. Hayek*, ed. Sandra J. Peart, vol. 16, *Hayek on Mill: The Mill-Taylor Friendship and Related Writings* (Chicago, IL: University of Chicago Press, 2014).
2. See Bruce Caldwell's assessment in "Editor's Introduction," in *Collected Works of F. A. Hayek*, ed. Bruce Caldwell, vol. 13, *Studies on the Abuse and Decline of Reason: Texts and Documents* (Chicago, IL: University of Chicago Press, 2010), 1–45: "The distinction between the hubris of the scientistic approach and the humility of individualism would be a major theme of Hayek's 'Individualism: True and False,' and would reappear in later writings as the contrast between constructivist rationalism and the evolutionary way of thinking" (p. 13).
3. Hayek, "Individualism: True and False," 7.
4. Ibid., 10.

5. Ibid., 4. There was in Hayek's view yet another problem with such rationalism, its narrow conception of economic man. See Friedrich A. Hayek, *The Collected Works of F. A. Hayek*, ed. Ronald Hamowy, vol. 17, *The Constitution of Liberty: The Definitive Edition* (Chicago, IL: University of Chicago Press, [1960] 2011), 121: "in the view of those British philosophers, man was by nature lazy and indolent, improvident and wasteful, and that it was only by force of circumstances that he could be made to behave economically or would learn carefully to adjust his means to an end. The *homo oeconomicus* was explicitly introduced, with much else that belongs to the rationalist rather than the evolutionary tradition, only by the younger Mill." Leonidas Montes, "Is Friedrich Hayek Rowing Adam Smith's Boat?" in *Hayek, Mill, and the Liberal Tradition*, ed. Andrew Farrant (London: Routledge, 2011), 19, argues that Hayek suggests that Mill here departed from Adam Smith. In this respect, it now seems fair to say that Hayek was mistaken; Mill's conception of economic man is much more Smithian than that of economists late in the nineteenth century such as William Stanley Jevons. See also Sandra J. Peart, introduction to *W. S. Jevons: Critical Responses*, ed. Sandra J. Peart (London: Routledge, 2004) vol. I: 1–26.
6. Lorie Tarshis, *The Elements of Economics* (Boston, MA: Houghton Mifflin, 1947).
7. George H. Nash, *The Life of Herbert Hoover: The Engineer 1874–1914* (New York: Norton, 1983), 505.
8. Isaac Don Levine, "The Strange Case of Merwin K. Hart," *Plain Talk* 4 (February 1950): 1–9.
9. This is reported on the authority of manuscripts in the Merwin K. Hart papers in the Special Collections of the University of Oregon by John Moser, *Right Turn: John T. Flynn and the Transformation of American Liberalism* (New York: NYU Press, 2005), 169. John Chamberlain gives us the name of the privately financed staff member but not the funding source: "Percy Greaves was hired privately to help the minority Republicans who had no funds for a research staff." John Chamberlain, "Foreword," in Percy L. Greaves, Jr., *Pearl Harbor: The Seeds and Fruits of Infamy*, ed. Bettina B. Greaves (Auburn, AL: Ludwig von Mises Institute, 1991), xviii.
10. Karen Vaughn, *Austrian Economics in America: The Migration of a Tradition* (New York: Cambridge University Press, 1994).
11. John B. Judis, *William F. Buckley, Jr.: Patron Saint of the Conservatives* (New York: Simon and Schuster, 1988), 45, 122; Brian Doherty, *Radicals for Capitalism: A Freewheeling History of the Modern American Libertarian Movement* (New York: Public Affairs, 2007), 178, 314, 651, 675.
12. The 1952 study by the Anti-Defamation League emphasizes Hart's centrality. See Arnold Forster and Benjamin R. Epstein, *The Trouble-Makers: An Anti-Defamation League Report* (Garden City, NY: Doubleday, 1952), 199: "Hart is probably the most ubiquitous of the network figures. He is a registered lobbyist whose activities were closely examined by the House Select Committee on Lobbying Activities of the 81st Congress." The same judgment is found in their later *Danger on the Right*: "[he] was a focal point for much of the Extreme Rightist activity of the 1940s and 1950s." Quoted from Arnold Forster and Benjamin R. Epstein, *Danger on the Right* (New York: Random House, 1964), 107.

13. David C. Colander and Harry Landreth, eds., *The Coming of Keynesianism to America: Conversations with the Founders of Keynesian Economics* (Cheltenham, UK: Edward Elgar, 1996); Paul A. Samuelson, "Credo of a Lucky Textbook Author," *Journal of Economic Perspectives* 11, no. 2 (1997): 153–69; David M. Levy and Sandra J. Peart, "Soviet Growth and American Textbooks: An Endogenous Past," *Journal of Economic Behavior and Organization* 78, nos. 1–2 (April 2011): 110–25. See also David M. Levy, Sandra J. Peart, and Margaret Albert, "Economic Liberals as Quasi-Public Intellectuals: The Democratic Dimension," *Research in the History of Economic Thought and Methodology* 30, no. 2 (2012): 1–116.
14. William F. Buckley, Jr., *God and Man at Yale: The Superstitions of "Academic Freedom"* (Chicago, IL: Regnery [1951] 2002), 64. "I am also grateful to the National Economic Council for its telling analysis of the Tarshis book (*Review of Books,* August 1947)." Ibid., 221. Contemporary discussions linked Hart's *Review of Books* to Buckley, for example, [F. Porter Sargent], *Educational Directions: A Report–1951* (Boston: F. Porter Sargent, 1952), 93: "Some of Buckley's objections coincide with those of Rose Wilder Lane, whose review for Merwin K. Hart's National Economic Council he quotes. Miss Lane was formerly a writer of fiction." The public reaction of those who were attacked was very late in coming. See Colander and Landreth, *Coming of Keynesianism*; Samuelson, "Credo." The reviews and some items in the Hart campaign to rid the campus of the Tarshis text are reprinted in Levy, Peart, and Albert, "Economic Liberals."
15. The documentary record is found in Box 2, Folder 34, Merwin K. Hart Papers. Special Collections and University Archives, University of Oregon.
16. William F. Buckley, Jr. and L. Brent Bozell, *McCarthy and His Enemies* (Chicago, IL: H. Regnery, 1954).
17. William F. Buckley, Jr., *Up from Liberalism* (New York: McDowell Obolensky, 1959).
18. William F. Buckley, Jr., "Introduction to the Twenty-Fifth Anniversary Edition," in *God and Man at Yale: The Superstitions of 'Academic Freedom,'* ed. William F. Buckley, Jr. (Chicago, IL: Regnery, [1977] 2002), xiv–lviii. A less obvious moment to confront the past came when in the blast from the John Birch Society protesting *National Review's* attack, Buckley's discussion of the textbooks was singled out for praise. See John F. McManus, *William F. Buckley, Jr.: Pied Piper for the Establishment* (Appleton, WI: John Birch Society, 2002), 54: "a lengthy chapter crammed with passages from economics textbooks that were required reading. Buckley presented convincing evidence that the books promoted socialism, Keynesianism, and other collectivist nostrums while disparaging individualism, free enterprise, and limited government." Oddly enough the Hart linkage is not noticed by Nash. See George H. Nash, "*God and Man at Yale* Revisited," *Reappraising the Right: The Past and Future of American Conservativism* (Wilmington, DE: ISI Books, 2009), 133–47.
19. William F. Buckley, Jr., *In Search of Anti-Semitism* (New York: Continuum, 1992), 4–6.
20. Spencer's name does not appear in *The Road to Serfdom*. In Hayek, "Individualism: True and False," 11, Spencer is linked to Mill's "false" individualism on the basis

of their shared rationalism. In the exchange published in Mill's *Utilitarianism*, Spencer distinguished his utilitarianism from Mill's on the basis of his rationalism and Mill's empiricism. See Sandra J. Peart and David M. Levy, *The "Vanity of the Philosopher": From Equality to Hierarchy in Post-Classical Economics* (Ann Arbor, MI: University of Michigan, 2005), 214–15.

21. Albert J. Nock, review of *The Road to Serfdom*, by F. A. Hayek, *Economic Council Review of Books* 2 (October 1944): 1–2.
22. Charles Lam Markmann, *The Buckleys: A Family Examined* (New York: William Morrow, 1973), 90: "Buckley, who went to Chicago from Mexico for the radio appearance, was taken to lunch with Hayek, whom everyone expected to be basically in accord with Buckley and who deeply differed with him on academic freedom, which for Hayek, regardless of his personal conservatism, was or ought to be inviolate." Nash, *God and Man*, 143: "Friedrich Hayek, from whom Buckley badly wanted a blurb for the book, declined to give him one, the great economist objected strenuously to Buckley's chapter on academic freedom."
23. Provided to us by Angus Burgin from 3/25/1951, Hayek Papers, Box 24, Folder 19. Our thanks! We are grateful to the Estate of F. A. Hayek for permission to quote.
24. This ought not to be a surprise from the greatest of the J. S. Mill scholars of his generation. See Peart, Editor's Introduction to *Hayek on Mill*. Hayek's disagreement with Mill is very localized, Sandra J. Peart, "We're All 'Persons' Now: Classical Economists and Their Opponents on Marriage, the Franchise and Socialism," *Journal of the History of Economic Thought* 31, no. 1 (2009): 3–20.
25. Quoted in Colander and Landreth, *Coming of Keynesian Economics*, 43.
26. Friedrich A. Hayek, *The Collected Works of F. A. Hayek*, vol. 2, *The Road to Serfdom: Texts and Documents: The Definitive Edition*, ed. Bruce Caldwell (Chicago, IL: University of Chicago Press, [1944] 2007), 240. Recent scholarship has emphasized how important Henry Simons was in Hayek's plans for the future. See Angus Burgin, *The Great Persuasion: Reinventing Free Markets since the Depression* (Cambridge, MA: Harvard University Press, 2012).
27. Friedrich A. Hayek, "'Free' Enterprise and Competitive Order," in *Individualism and Economic Order* (Chicago, IL: University of Chicago Press, [1947] 1948), 117.
28. On the front flap of the dust jacket of Henry Simons, *Economic Policy for a Free Society* (Chicago, IL: University of Chicago Press, 1948). The practice of university libraries to discard dust jackets might perhaps be compared with the treatment by rare book dealers. We acknowledge helpful correspondence with Angus Burgin on this issue.
29. Hayek with evident amusement remembers acting as Eucken's translator at the 1947 MPS. "And I believe that Eucken's success in 1947—as the only German attending a scholarly international conference—contributed a little, if I may use this term, to the rehabilitation of German scholars on the international scene. Up to that time, my American friends in particular had been asking, 'Do you really dare to invite Germans too?'" F. A. Hayek, "The Rediscovery of Freedom," in *The Collected Works of F. A. Hayek*, ed. Peter G. Klein, vol. 4, *The Fortunes of Liberalism: Essays on Austrian Economics and the Ideal of Freedom* (Chicago, IL: University of Chicago Press, 1992), 192. Richard Ware remembered, after a

lapse of 60 years, Walter Eucken's impact (Richard Ware interview by Peart and Levy, 2008).

30. Hayek, "Individualism: True and False" disparaged such sanctification of the status quo as an impediment to "true" individualism. This is yet another reason to lament that he did not review *God and Man at Yale*.
31. Buckley, *God and Man*, 84–85.
32. John Chamberlain, "Foreword," in Buckley, *God and Man*, lxi.
33. Rose Wilder Lane and Jasper Crane, *The Lady and the Tycoon: Letters of Rose Wilder Lane and Jasper Crane*, ed. Roger Lea MacBride (Caldwell, ID: Caxton, 1973), 106.
34. Ibid., 78.
35. "It will be on Germans who have carried on in this manner... that our hopes must rest, and to them that we must give any assistance we can. The task of finding them and assisting them without at the same time discrediting them with their own people will be a most difficult and delicate one." Quoted from Friedrich A. Hayek, "Historians and the Future of Europe," in *Fortunes of Liberalism* [1944], 202. Recovery of a liberal tradition inside Germany "would be hopeless if there were in Germany no men or women at all who will adhere to the beliefs that we wish to see again victorious. But unless during the last two years they have all been killed, there is good reason to believe that we shall find in Germany such men and women, a small number it is true, but not so few in comparison with the number of people who think independently in any nation." Ibid., 224.
36. "Hayek notes that John Maynard Keynes had become a hero on the European continent by writing *The Economic Consequences of the Peace.* Keynes argued that the defeated Germany (and the Germans had come to regard themselves as not so much defeated as betrayed into a punitive armistice) could not pay the reparations which France demanded without exports at a level which the other powers would not tolerate." Quoted from Stephen Kresge and Leif Wenar, "Introduction," in *Hayek on Hayek*, ed. Stephen Kresge and Leif Wenar (London: Routledge, 1994), 9.
37. John Maynard Keynes, *The Economic Consequences of the Peace* (New York: Harcourt, Brace and Howe, [1919] 1920), 274. He concludes: "The ungrateful Governments of Europe owe much more to the statesmanship and insight of Mr. Hoover and his band of American workers than they have yet appreciated or will ever acknowledge. The American Relief Commission, and they only, saw the European position during those months in its true perspective and felt towards it as men should. It was their efforts, their energy, and the American resources placed by the President at their disposal, often acting in the teeth of European obstruction, which not only saved an immense amount of human suffering, but averted a widespread breakdown of the European system." Ibid.
38. The manuscript has a date of July 19, 1946. Its province is as follows. A collection of Hayek manuscripts, his postcards to Charlotte Cubitt, and memorabilia were sold at an auction at Bonham's (Sale 15231 Lot 42) on June 26, 2007. The lot was purchased by a British rare book dealer from whom we purchased all but the manuscript "The Marxian Theory of the Crisis." We hope to publish the

manuscript when we deal with the differences between the foreign policy views of Hayek and the individualists. Preliminary discussions with the specialists at the Hoover Presidential Library in 2012 have not led us to reject the hypothesis that the manuscript is authentic.

39. George H. Nash, introduction to *American Individualism and The Challenge to Liberty*, by Herbert Hoover (West Branch, IA: Herbert Hoover Presidential Library Association, 1989), 1–28; George H. Nash, "Foreword," in *Two Faces of Liberalism: How the Hoover–Roosevelt Debate Shapes the 21st Century*, ed. Gordon Lloyd (Salem, MA: M & M Scrivener, 2007), vi–x.
40. Herbert C. Hoover, *The Principles of Mining: Valuation, Organization and Administration Copper, Gold, Lead, Silver, Tin and Zinc* (New York: McGraw Hill, 1909), 163.
41. Nash, *Life of Herbert Hoover*, 505.
42. Roger C. Bannister notes Carver's role as satisfying the stereotype of the laissez-faire eugenicist. See Roger C. Bannister, *Social Darwinism: Science and Myth in Anglo-American Social Thought* (Philadelphia, PA: Temple University Press, 1979), 241.
43. Henry Hazlitt remained an industrious popularizer of Carver well into the 1960s. See Levy, Peart, and Albert, "Economic Liberals."
44. Bastiat's *The Law* was printed as the first of the Los Angeles *The Freeman* series. See Frederic Bastiat, *The Law, The Freeman* 1 (Los Angeles: Pamphleteers [1850], 1944) and then again, with a new translation by the Foundation for Economic Education, Frederic Bastiat, *The Law*, trans. Dean Russell Irvington-on-Hudson, NY: Foundation for Economic Education, [1850] 1950). The importance of getting Bastiat right can be judged by the fact that Bertrand de Jouvenel was engaged to check the new translation.
45. Thomas Nixon Carver, *Recollections of an Unplanned Life* (Los Angeles: The Ward Ritchie Press, 1949), 241.
46. Leonard E. Read, *Pattern for Revolt* (Santa Ana, CA: Register Publishing, 1945), 21.
47. Richard Hofstadter, *Social Darwinism in American Thought* (Boston: Beacon Press, [1944] 1992).
48. Philip Mirowski and Dieter Plehwe, eds., *The Road from Mont Pèlerin: The Making of the Neoliberal Thought Collective* (Cambridge, MA: Harvard University Press, 2009).
49. Watts is described in *Road from Mont Pèlerin*, 21, 198, as a FEE executive. His tenure was quite short; by 1950 when he was writing for Hart's *Economic Council Reviews*, he was no longer at FEE. See Levy, Peart, and Albert, "Economic Liberals." Samuelson gives a Knightian reading of Watts and Carver: Paul A. Samuelson, review of *Do We Want Free Enterprise*?, by Orval Watts, *The Annals of the American Academy of Political and Social Science*, 236 (November 1944): 198–99. Watts's role in the textbook controversy of the early 1950s seems to have been generally overlooked. In the correspondence between Lane and Crane, Watts's name comes up as often as Hayek's and von Mises's. See Lane and Crane, *Lady and the Tycoon*. The correspondence is important for insight into "business

conservatives" and the MPS. See Kim Phillips-Fein, "Business Conservatives and the Mont Pèlerin Society," in *The Road from Mont Pèlerin*, 280–301.

50. E. Böhm-Bawerk, "Capital and Interest Once More: I, Capital vs. Capital Goods," *The Quarterly Journal of Economics* 21 (November 1906): 1–21.
51. Carver, *Recollections*, 253–54.
52. Thomas Nixon Carver, [Remarks], *Ninety-Second Annual Conference of the Church of Jesus Christ of Latter-day Saints* (Salt Lake City, UT: Church of Jesus Christ of Latter-day Saints, 1922).
53. Thomas Nixon Carver, "The Demand for Money," *Economic Journal* 44, no. 174 (June 1934): 188–206.
54. Carver, *Recollections*, 236, 240–44.
55. Ward Ritchie, *Fine Printing: The Los Angeles Tradition* (Washington: The Library of Congress, 1987).
56. Armen Alchian and Friedrich A. Hayek, interview included in *Nobel Prize Winning Economist: Friedrich A. von Hayek* (Los Angeles: University of California, Oral History Program, 1983). http://www.archive.org/stream/nobelprizewin nin00haye/nobelprizewinnin00haye_djvu.txt (accessed May 6, 2013).
57. Thomas Nixon Carver, *Essential Factors in Social Evolution* (Cambridge, MA: Harvard University Press, 1935), 344.
58. Thomas Nixon Carver, *Essays on Social Justice* (Cambridge, MA: Harvard University Press, 1915), 99.
59. Thomas Nixon Carver, *The Religion Worth Having* (Boston, and New York: Houghton Mifflin, 1912), 79–80.
60. Ibid., 82.
61. Levy, Peart, and Albert, "Economic Liberals."
62. Thomas Nixon Carver, *Principles of National Economy* (Boston: Ginn, 1921), 601–02.
63. Ibid., 603.
64. Ibid.
65. Ibid.
66. Thomas Nixon Carver, *What Must We Do to Save our Economic System?* (Los Angeles: [self-published?] 1935).
67. Ibid., 4.
68. Ibid., 6.
69. Ibid., 10.
70. Ibid., 12.
71. Ibid., 20.
72. Ibid., 21.
73. Ibid., 65–66, emphasis added.
74. Ibid., 68–69.
75. Ibid., 70.
76. Ibid., 71. Carver's 1945 defense of population planning, along with a possible defense of the Hitler regime's sterilization of the unfit is reprinted in Levy, Peart, and Albert, "Economic Liberals."

77. Carver, *Save our Economic System,* 70–72.
78. *Baltimore Sun*, May 1, 1936, p. 14.
79. *Los Angeles Times*, June 2, 1936, p. A1.
80. Leonard E. Read, *The Romance of Reality* (New York: Dodd, Mead, 1937), 111–12.
81. *Los Angeles Times*, January 14, 1939, p. A1.
82. Ibid., July 7, 1941, A13.
83. Ibid., April 27, 1945, A1.
84. Thomas Nixon Carver, "How Can There be Full Employment after the War?" *The Economic Sentinel* 3 (Los Angeles Chamber of Commerce, Los Angeles, 1945).
85. Doherty, *Radicals*, 152.
86. Hayek, *Road to Serfdom,* 61: "We shall never be successful in our dealings with the Germans until we understand the character and the growth of ideas which now govern them. The theory which is once again put forth, that the Germans as such are inherently vicious, is hardly tenable and not very creditable to those who hold it. It dishonors the long series of Anglo-Saxon thinkers during the last hundred years have gladly taken over what was best, and not only what was best, in German thought. It overlooks the fact that, when 80 years ago John Stuart Mill was writing his great essay *On Liberty*, he drew his inspiration, more than from any other men, from two Germans—Goethe and Wilhelm von Humboldt—and forgets the fact that two of the most influential intellectual forebears of National Socialism—Thomas Carlyle and Houston Stewart Chamberlain—were a Scot and an Englishman. In its cruder forms this view is a disgrace to those who by maintaining it adopt the worse features of German racial theories."
87. Hayek, "Tribute to Röpke," *Fortunes of Liberalism*, 195.
88. More recent studies of the linkage between social Darwinism and Nazi ideology are found in Hans-Gunter Zmarzlik, "Social Darwinism in Germany, Seen as a Historical Problem," trans. Ralph Mannheim, in *Republic to Reich: The Making of the Nazi Revolution*, ed. Hajo Holborn (New York: Pantheon, [1963] 1972), 435–74; Daniel Gasman, *The Scientific Origin of National Socialism: Social Darwinism in Ernst Haeckel and the German Monist League* (London: MacDonald, 1971); Mike Hawkins, *Social Darwinism in European and American Thought, 1860–1945* (Cambridge: Cambridge University Press: 1997); Neil MacMaster, *Racism in Europe: 1870–2000* (New York: Palgrave, 2001). Charles Kingsley's role in combining Thomas Carlyle with Charles Darwin and putting forward a theology of extermination should not be overlooked. See David M. Levy and Sandra J. Peart, "Charles Kingsley and the Theological Interpretation of Natural Selection," *Journal of Bioeconomics* 8, no. 3 (November 2006): 197–218.
89. Jacob Viner, "Hayek on Freedom and Coercion," *Southern Economic Journal* 27 (1961): 230–36.
90. James M. Buchanan, Workshop Discussion of F. A. Hayek (Fairfax, Virginia, April 6, 2005).
91. Buchanan, Workshop Discussion, points to the importance of Richard Ware's insistence that Hayek's evolutionary move would undermine Hayek's earlier

contributions. Ware was close to Warren Nutter on whose thinking Knight had an enormous impact (Richard Ware interview by Peart and Levy, 2008). Knight's opposition to Carver is found in Frank H. Knight, review of *The Economy of Human Energy*, by Thomas Nixon Carver, *Journal of Social Forces* 3, no. 4 (May 1925): 777–78, and the larger link between efficiency and ethics is of great importance here. John Rawls's annotation of Knight's *Ethics of Competition* brings out the connection between the Knightian era at Chicago and later Rawlsian thinking as seen in Frank H. Knight, *Ethics of Competition and Other Essays* (New York: Augustus Kelley, [1935] 1951) with annotations by John Rawls. (Now in the possession of Levy and Peart.) See also James M. Buchanan and John Rawls, "The Buchanan-Rawls Correspondence," in *The Street Porter and the Philosopher: Conversations in Analytical Egalitarianism*, ed. Sandra J. Peart and David M. Levy (Ann Arbor, MI: University of Michigan, 2008), 397–418.

92. Karl R. Popper, *The Open Society and Its Enemies* (Princeton, NJ: Princeton University Press, 1945); Ludwig von Mises, *Human Action: A Treatise on Economics*, ed. Bettina Bien Greaves (Indianapolis: Liberty Fund, [1949] 2007): 171–74.
93. Friedrich A. Hayek, *The Fatal Conceit: The Errors of Socialism*, ed. W. W. Bartley III (Chicago, IL: University of Chicago Press, 1988).
94. Alan Ebenstein, *Hayek's Journey: The Mind of F. A. Hayek* (New York: Palgrave, 2003), 220–32; Bruce Caldwell, *Hayek's Challenge: An Intellectual Biography of F. A. Hayek* (Chicago, IL: University of Chicago Press, 2004), 314–19.
95. Viktor J. Vanberg, *The Constitution of Markets* (London and New York: Routledge, 2001).
96. Gerald F. Gaus, "Social Complexity and Evolved Moral Principles," in *Liberalism, Conservativsm, and Hayek's Idea of Spontaneous Order*, ed. Louis Hunt and Peter McNamara (New York: Palgrave, 2007), 149–76.
97. John Gray, *Hayek on Liberty*, third edition (London: Routledge, [1984] 1998), 103–10.
98. Erik Angner, *Hayek and Natural Law* (London and New York: Routledge, 2007).
99. Viner, "Hayek on Freedom."
100. Sandra J. Peart and David M. Levy, "Hayek's Sympathetic Agents," in *Hayek and Liberalism*, ed. Andrew Farrant (London: Routledge, 2011), 39–56.
101. Friedrich A. Hayek, "The Changing Range and Content of Individual Responsibility." The manuscript from which we quote was part of the Bonham's lot (discussed in endnote 38) and has an attributed date of 1981. We are grateful to the Estate of F. A. Hayek for permission to quote from the manuscript in our holding.
102. Friedrich A. Hayek, "Economics and Knowledge," in *Individualism and Economic Order* (Chicago, IL: University of Chicago Press, [1937] 1948), 33–56; "The Use of Knowledge in Society," in *Individualism and Economic Order* (Chicago, IL: University of Chicago, [1945] 1948), 77–91.
103. Metcalfe's Law. http://en.wikipedia.org/wiki/Metcalfe's_law.
104. Friedrich A. Hayek, "The Meaning of Competition," in *Individualism and Economic Order* (Chicago, IL: University of Chicago Press, [1946] 1948), 92–106.

105. Hayek, *Fatal Conceit*, 120–21.
106. For Buchanan's exposition of Smith's increasing returns to scale argument see James Buchanan, "Let Us Understand Adam Smith," *Journal of the History of Economic Thought* 30, no. 1 (2008): 21–28.
107. Peart and Levy, *Vanity of the Philosopher.*

PART II

Contributions to Political Economy in Theory and Practice

CHAPTER THREE

The Evolution, Evaluation, and Reform of Social Morality: A Hayekian Analysis

Gerald Gaus

The Fundamental Philosophical Question about the Evolution of Morality

Two Senses of "Morality"

Like Darwin, I "fully subscribe to the judgment of those writers who maintain that of all the differences between man and the lower animals, the moral sense is by far the most important."[1] A fundamental project in evolutionary science is to understand how this distinctive capacity, which appears to require that an individual sometimes refrain from the course of action that maximizes his fitness,[2] could have evolved. We have recently witnessed powerful analyses of the evolution of biological and psychological altruism, reciprocal cooperation, of our ability to follow rules and to socially enforce them, and of the development of conscience. Most, but not all, of this work has focused on biological evolution, employing both natural and social selection models, and increasingly employing some version of multilevel selection. This important work has made great progress in helping us understand the evolution of the building blocks of cooperation and morality. And until we know how our basic moral sense could have evolved, the entire moral enterprise—and by extension, the nature of human social life—remains an evolutionary mystery.

As important as this work is, I shall largely put it aside here, and focus instead on another line of analysis: the evolution of social-moral rules or, we might say, systems of social morality. Suppose, as I think is the case, that not only our basic moral capacities have evolved but, through cultural evolution (or gene–culture coevolution), so has the content of our social morality—the system of moral rules and norms that forms the basis of our normative and empirical expectations, and which are enforced through general social disapproval of violations.[3] The simple yet fundamental philosophical question arises: *so what?* From the perspective of the social scientist it might be of utmost importance that culture evolves, and that our social-moral rules are a fundamental part of culture. Yet the moral philosopher wants to know what this *fact* about the history of our accepted social morality tells us about what our social rules *ought* to be. "[T]alk of morality," Anthony O'Hear points out, "is itself ambiguous. Do we mean morality as that which is done and enforced within a particular group? Or do we mean that which in some absolute sense simply ought to be done, regardless of group norms and loyalties? And what, if anything, is the connection between the two?"[4] If the first sense of morality does not tell us anything about the second, then the evolutionary theorist appears unable to shed any light on the moral philosopher's question: What rules ought we to have? Too often the evolutionist has simply dismissed the philosophers' concern. Ken Binmore, for instance, insists that "orthodox moral philosophy has gotten us nowhere because it asks the wrong questions. If morality evolved along with the human race, asking how we ought to live makes as much sense as asking what animals ought to exist, or which language we ought to speak."[5] This, though, seems more evasive than helpful. Surely, we can and do step back from our evolved morality and ask whether it is the one we ought to have.

The Allure of Progress

Moral and political philosophers committed to an evolutionary analysis of culture have often sought to connect O'Hear's two meanings of "morality" through a claim that evolution is morally progressive: the evolution of *positive morality* as that which is done and enforced within a particular group tends to increasingly approximate *true morality* in the sense of what truly ought to be done (or, let us say, the rules that are normatively justified). Nineteenth-century evolutionary accounts of morality invariably associated evolution with development or progress.[6] L. T. Hobhouse—perhaps the preeminent English political philosopher at the close of the century—applied evolutionary thought to social systems, seeking to show that evolution led to an increase in social integration and harmony, a research program that his student, Morris Ginsberg, continued throughout the first part of the twentieth century.[7]

A remarkably similar account of moral progress has recently been advanced by Philip Kitcher, one of today's leading philosophers of science. On Kitcher's analysis, the "ethical project" has its roots in our altruism failures—failures that lead to social conflict. Morality evolved as an adaptive response to such failures. The function of social morality throughout its evolutionary history has been, and remains, to remedy these failures. Echoing Hobhouse, Kitcher insists that "[e]thics must continue to promote social harmony through remedying altruism failure."[8] As Kitcher understands it, ethical progress is characterized by refinements in this function of social morality, leading to enhanced social harmony and, it seems, equality.[9] To be sure, Kitcher rejects what he calls "crude evolutionary reductionism" according to which, apparently, there is a one-to-one mapping of evolved positive group morality to progress in justified morality.[10] Ethical progress can be "unsteady," and evolutionary adaptations can be morally regressive yet, it seems, the evolution of positive and justified morality are closely tied.

Despite its allure, most careful analyses of social and moral evolution have long refused to associate the evolution of positive morality and moral progress. A fundamental concern has always been that progressive views often misunderstand evolution as a teleological process aiming at a goal, rather than a causal process driven by variation, selection, and transmission. Leaving aside this fundamental error, moral philosophers have been especially critical of more orthodox Darwinian accounts of morality via natural selection, pointing out that Darwin stressed the "struggle for existence" as a central organizing idea of his theory.[11] Many moral philosophers have been skeptical that this Malthusian selection mechanism systematically maps on to what is highest for humans.[12] Indeed, it was the moral valorizing of the struggle for existence and its outcomes that was so objectionable in the hands of nineteenth-century Darwinian sociologists such as William Graham Sumner.[13] So even if, say, evolution was "progressive" in some way, such as the development of complexity, many philosophers have insisted that there is no reason to think that this sort of progress constitutes, or implies, moral progress.[14]

Hayekian Analyses of the Evolution of Rules and Order

Cultural Evolution: Variation and Transmission

My aim in this essay is to take some preliminary steps toward understanding the conditions under which the evolution of positive morality is informative about true or justified morality, without appeal to vague claims that evolution is morally progressive. We cannot make headway on this problem, however, without being clearer about the idea of moral evolution, as I hope to show that different accounts have very different resources for answering our fundamental philosophical question. I suppose here an account of moral evolution as a feature of cultural evolution, a type of analysis pioneered by F. A. Hayek, and more recently advanced by, among others, Robert Boyd and Peter J. Richerson.[15] Hayek insisted that social evolution, though it was a path-dependent process[16] that relied on competitive selection, did not rely on Darwinian natural selection.[17] Cultural evolution, says Hayek, "simulates" Lamarckian evolution because acquired characteristics—rules and institutions—are transmitted from earlier to later generations.[18] This is accomplished, he argues, through individual-to-individual transmission of social-moral rules, crucially through imitation.[19] The more recent, and much more sophisticated, work of scholars such as Boyd and Richerson has greatly added to our understanding of cultural transmission, distinguishing conformity bias (doing as most others do), prestige bias (copying high status individuals), unbiased transmission, and various content-biased transmissions such as those having more vivid content.[20] It is important to appreciate that the teaching and preaching of social-moral rules is an important form of transmission.[21]

An evolutionary analysis requires, in addition to a *transmission* mechanism, sources of *variation* and *selection*. In cultural evolution, variation in social-moral rules can come from random changes, errors in transmission, drift, or explicit revision.[22] This last factor is especially important: There is no reason why a theory of cultural evolution cannot appeal to explicit efforts to improve social-moral rules; in this sense, cultural evolution is by no means simply "blind." Some might decide that a current moral rule is objectionable, and so, say start preaching an alternative. Although Hayek's evolutionary account is often criticized as having no room for conscious attempts at innovation, an evolutionary analysis *requires* variation, and Hayek certainly accepts that rules can be consciously altered.

Selection, Macro and Micro

Hayek's account of the selection mechanism is complicated, indeed more so than he often suggests. Selection occurs at both the macro- and microlevels.[23]

At the macro-level, "the selection process of evolution will operate on the order as a whole"; what is selected, Hayek argues, is an "order of actions" that arises from numerous interacting rules, other elements of the social system, and the wider environment.[24] At the macro-level selection pressures operate directly on "the order of actions of a group."[25] This distinction between a set of rules and the order of actions to which it gives rise is a fundamental insight of Hayek's, which allows us to distinguish the focus of selective pressure and the underlying rules, which are transmitted. On Hayek's analysis, a group of individuals living under a set of social rules *R*, composed of rules $\{r_1 \ldots r_n\}$, will give rise to a certain abstract pattern of social interactions, *O*, on which macro selection operates.[26] Hayek advanced a rather strong emergentist relation between *R* and *O*, seeing *R* as a complex system with *O* as an emergent property.[27] We need not follow him quite that far. What is fundamental to the analysis is that a specific order O_X is an abstract pattern of a large number of human interactions, which does not arise from any specific rule *r*, or the aggregated effects of a set of independent rules, but from a set of interacting rules in an environment *E*. Hayek described this as a sort of holism: "systems of rules of conduct will develop as a whole."[28] We need, though, to distinguish two aspects of this "holism." One is simply a restatement of the idea that *O* as a whole is the focus of macro selection; the other is that every rule in *R* is dependent on every other rule. This second claim is, once again, overly strong, and in any event not required for a Hayekian analysis; so long as there are considerable interdependencies in *R*, *O* will possess the sort of complex, nonaggregative relation to $\{r_1 \ldots r_n\}$ that characterizes adaptive landscapes, and, as we shall see, sets the stage for some of Hayek's crucial insights.

On Hayek's analysis, macro social evolution is based on a form of group selection. "The rules of conduct have . . . evolved because the groups who practiced them were more successful and displaced others."[29] Just what is meant by "group selection" is a vexed issue; models with very different dynamics are often categorized under this rather vague term.[30] Leaving nomenclature aside, a crucial claim is that if society S_1, characterized by order of actions O_1, is more productive than S_2 based on O_2, society S_1 will tend to win conflicts with S_2, a mechanism akin to natural selection.[31] But perhaps more importantly, the members of S_2, seeing the better-off participants in S_1 characterized by O_1, may either immigrate to S_1, or seek to copy the underlying rules R_1, thus inducing differential rates of reproduction between the two sets of underling rules.[32]

Although in some statements Hayek seems to suggest that all selection occurs at this macro-level, his more nuanced view is that, while the macro-level is the primary locus of selection, rule selection also takes place in the form of competition between rules within a society.[33] For a rule *r* to be selected, it must be contributory to a selected order, *O*, but it must also attract allegiance within the group of individuals who coordinate via *r*. Individuals are constantly testing rules to determine whether conformity suits their overall concerns; "it is, in fact, desirable that the rules should be observed only in most instances and that the individual should be able to transgress them when it seems to him worthwhile to incur the odium this will cause... It is this flexibility of voluntary rules which in the field of morals makes gradual evolution and spontaneous growth possible, which allows further modifications and improvements."[34] Although Hayek himself disparaged rule selection based on how well a rule conformed to one's social or moral ideals,[35] any plausible account of the selection of moral rules within a group must accord weight to how well those rules conform with the moral sense and judgment of different individuals.[36] One of the factors that determine within-group fitness of a moral rule is its ability to secure allegiance and be taught to the next generation. This is a case of content bias: Rules that accord with people's moral sensibilities are more apt to be learned and transmitted. Hayek was certainly right to model micro-evolution into his account, but he was needlessly restrictive of the factors that affect cultural success and transmission.

Two Landscapes

Adaptive Landscapes in Social Evolution

Having some idea of the outlines of a Hayekian account of social evolution, we can model it a bit more rigorously as a type of "rugged landscape." Consider a simplified version of Hayek's analysis, a set *R* with only two rules, r_1 and r_2. As Hayek stressed, the rules interact, such that their effects on *O* are not simply aggregative. The fitness of *O* is a nonadditive function of r_1 and r_2, thus giving rise to what is known as

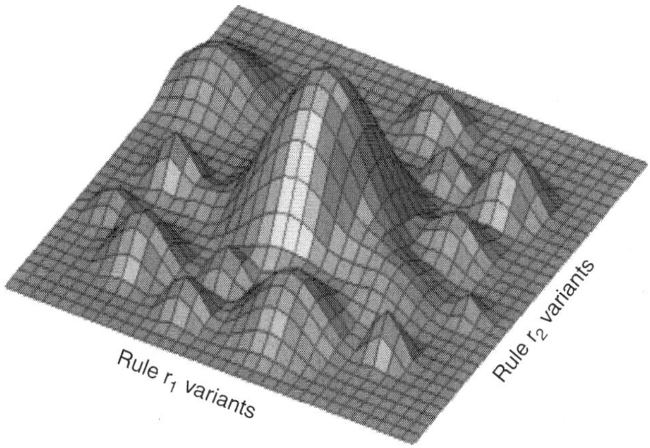

Figure 3.1 A Hayekian adaptive landscape.

Source: http://cairnarvon.rotahall.org/2007/01/02/on-fitness-landscapes. Used with permission.

an *NK* optimization problem, which characterizes many evolutionary adaptive landscapes. Figure 3.1 illustrates a highly simplified version of such a landscape.

I suppose for now (I shall relax this assumption later) an environment that is sufficiently stable such that the landscape does not significantly change. I suppose also that r_1 and r_2 are each classes of rule variants regulating some area of social life that can be arrayed along a dimension of similarity.[37] The topography of the landscape represents the fitness of the resulting *O*.[38] The ruggedness of the landscape results from the adaptive optimization problem possessing multiple *N* dimensions of evaluation with *K* interdependencies. When $K = 0$, that is, when there are no interdependencies between the dimensions, the landscape will not be rugged. Hayek's claim that selection operates on *O*, which emerges from *multiple interdependent rules*, however, commits him to the type of rugged adaptive landscape depicted in Figure 3.1.[39]

We can now see why a Hayekian cannot be a simple believer in social evolution as always leading up, up, and onward.[40] To take a simple case: If evolutionary selection focuses on two traits that are not interrelated, we can model the fitness landscape as having a single peak, as in Figure 3.2.

In this "Mount Fuji landscape," the global optimum will be reached by a series of selected variations, no matter where on the landscape society is. In Figure 3.2, we suppose that there is one trait that regulates

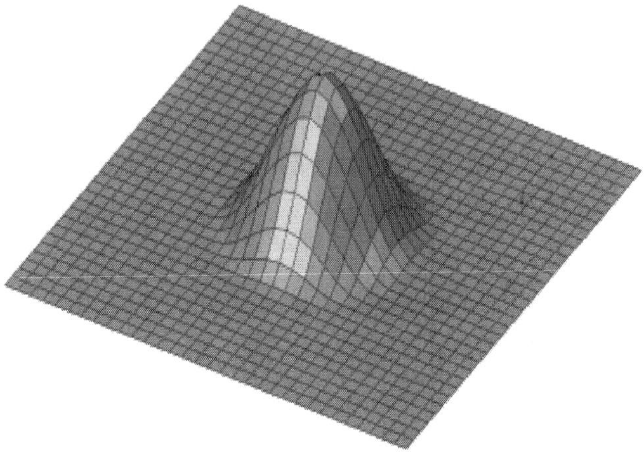

Figure 3.2 A Mount Fuji "progressive" landscape.

Source: http://cairnarvon.rotahall.org/2007/01/02/on-fitness-landscapes. Used with permission.

the functional capacity of the rules to resolve altruism failure, and that this is the only feature that is selected for. This results in constant gradients from all points to the global optimum. In contrast, in a rugged landscape it is possible for selection to get stuck at a local optimum that is far short of the global optimum. Occupying a local optimum—in Figure 3.1, the top of a small hill—any near variation in either r_1 or r_2 results in a less fit order of actions.

None of this is to say that orders cannot evolve to the global optimum in a rugged landscape. One important consideration (to which we shall return), is the size of the basin of attraction of the global optimum. In Figure 3.1 the basin is large: that is, from a number of different initial pairs of variations, there is a steady gradient to the global optimum. In other landscapes, as we shall see, the basin of attraction of the global optimum is much smaller. More generally, if different orders are spread over the landscape, some will climb to the top of higher local optima; under some conditions an order that climbs to a higher optimum (i.e., is more fit) could displace one stuck at a less fit one; if the less fit order observes the more fit, it may copy its $\{r_1, r_2\}$ variants and, perhaps, "jump" to the higher optimum. But observe also that even if *O*, stuck at a poor local optimum, can jump to a better local optimum, this could move *O further* away from the global optimum. The conditions under which *O* will find the global optimum is a fundamental issue in evolutionary modeling; we shall consider some of these matters later when we ask whether adaptive and evaluative landscapes are correlated.

Evaluative Landscapes

A striking development in the last 20 years has been the application of *NK* optimization analysis to a wide variety of evaluative problems. Rugged landscape models have been employed in management and other organizational contexts as an analysis of complex problem solving,[41] in epistemology and the philosophy of science as a way of understanding how diverse communities can best maximize a complex objective function,[42] and in the theory of collective deliberation and democracy.[43] I have explored how it can be applied in more explicitly social-moral theoretical contexts.[44]

Most large-scale moral evaluative problems in social and political philosophy readily fit the requirements of *NK* analysis. Consider, for example, questions of just distribution. Amartya Sen tells a parable of three children quarreling over a flute.[45] If, says Sen, we consider only claims based on who can best use the flute, it goes to Anne who alone can play it; if we consider only claims of need, it goes to Bob who is so impoverished that he has no other toys; if we consider only claims to desert and self-ownership, it goes to Carla, who made the flute. All three standards, Sen argues, qualify as impartial principles of justice. "At the heart of the particular problem of a unique impartial resolution of the perfectly just society is the possible sustainability of plural and competing reasons of justice, all of which have claims to impartiality and which nevertheless differ from—and rival—each other."[46]

If we follow Sen (and on this point I certainly think we should), justice is *multidimensional*. It also seems uncontroversial that these dimensions display *interdependencies*. For example, the "justice value" of a social state in which people generally deserve what they need—a wonderful condition—may be much higher than simply an aggregation of its need-satisfaction and desert-satisfaction scores; alternatively, a condition in which need and desert are balanced may be much more just than one that scores extraordinarily highly on one dimension but very low on the other. If optimizing justice is this sort of complex task, we are again confronted with an *NK* optimization problem, and so we are again confronted with a rugged landscape. Thinking back to our simple case of Figure 3.1, with simply two rule variants $\{r_1, r_2\}$, the topography is now determined not by Hayekian fitness, but by the justice score of each combination of variants.[47]

I thus model "justified morality" as a function that generates a "justified morality (or justice) score" for every order of actions that emerges from various rule combinations. Some philosophers may resist this, insisting that "true" or "justified morality" is a single unique point (on the modeling employed here, the global optimum). So some philosophers might maintain that the global optimum is all that counts: If we are not there, we are nowhere. Attractive as this may be to many philosophers, I set aside this rather austere depiction of our moral thinking. My concern is with those philosophers willing to adopt Sen's imagery of a moral mountain range, where we are trying to climb upward to increasingly just arrangements, while also recognizing that in some cases moving to a "more just" state of affairs may in some sense lead us further from the "most just" order.[48] It is this conception of "true" morality that is captured by the evaluative landscape model.

Conditions for the Correlation of the Two Landscapes

The Correlation View

We now see that for the theorist of social-moral evolution to reply to the philosopher's "so what?" challenge she need not appeal to some vague idea that evolution is a mechanism of moral progress. The question is: Are the adaptive and evaluative landscapes correlated? To the extent to which we have reason to suppose that the topographies of the two landscapes are positively correlated, we then have grounds for supposing that our evolved positive morality is indicative of true morality or justice. This is not to say that the fact of evolution is in itself a basic justificatory ground for claims about true morality or justice, but it is to say that the fact that our positive morality has evolved can ground a confidence that, to some extent, we also have made some headway toward true morality or justice.

Suppose we are at some point *a* on the adaptive landscape. If the two landscapes are significantly positively correlated, we know that how "well we have done" from the evolutionary perspective is indicative of how "well we have done" morally—our current position *m* on the moral landscape. This does not entail that either *a* or *m* is a local, much less a global, optimum, though evolutionary selection drives us toward local optima, and in some cases the global optimum; neither does correlation imply that, if *a* is a local or global optimum on the adaptive landscape, *m* will be one on the moral landscape.[49] And most importantly, the correlated landscapes view does not suppose that evolutionary and moral progress march hand-in-hand (the correlation need not be 1), much less that we are climbing perfectly correlated Mount Fuji landscapes. Because of this, the correlation view avoids one of the most dubious aspects of (some statements of) Hayek's analysis, which elsewhere I have called the "sufficiency claim"—that order *O* has evolved is sufficient reason for us to endorse it as moral, or at least not to question it.[50] As we shall see, moral evaluation, criticism, and reform make perfect sense on the correlation view. Yet it also captures Hayek's important insight that we do not know the full conditions for a perfectly just social order and could not plan one from scratch. We approach justice through an evolutionary process, but that does not mean an entirely blind or unconscious one.

The Substantive Condition for Correlation: Dancing in the Right Way

The Endogeneity of True Morality

The correlation view is compelling when two conditions hold. The first, which I explore in this section, is substantive: that we have available some plausible account such that one landscape causally affects the other, producing the positive correlation. Under this condition, an observed correlation would not be spurious, and we could have confidence that one landscape is in some way truly tracking the other. An important insight of Hayek is that the evaluative landscape tracks the adaptive landscape because, at any given time *t*, what we believe about true justice or morality (the evaluative landscape) is a function of our current cultural evolution (the adaptive landscape).

From the perspective of social and cultural evolution, we currently possess an evolved system of social morality. Now, Hayek argues, we certainly can criticize and reform this morality, but our resources for thinking this criticism through will crucially depend on our presently evolved morality. Hayek's rejection of proposed revolutions based on radical moral views is not that they criticize the current evolved morality, but that they fail to consider the entire evolved system, building on only some bits of it. "I wish neither to deny reason the power to improve norms and institutions nor even to insist that it is incapable of recasting the whole of our moral system in the direction now commonly conceived as 'social justice.' We can do so, however, only by probing every part of the system of morals."[51] On this account, then, our views of true morality (*i*) must commence with our currently evolved positive morality and (*ii*) an adequate criticism and reform must have some grounds for thinking that a revised system is, from the moral point of view, better. Recall that Hayek conceives of moral rules as producing an order of actions, which is a type of emergent property, on the system of moral rules; it is ultimately the pattern of human interactions, *O*, that we are interested in from the normative perspective. A proposed global moral reform that was only based on a fragment of positive morality (say, our devotion to equality), would have no grounds for predicting what order of actions could possibly result—except, perhaps, a reasonably certain knowledge that no order of actions at all would result, because the moral system had become too simplified.

This analysis of moral evaluation and reform has much in common with coherence analyses of justified belief. On a standard coherence view, one starts with a system of belief $\{b_1 \ldots b_n\}$, which forms a system of mutual inferences with a degree of coherence, *C*.[52] The aim of epistemic improvement—a body of better justified beliefs—is to improve *C* by alternations (basically, deletions and additions to) $\{b_1 \ldots b_n\}$, producing $\{b^\star_1 \ldots b^\star_m\}$. Now we can see that $\{b_1 \ldots b_n\}$ and $\{b^\star_1 \ldots b^\star_m\}$ will be strongly correlated. This is not to say that every case of belief change will result in marginal changes, such that the two sets always will be very similar; in some cases $\{b^\star_1 \ldots b^\star_m\}$ may be a rather large jump from $\{b_1 \ldots b_n\}$, for example, where some central organizing belief of the latter had to be dropped. But over the run of revisions, the two will be strongly correlated because $\{b^\star_1 \ldots b^\star_m\}$ is largely endogenous to $\{b_1 \ldots b_n\}$; the former is, to a large extent, the outgrowth of the latter. Not too surprisingly, just as Hayek's view has been deemed "conservative"[53] so have coherence theories; both see the current body of rules/beliefs as assets to be conserved while improving upon them. For both, the core insight is that we can only start our thinking from where we are, so an improvement typically will be a type of conservative modification of where we are.

To be sure, many moral theories deny (*i*) and (*ii*). Many assert that moral knowledge is entirely independent of current positive morality (e.g., some follow Plato in claiming to possess direct intuition of an objective, mind-independent, moral truth), or that moral improvement need not take into account the entire current system, but can select simply one part of our positive morality and employ it as the basis of a revolution in morals (as Godwin and Bentham sought to do with the greatest happiness principle). Our concern here is not to show that all proposed moral theories endorse correlation (that would be absurd) but to gain a better understanding of the sort of accounts of morality that do so.

How True Morality Affects Evolved Morality

We have seen that on a Hayekian account, at any given time *t*, what we believe about true justice or morality is a function of our current cultural evolution. Causal influence also runs in the other direction, for the positive morality evolved at *t* is to some extent the result of the population's views on true morality at *t*-1. As we have seen, on the Hayekian analysis, social evolution occurs at the micro- and macro-levels; especially important here is the former. At the microlevel, whether any specific rule variant *r* survives as part in the system of moral rules partly depends on *r*'s tendency to be internalized and followed by the population. Again, this depends on two key claims: (*i*) the population as a whole tends to have a reasonable grasp of justified or true morality and (*ii*) the tendency of individuals to internalize and act on rule variant *r* is significantly influenced by their understanding of true or justified morality. This second claim does not presuppose that this understanding is the sole factor influencing internalization and conformity. It is nearly universally acknowledged that normative guidance evolved, as it were, on top of an essentially egoistic motivational system;[54] the factors influencing rule conformity are certainly complex. We need only suppose here that reflective normative deliberation is an important factor in determining rule conformity: rules that strike many as mistaken, unjust, or unjustifiable, will tend to fail to attract sufficient conformity to survive in the moral system.[55] Striking examples are moral rules against homosexuality and homosexual parenting; they have been abandoned with breathtaking rapidity.

Many moral philosophers are apt to resist the first claim, that the population generally has a pretty good understanding of justified or true morality. From Plato to the present, moral philosophers have often insisted that inquiry into "true morality" is a specialized and technical endeavor for which only some (i.e., they) have adequate competence. Importantly, endorsing claim (*ii*) does not require denying that philosophers have expert knowledge.[56] Scott E. Page's analysis of optimization on rugged evaluative landscapes indicates that while a group of homogeneous experts (those conceiving of the problem in similar ways and employing similar approaches) will seldom get stuck at poor local optima, they do tend to get caught on "high" but suboptimal peaks. In contrast, in a diverse population of less (but not in-) competent searchers, some in the group will tend to (under certain assumptions, they definitely will) find the global optimum.[57] More generally, competent diversity rather than expertise is generally the best way to explore rugged evaluative landscapes.

This has fundamental implications for understanding Hayekian morality. As Hayek stressed, his main focus was on the evolution of morality in what he called "the Great Society,"[58] a large-scale diverse society. It is such diverse societies that provide the basic dynamics for efficient searching of rugged evaluative landscapes *if* one person's discoveries are taken up by others. To exploit the exploration of others[59] we need to learn from them or, more generally, copy them.[60] Conformity and prestige bias are no doubt important ways in which this occurs. In any event, we have reason to suppose that in certain sorts of diverse societies with significant copying of the successful, claim (*ii*) is warranted: The general population will have a good grasp of improvements on the evaluative landscape, and this will affect the fitness of rule variants.

Coupled Landscapes

The analysis of this section leads to the conclusion that in certain Hayekian views the adaptive and evaluative landscapes are coupled. Coupling of two adaptive landscapes is by no means unusual. If two species are interdependent, their adaptive landscapes will be coupled: A change in one species' adaptive landscape will produce changes in the landscape of the other. When this type of coevolution occurs we have dancing landscapes.[61] So too with the evolutionary and evaluative landscapes. Social evolution affects our views of what is morally justifiable and so changes the evaluative landscape, and these understandings of moral justifiability feed back into the adaptive landscape, changing the fitness of orders of actions. It is this dance that is the foundation of the moral relevance of social evolution.

Once two systems are coupled in this way, optimization dynamics become much more complex; neither system can be strictly modeled as having local optima that serve as steady attractors. Indeed, it can be difficult to model such systems in terms of optimization at all.[62] Modeling depends here on the nature of interactions and, as we shall presently see, characteristics of each landscape. Under some conditions couplings of rugged landscapes can lead to chaotic fluctuations in each landscape.[63] Crucial to whether the coupled systems are chaotic or display order is the complexity of each maximization problem, a question to which we will now turn.

The Formal Condition for Correlation: Modest Interdependence (No Radical Holism)

Critical to whether a rugged landscape has significant optima to which the system gravitates or, instead, displays chaotic features, is the complexity of the optimization problem. Recall that rugged landscapes are created by *NK* optimization problems: We are seeking to optimize over *N* dimensions with *K* interdependencies between the dimensions. Recall also that if $K = 0$, the *N* dimensions are independent, and we are faced with a simple aggregation problem. As we increase our success on any dimension we move higher on the landscape. However, as Kauffman stressed in his analysis, if we have a number of dimensions, and interdependencies are very high, the landscape will be fully random.[64] Let us call a *high-dimensional landscape* one in which many dimensions display a large number of interdependencies, at the limit each dimension is affected by all others ($K = N - 1$). In terms of social evolution, in a maximally high-dimensional landscape there is no systematic relation between the fitness of *O* and its one-rule variant mutation. Such landscapes have a very large number of poor local optima.[65]

The crux of such high-dimensional landscapes is that the fitness (or, more generally, value) of any one rule is a function of all others, producing what Kauffman called "a complexity catastrophe."[66] Now as we saw earlier, Hayek is attracted to a type of holism, as are many philosophers. "A sensible contractualism," writes T. M. Scanlon, "like most other plausible views, will involve holism about moral justification."[67] According to such holist views, the justification of every element of a system of values or beliefs is dependent on many others—such systems are often depicted as "webs," indicating a very high degree of interdependence among many variables. At the limit, each of the *N* elements is related to the $N - 1$ others. It is precisely such systems that give rise to complexity catastrophes; a small variation in one value can jump the system to a radically different state. Coupling two such systems produces a highly chaotic dance.

As *K* decreases (*i*) the number of local peaks decreases, (*ii*) the slopes lessen, so that the basin of attraction of the optima is wider (the same optimum is reached from a wider array of starting points), and (*iii*) the peaks are higher.[68] Additionally, in low-dimensional landscapes (*iv*) the highest optima tend to be near each other[69] and (*v*) the highest optima tend to have the largest basins of attraction.[70] As *K* decreases, the landscape becomes correlated within itself. In the case of the adaptive social evolutionary landscape, one-rule variants will yield orders of action *O** that have overall values that are correlated with that of the current order *O*. In a low-dimensional evaluative landscape, one-rule variants produce overall moral changes that are incremental vis-à-vis the current order.

Correlation of the adaptive and evaluative landscapes thus requires social evolutionary and moral evaluative theories that possess multiple dimensions with a modest degree of interdependence. In such correlated landscapes adaptive heights are associated with evaluative heights, and such heights have large basins of attraction; small changes do not drive either system to radically different values. What is required is that the landscapes waltz, not jitterbug.

All of this constitutes something like a possibility proof; under some conditions the two landscapes are correlated, and when this occurs, knowing that our social morality is adaptive tells us something important about true morality. The conditions for the correlated landscape answer to the philosopher's fundamental question are certainly nontrivial—but not, I think, implausible. I have argued elsewhere that evaluative judgments have modest interdependencies.[71] Whether the social evolutionary adaptive landscape is low/modest or high-dimensional is a critical issue to be investigated. On the one hand, it certainly is plausible to suppose that cultural traits are highly interconnected, forming complex systems with extremely rugged landscapes.[72] Yet relatively simple models and analyses that focus on the adaptive value of single traits have been extremely enlightening. And, indeed, insofar as cultural evolution postulates selection through copying useful traits, it must be possible to identify a trait (or small number of allied traits) as useful independently of the adaptiveness of the entire order, *O*, which results from their inclusion. While theorists such as Boyd and Richerson rightly insist that simple models can be useful steps in a cumulative understanding of more complex phenomena, this has its limits:[73] If the adaptive value of a very small variation in *O* is uncorrelated with *O*'s present value, models of the adaptive value of single traits become less enlightening.

Social Evolution and Moral Reform

Does Social Evolutionary Analysis Condemn Intentional Moral Change?

Focusing on the formal features of the landscapes also helps us make progress on a second question that is repeatedly raised about evolutionary accounts such as Hayek's: Do they provide a basis for deliberative criticism and intentional reform of our morality? Hayek depicts an order of actions *O* as an emergent property that arises out of a complex and self-organizing system of moral rules, *R*. He repeatedly stresses that because *R* is a complex system, its behavior cannot be predicted or controlled.[74] It is because of this complexity, and our resultant inability to engineer the system, that Hayek so stresses self-organization and evolution.[75] That we can rationally design a moral system, he famously argued, is a fatal conceit.[76] But all this would appear to undermine the efficacy of conscious criticism and reform; if we cannot predict the consequences of changes in our moral system, all moral reform would seem to be a shot in the dark. Thus, many believe that Hayek is committed to a Burkean reverence for traditional moral rules, which have critical functions in our order of actions that we cannot fully understand.[77] Indeed Hayek associates himself with the Whig tradition, which includes Burke,[78] but Burke was suspicious of moral change; it would seem that an evolutionary view such as Hayek's, despite its protestations, must follow suit.

The analysis of the previous section helps us sort out this problem. If R is a highly complex system characterized by a very high-dimensional landscape, then indeed a small variation in one rule r can result in an order O with a drastically different height (value). This may lead to caution about changing our existing moral rules; any small change in R and we could fall far down.[79] However, under these circumstances, the observation that our current morality has evolved (i.e., is adaptive) would not itself provide much support for "moral reverence" toward our existing order. Unless this chaotic moral landscape is tied extraordinarily closely to the adaptive landscape—unless, essentially, every point a on the adaptive landscape is linked to a unique m on the moral landscape—the same level a of evolutionary adaptation will display significant degrees of freedom in relation to a set of points $\{m_1 \ldots m_n\}$ with which it is correlated. But if the evaluative system suffers from complexity catastrophe, the points within $\{m_1 \ldots m_n\}$ are not correlated with each other; thus any given a is linked to a set of uncorrelated evaluative points. If this is so, we cannot infer anything about the goodness of the current rules from the adaptiveness of a, even if we are currently high on the adaptive landscape.

Assume instead that the evaluative landscape models a system with low/modest interactions that is correlated with a low/modest dimensional adaptive landscape. In such an evaluative landscape the basins of attraction of good optima are large, the slopes gentle. Here we need not be worried that moral change will have disastrous results. We could get it wrong and descend a bit on the evaluative landscape, or we could get it right and ascend. But the fact that our current morality has evolved will not lead us to be terrified of the moral results of moral reform. And when the adaptive landscape is similarly low dimensional, we will not fear the social fitness consequences of moral change. It is certainly possible that moral change could move us down an adaptive gradient,[80] but if the adaptive landscape is not highly rugged (i.e., highly dimensional), even if the evaluative and adaptive landscapes are highly correlated, we would not expect sudden losses in social fitness.

Reform versus Revolution: The Importance of Neighborhoods

Given this, however, we might be driven to ask: What is left of the Hayekian project? While in my view his work on social and moral evolution is independently valuable, in his larger project these elements were marshaled in support of his master claim in social and political philosophy that planning is infeasible. A standard criticism of the infeasibility claim is that his support of deliberate moral criticism and change shows that we can, after all, predict the consequences of social change, and so planning is, after all, possible.

I have argued that, if Hayek's analysis is to avoid a complexity catastrophe, the landscapes must be low/modest dimensional, which does indeed allow moral reform, and so "reverence" for current positive morality is indeed inappropriate. This, though, does not lead to "planning" if, as did Karl Popper, we mean by it a synoptic social engineering that seeks to build the entire system according to some blueprint. Popper contrasted such utopian planning to "piecemeal" reform, seeing Hayek as an opponent only of the former.[81] Our question, then, is: Does Hayek's evolutionary analysis provide grounds for this distinction, allowing "piecemeal" reform of our morality, but not utopian reconstruction from the ground up? It should be stressed that while utopian economic plans have faded since Hayek wrote *The Road to Serfdom*,[82] contemporary moral and political philosophy is to a large, and perhaps increasing, extent committed to the production of utopian moral schemes.[83] So if his analysis speaks against them, this is of some importance.

And it does. I have stressed that in low-dimensional evaluative landscapes where slopes are modest and basins of attractions for high peaks are large, moral reform is well-grounded. We only have to make small variant decisions, and our concern is usually to climb a gradient (more of this anon). We do not need really powerful predictive tools about the overall effects of moral changes on the order of actions; as Popper stressed, if we get a piecemeal change wrong, we can climb back to where we were, and try again to move in an ascending direction. The costs are apt to be modest. However, even in low-dimensional landscapes, correlation pertains only in some neighborhood; locations outside the correlation neighborhood are fully uncorrelated with respect to one's present location.[84] Thus, in any move outside one's present neighborhood to a utopian position *u*, the value of one's current order of actions (on the evaluative landscape) provides no information about the moral value of *u*. Thus, accuracy in determining the value of *u* depends entirely on the power of the predictive models employed.

This is the heart of the Hayekian critique of utopian moral change; it is purely rationalistic in the sense that its success entirely depends on models for predicting the order of actions *O* that will emerge from a set of rules *R*. Although emergentist language tends to suggest that it is well-nigh impossible to predict the order which a given *R* produces, we certainly need not go that far. It is enough to observe that the predictive models have large variances, and different perspectives employ different predictive models.[85] To rely entirely on such models can lead us to unexpectedly awful parts of the adaptive and evaluative landscapes. Thus, because as we move further from our current location (on both the adaptive and moral landscapes), the value of our present state is decreasingly informative of the value of the proposed change, we are thrown back entirely on predictive models of at best uncertain accuracy; utopian schemes of moral revolution are much too like shots in the dark.

A caveat is in order. I said earlier that moral reform will typically be a matter of gradient climbing, and in low-dimensional landscapes with large basins of attraction of high peaks, this will indeed usually be the case. But a society that only climbs gradients is also one that is apt to get caught at local optima.[86] In some cases we may occupy a poor local optimum and have a not-so-distant better moral optimum that is sufficiently approximate in its social and institutional character that we can have reasonable confidence in our predictive models. From the *perspective of simply the moral landscape*, risking more radical innovations by seeking to jump to a new optimum may be the only way out, hoping that the predictive models are up to the task, and we do not land in an evaluative gully. However, *from the perspective of the adaptive landscape*, we should recall that the order of actions is also subject to adaptive pressures, which may induce changes in *O*. If the current poor local optimum on the evaluative landscape is such that *O* is ill-adapted, given that the adaptive and evaluative orders are coupled, movement in the adaptive landscape will produce changes in the moral landscape. This can result in a new evaluative landscape with a gradient to a morally better location. Indeed, a great attraction of an account that employs coupled adaptive and moral landscapes—in addition, of course, to the fundamental one that it both distinguishes and relates fitness and moral evaluation—is that dancing landscapes are less liable to get caught at local optima, as movement in one changes the terrain of the other.

To see this more clearly, consider Figure 3.3. In panel I, *O* is presently at a moral local optimum (*m*), with a higher optimum "near by"; the adaptive point is *a*, not a local optimum. In panel II, *a* has climbed its local gradient, but because the moral landscape is coupled, the moral landscape has shifted, putting *m* on an upward gradient.[87] A nice example of this type of analysis is John Stuart Mill's discussion of capitalism and socialism.[88] To Mill, from the perspective of justice, Victorian capitalism was far below the moral optimum; but, in his eyes, even if it climbed its local gradient to the top, and so became something like the best it could be, it would still be suboptimal from the perspective of justice. On the other hand, forms of socialism looked as if they could be morally attractive alternatives from the perspective of justice, but Mill adamantly opposed a revolutionary leap to such orders. This would require a complete restructuring of the society and economy; not only would the results be highly uncertain, but the transition period may be worse than either alternative. However, Mill insisted that the evolution of new forms of partnerships and corporations (that render capitalism more efficient) would also allow competitive market processes within capitalism to test the viability of socialist experiments and provide a

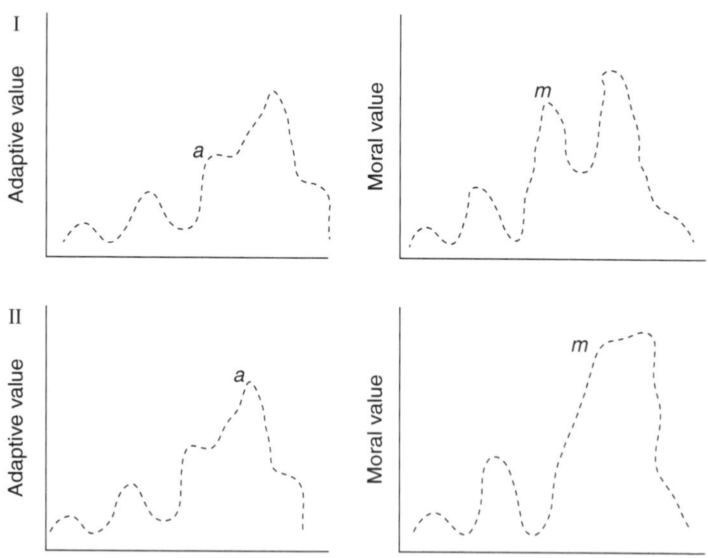

Figure 3.3 Dancing landscapes.

smooth moral gradient from capitalism to what he saw as a more just, cooperative, order.

Moral Deliberation and Predictive Modeling

Fundamental to the analysis of the previous section is the claim that all moral reform relies on predictive models, and utopian reform entirely on them (i.e., they cannot suppose correlation with present values). This may seem odd on a rule-based account of morality. On what we might call a strict "morality-as-rules" view,[89] in reforming a moral order we simply examine some constituent rule *r*, and ask whether we approve of it, whether it is justified, or whether it is part of true morality. If we decide that it is not, we look for some variant *r*★ that passes some test of moral justifiability, and replace *r* with *r*.★ We could, in principle, perform this deliberation in relation to any order, regardless of how different it is from ours. We could simply reflect on the rules and give our judgment (an all-too-common method in moral philosophy). For Hayek, of course, this is not sufficient; our ultimate concern is the order of actions that emerges from the system of rules. And that means that our decision whether to replace *r* with *r*★ depends on the application of a predictive model, which tells us what an order *O*★ with *r*★ would look like.

This is not really an unusual form of rule-based moral evaluation. John Rawls proposes a similar procedure in his interpretation of Kantian ethics.[90] As is well-known, one of Kant's formulations of his famous categorical imperative requires that a person test the maxim of her act by seeing whether she could will it as a law of nature. Rawls reinterprets this in terms of a four-step CI (Categorical Imperative) procedure. The first three steps on the CI procedure are fairly straightforward. One commences by adopting a maxim:

1. I am to do *X* in circumstances *C* in order to bring about *Y*. (Here *X* is an action and *Y* a state of affairs.)

   The second step generalizes the maxim at the first to get:

2. Everyone is to do *X* in circumstances *C* in order to bring about *Y*.

   At a third step we are to transform the general precept at (2) into a law of nature to obtain:

3. Everyone always does *X* in circumstances *C* in order to bring about *Y* (as if by a law of nature).[91]

It is the fourth step that leads us to predictive modeling. We are to consider the "perturbed social world" that would result from the addition of this new law of nature, and seek to understand the new "equilibrium state" on which this perturbed social world would settle. This social world emerges upon the new law of nature in the context of the rest of the present order. We are then to ask ourselves whether, when we regard ourselves as a member of this new social world, we can "will this perturbed social world [order] itself and affirm it should we belong to it."[92] The ultimate concern here is the social world—the order of actions—that would result under the assumptions of the model.

Conclusion

The uncompromising advocate of evolutionary ethics insists that our evolved positive morality *is* our current best approximation of true morality; seeking to depart from it by appeal to critical moral ideals can only lead to disaster. The uncompromising moral philosopher seeks to repel this assault on her domain by drawing a clear line in the sand—that between *is* and *ought*. Evolutionary analysis can explain what our positive morality *is* and how it came about, but this tells us nothing useful about what *ought* to be done. Indeed, leading philosophers have recently proclaimed that true morality and true justice *could* be permanently outside the motivational horizon of humans. Darwin's fundamental insight—that morality is a distinctive evolutionary achievement of humans that made possible our form of eusocial life—has, the uncompromising moral philosopher tells us, no real normative significance. Both are simple views: for both there is only one landscape to be traversed.

Thoughtful philosophers such as Kitcher struggle to capture the normative significance of the fact that our evolved morality makes human social life possible while preserving the ethical project as a conscious, critical, stance that can reform our evolved morality according to our normative ideals. That is clearly the fundamental task for evolutionary ethics—indeed, for any plausible moral theory. In this chapter I have tried to take some initial steps to think a bit more carefully about how evolutionary and critical morality might be related. I believe that in this context *NK* models are helpful.[93] When we depict the problem in these terms, we can more clearly see the conditions under which adaptive and moral landscapes are plausibly correlated. And this, in turn, places us in a position to more rigorously deal with other recurring questions, about what an evolutionary analysis implies about the respect for our current morality and its reform, based on our normative thinking. By focusing on Hayek I have tried, first, to bring out the surprising richness and subtlety of his analysis of evolved morality (things that are still not sufficiently appreciated) but, more importantly, to demonstrate that the sort of correlation I analyze is not a mere abstract possibility, but one which, if not precisely implicit in his thought, can be easily reached from it. Like all living things, the Hayekian project is subject to evolutionary pressures; here, at least, I hope evolution and progress march together.[94]

Notes

1. Charles Darwin, *The Descent of Man*, second edition (New York: Penguin, [1871] 2004), 120.
2. Whether this is *mere* appearance—and, importantly, just what it could mean—is a crucial issue. The work of the last 20 years, I believe, inclines to the view that it is not simply appearance, and true biological altruism may evolve. But this is still a matter of controversy.
3. For general analyses of such rules, see Cristina Bicchieri, *The Grammar of Society: The Nature and Dynamics of Norms* (Cambridge: Cambridge University Press, 2006); Gerald Gaus, *The Order of Public Reason* (Cambridge: Cambridge University Press, 2011), Ch. 3 and 4.
4. Anthony O'Hear, *Beyond Evolution: Human Nature and the Limits of Evolutionary Explanation* (Oxford: Oxford University Press, 1997), 101.
5. Ken Binmore, *Natural Justice* (Oxford: Oxford University Press, 2005), 1.
6. See, for example, Herbert Spencer, "Progress: Its Law and Cause," in *Essays: Scientific, Political, and Speculative. Library Edition, Containing Seven Essays Not before Republished, and Various Other Additions* (London: Williams and Norgate, 1891), 2. This essay, sketching Spencer's evolutionary theory, pre-dates the publication of *The Origins of Species*.
7. See, for example, L. T. Hobhouse, *Mind in Evolution* (London: Macmillan, 1901); L. T. Hobhouse, *Development and Purpose* (London: Macmillan, 1927); L. T. Hobhouse, *Social Evolution and Political Theory* (New York, Columbia University Press, 1911); Morris Ginsberg, "The Concept of Evolution in Sociology," *Proceedings of the Aristotelian Society*, n.s. 31 (1930–31): 201–24.
8. Philip Kitcher, *The Ethical Project* (Cambridge, MA: Harvard University Press, 2011), 239.
9. On progress and equality, see especially ibid., Ch. 6; on equality, see ibid., Ch. 8.
10. Ibid., 213.
11. "A struggle for existence inevitably follows from the high rate at which all organic beings tend to increase." Charles Darwin, *On the Origins of Species* (Oxford: Oxford

University Press, 2009), Ch. 3. Darwin explicitly credits Malthus with the idea. See *The Autobiography of Charles Darwin 1809–1882, with the Original Omissions Restored*, ed. Nora Barlow (London: Collins, 1958), 120.

12. See, for example, David G. Ritchie, *Darwinism and Politics*, 2nd ed. (London: Swan Sonnenschein, 1891), 1ff. Nevertheless, even Ritchie attempted to link evolution and progress in the second essay in the volume. Compare O'Hear's skepticism, *Beyond Evolution*, 2ff.
13. See, for example, William Graham Sumner, "Sociology," in *War and Other Essays*, ed. Albert Galloway Keller (New Haven, CT: Yale University Press, 1919), Ch. 7.
14. See O'Hear, *Beyond Evolution*, p. 74. See also John Tyler Bonner, *The Evolution of Complexity by Means of Natural Selection* (Princeton, NJ: Princeton University Press, 1988).
15. It is appropriate to commence with Hayek not simply because of the present occasion, but far more importantly, because Hayek was developing subtle accounts of moral and social evolution, complex systems, and social morality from the 1950s through to the 1980s, when few social theorists would go anywhere near these topics. Well into the 1980s the application of evolutionary thought to society was commonly associated with eugenics, imperialism, and fascism. Recall the abuse heaped on Edward O. Wilson for his *Sociobiology: The New Synthesis* (Cambridge, MA: Harvard University Press, 1975).
16. See Friedrich A. Hayek, "Notes on the Evolution of Systems of Rules of Conduct," in *Studies in Philosophy, Politics, and Economics* (Chicago, IL: University of Chicago Press, 1967), 75. See also Douglas Glen Whitman, "Hayek contra Pangloss on Evolutionary Systems," *Constitutional Political Economy* 9, no. 1 (1998): 450–66.
17. Hayek suggests a gene–culture coevolution thesis, but I shall not explore it here. See his "Evolution of Systems," 71.
18. Friedrich A. Hayek, *The Fatal Conceit*, ed. W. W. Bartley III (Chicago, IL: University of Chicago Press, 1988), 25. For a contemporary discussion of whether cultural evolution is "Lamarckian" (allowing for the inheritance of acquired characteristics), see Alex Mesoudi, *Cultural Evolution: How Darwinian Theory Can Explain Human Culture and Synthesize the Social Sciences* (Chicago, IL: University of Chicago Press, 2011), 43–44.
19. Hayek, "Evolution of Systems," 67; Friedrich A. Hayek, *Law, Legislation and Liberty*, vol. 3, *The Political Order of a Free People* (Chicago, IL: University of Chicago Press, 1979), 156–57.
20. For an easily accessible version of their work, see Peter J. Richerson and Robert Boyd, *Not by Genes Alone: How Culture Transformed Human Evolution* (Chicago, IL: University of Chicago Press, 2005), Ch. 3. Their groundbreaking modeling of cultural evolution was presented in Robert Boyd and Peter J. Richerson, *Culture and the Evolutionary Process* (Chicago, IL: University of Chicago Press, 1985). For an overview see Mesoudi, *Cultural Evolution*, Ch. 3. Hayek notes prestige bias: "Evolution of Systems," 79.
21. This form of transmission has recently been stressed by Christopher Boehm, *Moral Origins: The Evolution of Virtue, Altruism and Shame* (New York: Basic Books, 2012), Ch. 7.

22. Mesoudi, *Cultural Evolution*, Ch. 3; Richerson and Boyd, *Not by Genes Alone*, 68ff.
23. On the contrast between micro and macro social evolution, see Mesoudi, *Cultural Evolution*, Ch. 3–5.
24. Hayek, "Evolution of Systems," 71. On Hayek's notion of the order of actions, see Eric Mack, "Hayek on Justice and the Order of Actions," in *The Cambridge Companion to Hayek*, ed. Edward Feser (Cambridge: Cambridge University Press, 2006), 259–86.
25. Hayek, "Evolution of Systems," 72.
26. Friedrich A. Hayek, "The Theory of Complex Phenomena," in *Studies in Philosophy, Politics, and Economics*, 23–24.
27. I have analyzed this thesis in "Hayek on the Evolution of Society and Mind," in *The Cambridge Companion to Hayek*, 232–58.
28. Hayek, "Evolution of Systems," 71.
29. Friedrich A. Hayek, *Law, Legislation and Liberty*, vol. 1, *Rules and Order* (Chicago, IL: University of Chicago Press, 1973), 18; Hayek, *Fatal Conceit*, p. 25. Sewall Wright participated in Hayek's evolution seminar at Chicago. See Bruce Caldwell, *Hayek's Challenge* (Chicago, IL: University of Chicago Press, 2004), 299. Hayek certainly advances what might be called a genuine multilevel selectionist account, in which the success of a group affects the selection of individual traits within it, allowing traits that have an in-group disadvantage to be selected. "Although the existence and preservation of the order of actions of a group can be accounted for only from the rules of conduct which individuals obey, these rules of conduct have developed because the individuals have been living in groups whose structures have gradually changed. In other words, the properties of the individuals which are significant for the existence and preservation of the group, and through this also for the existence and preservation of the individuals themselves, have been shaped by the selection of those individuals from the individuals living in groups which at each stage of evolution of the group tended to act according to such rules as made the group more efficient." Hayek, "Evolution of Systems," 72. This sort of group selection hypothesis is not supposed in this chapter.
30. While the importance of forms of multilevel selection in biological evolution is still hotly disputed, I think there is conclusive reason to view multilevel selection as fundamental in cultural evolution. For a very helpful discussion, see Samir Okasha, *Evolution and the Levels of Selection* (Oxford: Oxford University Press, 2006).
31. On modeling group conflict as fundamental to social evolution, see Samuel Bowles and Herbert Gintis, *A Cooperative Species: Human Reciprocity and Its Evolution* (Princeton, NJ: Princeton University Press, 2011).
32. Hayek, *Political Order*, 26, 159; Hayek, *Rules and Order*, 3, 17–18; Hayek, *Fatal Conceit*, 6, 25, 43. For a general analysis of different forms of cultural group selection and the plausible time spans under which they might operate, see Robert Boyd, Peter J. Richerson, and Joseph Soltis, "Can Group-Functional Behaviors Evolve by Cultural Group Selection?" in *The Origin and Evolution of Cultures*, ed. Robert Boyd and Peter J. Richerson (Oxford: Oxford University Press, 2005), 204–26.
33. "[C]ultural evolution operates *largely* through group selection." *Fatal Conceit*, 23, emphasis added.

34. Friedrich A. Hayek, *The Constitution of Liberty* (Chicago, IL: University of Chicago Press, 1960), 63.
35. On page 161 of the Epilogue to *The Political Order of a Free Society* (the last volume of *Law, Legislation and Liberty*), Hayek argues that the steps in cultural evolution toward large-scale coordination "were made possible by some individuals breaking some traditional rules and practising new forms of conduct—not because they understood them to be better, but because the groups which acted on them prospered more and grew." For a general analysis of the role of conscious deliberation and choice of rules in Hayek, see Sandra J. Peart and David M. Levy, "Discussion, Construction and Evolution: Mill, Buchanan and Hayek on Constitutional Order," *Constitutional Political Economy* 19, no. 1 (2008): 3–18.
36. It does no good for Hayek to claim that this moral sense is atavistic, as it was formed under conditions of living in small bands, and so should be ignored. We must remember that this is an account of the mechanisms of cultural evolution; we cannot rule out processes on evaluative or moral grounds. See Hayek, *Political Order*, 153–59.
37. I consider the idea of rule variants in my *The Order of Public Reason*, 270–71.
38. In many models of adaptive landscapes the points represent population average fitness; in others the points represent individual fitness, and populations are groups of points. In evolutionary modeling these different versions can lead to very different insights and problems. In the present social evolutionary context, *O* is an individual order, not a population average. See further Sergey Gavrilets, "Evolution and Speciation on Holey Adaptive Landscapes," *Trends in Ecology & Evolution* 12, no. 8 (August 1997): 307–12.
39. For an important pioneering analysis, see Stuart A. Kauffman, *The Origins of Order* (New York: Oxford University Press, 1993), especially Ch. 2. See also Sergey Gavrilets, "High-Dimensional Fitness Landscapes and Speciation," in *Evolution—the Extended Synthesis*, ed. Massimo Pigliucci and Gerd B. Müller (Cambridge, MA: MIT Press, 2010), 45–80.
40. See Whitman, "Hayek contra Pangloss."
41. See for example, Daniel A. Levinthal, "Adaptation on Rugged Landscapes," *Management Science* 43, no. 7 (July 1997): 934–50 and, more generally, Scott E. Page, *The Difference* (Princeton, NJ: Princeton University Press, 2007). Especially important in management science has been the work of James G. March; see for example, "Exploration and Exploitation in Organizational Learning," *Organization Science* (Special Issue: Organizational Learning: Papers in Honor of (and by) James G. March) 2, no. 1 (1991): 71–87.
42. Fred D'Agostino, *Naturalizing Epistemology* (New York: Palgrave Macmillan, 2010), esp. Ch. 7; Fred D'Agostino, "From the Organization to the Division of Cognitive Labor," *Politics, Philosophy and Economics* 8, no. 1 (2009): 101–29; Michael Weisberg and Ryan Muldoon, "Epistemic Landscapes and the Division of Cognitive Labor," *Philosophy of Science* 76, no. 2 (April 2009): 225–52.
43. Hélène Landemore, *Democratic Reason* (Princeton, NJ: Princeton University Press, 2013), esp. chap. 4.

44. Gerald Gaus, "Social Contract and Social Choice," *Rutgers Law Journal* 43, no. 2 (Spring/Summer 2012): 243–76; Gerald Gaus, "Between Discovery and Choice: The General Will in a Diverse Society," *Contemporary Readings in Law and Social Justice* 3, no. 2 (2011): 70–95. In what follows I will call the landscapes, "evaluative," "moral," and "justice" landscapes. Although in some contexts it would be important to distinguish these, the analysis presented here is sufficiently general that we can treat these terms as synonymous.
45. Amartya Sen, *The Idea of Justice* (Cambridge, MA: Harvard University Press, 2009), 12–15.
46. Ibid., 12.
47. I assume here that each rule varies along one evaluative dimension.
48. See Sen, *The Idea of Justice*, 102; A. John Simmons, "Ideal and Nonideal Theory," *Philosophy & Public Affairs* 38, no. 1 (Winter 2010): 34–35.
49. We shall see presently that this point has important implications.
50. I consider a slightly different version of this claim in *The Order of Public Reason*, 420ff. As John Thrasher has pointed out to me, James Buchanan advanced similar criticisms of Hayek; see, for example, Geoffrey Brennan and James Buchanan, *The Reason of Rules* (Cambridge: Cambridge University Press, 1985), 9–10. See also Peart and Levy, "Discussion, Construction and Evolution." At various places, rather than endorsing the claim that the evolution of an order is sufficient for its moral endorsement, Hayek appears to suggest that the question of moral justification is rationalistic and so inappropriate: morality requires "following of moral traditions that are not justifiable in terms of the canons of traditional theories of rationality...The process of selection that shaped customs and morality could take account of more factual circumstances than individuals could perceive, and in consequence tradition is in some respects superior to, or 'wiser,' than, human reason" (*The Fatal Conceit*, p. 75). In one sense, this is consistent with the correlation analysis presented here (that we can use evolution as indicative of the adequacy of our morality, and so "in some sense" it is a source of justificatory wisdom), but in a more radical interpretation it seems to suggest that we cannot rationally morally evaluate our currently evolved order. O'Hear rightly criticizes this radical view, pointing out that Hayek himself engages in overall evaluative judgments; *Beyond Evolution*, p. 148. As Caldwell notes, caution must be exercised when relying on *The Fatal Conceit* in interpreting Hayek, as some of the final text seems to reflect the views of Bartley, who finished the manuscript because of Hayek's failing health. See *Hayek's Challenge*, 316ff.
51. Hayek, *Fatal Conceit*, 8.
52. I consider coherence theories in more detail in *Justificatory Liberalism* (New York: Oxford University Press, 1996), Ch. 6.
53. Cf. Friedrich A. Hayek, "Why I am not a Conservative," in *The Constitution of Liberty*, 397–411.
54. Kitcher makes much of this in *The Ethical Project*, Part I. For a fascinating narrative of this evolution, see Boehm, *Moral Origins*. For more rigorous modeling, see Bowles and Gintis, *A Cooperative Species*.

55. This supposes, *pace* the well-known work of Jonathan Haidt, that reflective moral consciousness in an important variable in action. See his "The Emotional Dog and its Rational Tail: A Social Intuitionist Approach to Moral Judgment," *Psychological Review* 108, no. 4 (October 2001): 814–34. My understanding of Haidt's work owes much to Piper Bringhurst.
56. Of course neither does it imply that this claim of philosophers should be accepted!
57. Page, *The Difference*, Parts II and III. Page's book is based on formal theorems developed with Lu Hong. See Lu Hong and Scott E. Page, "Problem Solving by Heterogeneous Agents," *Journal of Economic Theory* 97, no. 1 (March 2001): 123–63; Lu Hong and Scott E. Page, "Groups of Diverse Problem Solvers Can Outperform Groups of High-Ability Problem Solvers," *Proceedings of the National Academy of Sciences of the United States of America* 101, no. 46 (November 16, 2004): 16385–89.
58. Hayek, *Rules and Order*, 1–8, and 146ff. where he talks of the "open society."
59. See March,"Exploration and Exploitation in Organizational Learning"; Scott E. Page, *Diversity and Complexity* (Princeton, NJ: Princeton University Press, 2011), 122–24.
60. On the importance of imitative learning to the evolution of morality, see Hayek, *Fatal Conceit*, 21.
61. Page, *Diversity and Complexity*, 94.
62. Kauffman, *The Origins of Order*, 238.
63. Ibid.
64. Ibid., 45ff.
65. Ibid., 47. In deliberative searches groups will tend to get caught at a local optima since they abound (but see note 86). Crucial to Hong and Page's fundamental theorem is that only the global optimum is shared by all perspectives; if a local optimum is shared, collective search may end there. In high-dimensional landscapes poor local optima abound, and everyone is likely to share one, thus halting the collective search. Hong and Page, "Diverse Problem Solvers," 16387ff.
66. Kauffman, *The Origins of Order*, 52.
67. T. M. Scanlon, *What We Owe Each Other* (Cambridge, MA: Harvard University Press, 1998), 214.
68. Kauffman, *The Origins of Order*, 243. D'Agostino notes these features in *Naturalizing Epistemology*, 118–19.
69. Kauffman, *Origins of Order*, 60.
70. Ibid., 62–63.
71. See my *Order of Public Reason*, 495–97.
72. As did Hayek in "The Theory of Complex Phenomena." I explore this claim in some depth in my "Social Complexity and Evolved Moral Principles," in *Liberalism, Conservatism, and Hayek's Idea of Spontaneous Order*, ed. Louis Hunt and Peter McNamara (London: Palgrave Macmillan, 2007), 149–76.
73. Boyd and Richerson, *The Origin and Evolution of Cultures*, Ch. 19.
74. Hayek, "The Theory of Complex Phenomena." See also my "Social Complexity and Evolved Moral Principles."
75. Hayek repeatedly refers to "the twin ideas of evolution and spontaneous order." See Hayek, "Evolution of Systems," 77; Friedrich A. Hayek, "Dr. Bernard

Mandeville," in *New Studies in Politics, Economics and the History of Ideas* (London: Routledge, 1987), 250; Hayek, *Rules and Order*, 23, 158; Hayek, *Fatal Conceit*, 146. It should be noted that Kauffman's aim in *Origins of Order* was to account for self-organization within an evolutionary framework.

76. Hayek, *Fatal Conceit*, 7.
77. Hayek himself commends "the reverence of the traditional," invoking Hume's doctrine that the rules of morality are not the conclusions of our reason. Hayek, *The Constitution of Liberty*, 63. See further my "Social Complexity and Evolved Moral Principles," 166ff. O'Hear complains about this; *Beyond Evolution*, 154ff.
78. Hayek, "Why I am not a Conservative." But see p. 400 where Hayek distinguishes the liberal and conservative attitudes toward change.
79. Or, then again, also way up. On this model we need to add risk aversion to get reverence. Of course other, more specific, models could lead to Burkean reverence. Consider a landscape that has few high peaks that are far apart, each with very sharp slopes, with the rest of the terrain being low and flat. If one thought we are currently at a local optima we would not budge, for fear of falling off a cliff.
80. This is a way of modeling O'Hear's point that the best norms may run "counter to survival." O'Hear, *Beyond Evolution*, 3. This clearly has limits.
81. Karl R. Popper, *The Poverty of Historicism*, 2nd ed. (London: Routledge and Kegan Paul, 1961), Ch. 20–25. Popper insightfully analyzes the way that holism undermines social experimentation.
82. F. A. Hayek, *The Road to Serfdom* (Chicago, IL: University of Chicago Press, 1944).
83. For just two of many examples, see David Estlund, *Democratic Authority* (Princeton, NJ: Princeton University Press, 2008), Ch. 14; G. A. Cohen, *Rescuing Justice and Equality* (Cambridge, MA: Harvard University Press, 2008), Part II.
84. Kauffman, *The Origins of Order*, 70.
85. Hong and Page ("Problem Solving by Heterogeneous Agents") include in their theorem the way that a group employing diverse predictive models will outperform a single, even very good, model.
86. I have stressed that low-dimensional landscapes have many attractive features given the type of problems we have been analyzing. But as has been recognized since Sewall Wright, they pose this problem of getting caught on suboptimal peaks. Suboptimal traps can be avoided in some high-dimensional landscapes. If we consider landscapes in which points are individuals and species are groups of points spread over a *N*-dimensional area (see note 38), high-dimensional landscapes can display fitness ridges that provide paths from one optima to another. See Gavrilets, "High-Dimensional Fitness Landscapes and Speciation."
87. Of course the effect can work in the other direction as well, with movement on the moral landscape changing the adaptive landscape.
88. I draw here on Mill, *Principles of Political Economy*, Books II and IV, in *The Collected Works of John Stuart Mill*, ed. John M. Robson (Indianapolis: Liberty Fund, 2006), vols. 2 and 3, and his "Chapters on Socialism," in John Stuart Mill, *Principles of Political Economy with Chapters on Socialism*, ed. Jonathan Riley (Oxford: Oxford University Press, 1994). I am not concerned here with whether Mill was correct about either his moral or social analysis.

89. Sen has called this "institutional fundamentalism," which he mistakenly believes is Rawls's view. See *The Idea of Justice*, 82–83. I supposed some such view in "Social Complexity and Evolved Moral Principles."
90. And, like Hayek, he believes it should be restricted to the neighborhood of the present order. See John Rawls, *Justice as Fairness, A Restatement*, ed. Erin Kelly (Cambridge, MA: Harvard University Press, 2001), 70.
91. John Rawls, "Themes in Kant's Moral Philosophy," in *John Rawls: Collected Papers*, ed. Samuel Freeman (Cambridge, MA: Harvard University Press, 1999), 499.
92. Ibid., 500.
93. Although of course they are not the only way to analyze this difficult problem. When we employ a good model we see things differently, and so we see things that would have escaped us. But the model can also blind us to important features of the phenomenon. Like any good tool, a good model helps greatly in the right context, but a one-tool toolkit quickly runs into problems. Clichés can be insightful: to one who only has a hammer, everything really can look like a nail.
94. My deep thanks to the members of my graduate seminars on diversity and on moral evolution at the University of Arizona for helping me think through some of these difficult issues. I am especially grateful for the comments and suggestions of Chad van Schoelandt, Stephen Stitch, John Thrasher, and Kevin Vallier. Special thanks to Fred D'Agostino and Ryan Muldoon for spurring me to think about these matters, and helping me do it.

CHAPTER FOUR

Hayek and the Conditions of Freedom

KENNETH MINOGUE

Hayek's work as a political theorist is both focused and diversified. As an economist, of course, Hayek was preoccupied with such issues as the socialist calculation debate, an issue inherited from von Mises. But his political focus is directly on identifying the character of freedom. One version of this focus argues that many supposed defects of capitalism are often functional to social progress. Thus, wealthy people, abused as privileged parasites in much socialist argument, explore and develop new and better forms of life that will be taken up more widely as the generations pass. Again, market prices ought not to be controlled by states because they are part of a discovery procedure indispensable to entrepreneurs. Markets generate prosperity, and people all over the world want to migrate toward wealth. The selfish striving for gain found among entrepreneurs, Hayek tells us, "enables him to do, precisely what he ought to do in order to improve the chances of any member of his society, taken at random."[1]

Here is a brisk disposal of popular tosh about putting "profit" before "people," and the general point is a standing theme of Hayek's argument. The valuable in commercial life as it spreads throughout the world is not the consequence of benevolence.

But in what way is he diverse? This feature of his work arises in a succession of varied arguments sustaining freedom. In his 1944 *The Road to Serfdom*, he was to some extent hobbled because he had to concentrate on Nazi Germany rather than on repression in our ally, at that time the Soviet Union. Here the obverse of freedom is to be found in the broad idea of totalitarianism. When we reach *The Constitution of Liberty* in 1960, we have a powerful statement of classical liberalism in which he is admirably clear on some of the familiar confusions in discussions of freedom, most notably, perhaps, the tendency to confuse freedom with power. But classical liberalism is here reinforced by Hayek's skeptical insistence on the place in economic activity of traditional rules and the inescapable ignorance of economic agents. It is an irony that this familiar theme of conservative politics appears in a volume to which Hayek has appended an essay explaining that he is not a conservative, because conservatives are merely timid in their responses to social problems.

He was, however, so persuaded of the abstract case for freedom that he moved on in the 1988 *The Fatal Conceit*[2] to explore further his preoccupation with catallaxy, the extended order in which economic agents find themselves involved. Hayek boldly compares the emergence of this important advance in human experience to the acquisition of sight by organisms in the process of evolution. It is here too that he wants to insist on the fact that the problem of central planning is not merely a political dispute arising from different values or preferences, but rather that of logical and scientific reality:

> The conflict between, on one hand, advocates of the spontaneous extended human order created by a competitive market, and on the other hand those who demand a deliberate arrangement of human interaction by central authority based on collective command over available resources is due to a factual error by the latter about how knowledge of these resources is and can be generated and utilised. As a question of fact, this conflict must be settled by scientific study...Thus socialist aims and programmes are factually impossible to achieve or execute; and they also happen, into the bargain as it were, to be logically impossible.[3]

This certainly raises the stakes of argument, shifting it from politics (which is, as it were, "essentially contestable") to the sphere of science, which is at least popularly supposed to be demonstrative. We move from policy (X leads to Y) to fact (now X causes Y). And in order to bring out the problem more sharply, let me move to Chapter 9 of *The Fatal Conceit* in which the issue raised is how the planet might be able to sustain the large population of human beings who now (late twentieth century) live on earth: "So many people already exist; and only a market economy can keep the bulk of them alive...Since we can preserve and secure even our present numbers only by adhering to the same general kinds of principles, [the "extended order" or catallaxy] it is our duty—unless we truly wish to condemn millions to starvation—to resist the claims of creeds that tend to destroy the basic principles of these morals, such as the institution of several property."[4] And this is unmistakably a policy prescription, even if the force of the consequence to be avoided is overwhelming.

It is, further, at this period that Hayek extends even further his use of the argument from evolution. Socialism is an "atavism" that reflects our hardwired response to the immemorial tribal forms of rationality we acquire in prehistoric terms. But the rationality reflecting this take on reality cannot realize that crucial information necessary to such rationality is unavailable in the new world of the extended order of social relationships. The rationality of the rules that have ended our range, and the signals of the desires and needs of the people cannot be known by the rational planner in modern times.

The evolutionary thesis is increasingly prominent in later writings, which I take to be a response of Hayek's pessimism about getting his argument across to the wider world of policy and public opinion. We remain, runs the argument, in some degree hardwired to understand modern societies in the same manner as the smaller tribal groups from which humanity emerged over many generations, and we have yet to recognize the new conditions of the extended order that is being created by the entrepreneurs whose pursuit of profit is leading toward the increasing internationality of trade in which we benefit from the activities of others so remote from us that no moral relationship is relevant to how we are connected to them. He is sensitive to the charge that he is engaged in Social Darwinism, but rejects it on the ground that Darwinism itself is merely the extension into biology of views that had already been cultivated in social and linguistic theory.

In his *Autobiographical Dialogue*, Hayek declares himself ultimately optimistic about the end of socialist illusions, but he does recognize that we are a long way from overcoming them so far.[5] He has no doubt that the basic end of central planning, as "social justice" or many of its synonyms, is vacuous, but he gives the impression of being baffled by the failure of intelligent agents to accept the argument, and move on. And his work becomes increasingly concerned with the evolutionary argument, which is highly speculative and actually remote from his intentions except as suggesting some powerful force standing in the way of recognizing reality on this point.

Let me suggest that an understanding of the attractions of social justice may be derived from much lower-level concerns. And in order to do this, I must make some remarks about the character of freedom in the modern European world.

Freedom versus Justice

In Hayek's seventies, his argument had developed as follows: As with other organisms, "the main 'purpose' to which man's physical make-up as well as his traditions are adapted is to produce other human beings...Life exists only so long as it provides for its own continuance."[6] For untold millennia, humans have lived in small groups to whose management a limited rationality of ends and means was appropriate. But in historic times, the extended order, the catallaxy, has evolved, partly out of the spread of commercial enterprise beyond tribal and national or social boundaries, and the result has been to connect a whole world of individuals whose cooperation in economic processes is not the less valuable because it is guided not by altruistic impulses but by the spread of rules such as those of several property, honesty, family loyalty, and so on. This extended order has not always been found attractive, but has been ever more widely supported because it has generated prosperity and sustained rising populations. The extended order rests upon all sorts of rules we follow from tradition or other motives but basically because they facilitate success. On the mechanics of this process, Hayek is notably vague. As one critic puts it: "the actual analysis of socio-economic evolution in Hayek's work appears sketchy and unfinished."[7] Yet we are still haunted, continues the argument, by the dream of controlling modern life by recourse to a rationality of a kind we inherit from the past, but which cannot work in modern circumstances because the information needed for decisions, along with the knowledge of why the rules we follow, are both lacking to us.

What Hayek has done, then, is to transpose a low-level ideological conflict into a remote echo of a higher-level evolutionary conflict between an old and dysfunctional development and a new (but perhaps rather chilly) form of life that alone can continue the vast successes (in prosperity and population growth) already achieved.

The essence of this argument is that it attempts to solve a lower-level problem (managed versus free societies) by invoking a very high-level and rather speculative explanation. Critics have taken it to be an instance of Social Darwinism, but Hayek claims that Darwinism itself emerges from earlier speculations about the development of society and of language, speculations that were then taken over into biology by

Darwin. The very term "evolution" is here being asked to do excessive work. This is overkill. Furthermore, as we have seen, it undermines the claim that the argument invalidating socialist calculation is logically and scientifically conclusive, because it makes the avoidance of socialism a managerial concern dependent upon the overriding purposes of prosperity and population. This is where Hayek's facts depend on evaluation.

The low-level conflict between socialism and capitalism, and central planning and free markets, has become absorbed in this larger evolutionary schema. And if Hayek is right, then socialism is indeed an "atavism," and he is probably right in arguing that socialist planning of our vastly populated world would hardly have any other consequence than the death of millions. But what seems to me eccentric about this whole scheme is that it is both vague and excessively ambitious, and I want to suggest much simpler ways of understanding the problem faced by those who support freedom.

The Ubiquity of Comprehensive Justice

Hayek thinks that human life has no other purpose than itself, and hence "success" in evolutionary terms may be taken as increase in population that does not drag everyone down into starvation. But what concerns Hayek (and the millions who want to migrate to the West) even more directly is the wealth and prosperity of the modern world. I take it therefore that the force of Hayek's refutation of central planning is linked to its "success" in generating prosperity. But the notion that certain kinds of society generate prosperity has not been a prominent object in managing most civilizations. They were concerned with justice, in ways that Europeans in recent centuries have not been.

Almost all past societies have arisen from conquest, and the result has generally been social hierarchy and political despotism. Conquerors generally want power to exploit their gains; they seldom give much thought to the question of whether the society they rule is best organized for creating general wealth. What is most immediately important to any regime of this kind is not prosperity but legitimacy, which emerges over time, from the interplay of custom, religion, and always, of course, power. Successful legitimation consists in diffusing the conviction over time that whatever hierarchy has emerged constitutes a just society from top to bottom. Such societies are thought to be *comprehensively* just when each individual is allocated a status according to how his or her characteristic function is thought to contribute to the common good of the whole. Societies of this kind are forms of order that sociologists used to call "traditional," and most people have hitherto lived in some version of this world. The Muslim Sharia notionally corresponds to the way in which Allah thinks we ought to live. The Hindu caste system reflects the just condition of an individual in terms of his conduct over many lives, while the hierarchies of Asian societies similarly put a value on this or that activity. Women, notoriously, generally come at the bottom of these hierarchies, along with slaves.

The twentieth century was notably a period when various parodies of comprehensive justice afflicted the world, in communism, Nazism, and Fascism. In recent centuries, of course, this type of social experience that I have so roughly sketched has been shaken in various degrees by the fact that increasing numbers of non-Europeans are learning that "there is a world elsewhere," and some familiarity with Western models has had a powerfully destabilizing effect on how human beings live. Tribal cultures are special versions of this very broad experience. Each person has recognized status in terms of age, sex, race or tribe, lineage, and much else. From the inside, all these forms of justice are imagined to be the way all human beings ought to live. From the outside—which is to say from our point of view—they are universally to be regarded as preposterous, and in some cases deeply deplorable. And the basic reason, as we shall see, is that, as Sir Henry Maine observed, our relations largely reflect contract rather than status.

All of these societies are forms of despotism, and that means that while the ideal of comprehensive justice is powerful, the realities of living in such a society may well be (and in fact are) very different from the ideal of justice in terms of which they are understood. In principle, the right conditions for each status are well known, and respected, but much inevitably remains indeterminate, and higher status is (more or less unchecked) also higher power. And while all societies have one or another set of institutions that will resolve disputes, none of them has in the European sense an established system of law to which appeal can seriously be made against the arbitrary dictates of the ruler. Justice is largely absorbed into the structure of power. Status determines the right of judgment, and the higher the status, the greater the power to do so.

The great virtue offered by comprehensively just societies has always been harmony, and that requires a strong management of the beliefs subjects may be permitted to express. There is no question of toleration of deviant forms of life, because such toleration might generate conflict. What might in Western states be tolerated is in these societies either forbidden, or embraced and appreciated. Everything recognized must either fit the system, or be deplored and punished. Nor is freedom of speech an issue, since there is no class of individualists who might claim it. This does not mean, of course, that a great multiplicity of opinions about life in these societies will not be held, but merely that such opinions will be controlled as threatening social harmony. Again, in this world the activity of politics in the Western sense will not be known. Rule comes from the despot and is mitigated by custom and the advice of whoever the ruler chooses to consult, but there is no public discussion and accountability. As the world has been increasingly absorbed into the Western international system, of course, presidents, assemblies, and even papers described as "constitutions" have come into being nearly everywhere. Sometimes, these have been a great success, sometimes a mere charade.

Now the point of this excursion into what I take to have been, in the broadest terms, the way people generally lived in earlier societies and civilizations is to recognize that "social justice," while it may be as vacuous an idea as Hayek believes, is very far from being unthinkable. Most people have lived under some system of comprehensive freedom, and however remarkable to us, it has provided them with a security they have valued. Modern European societies, by contrast, have been based on freedom, which carries with it the dangers of risk and insecurity. Let us then distinguish modern Europe as the only free civilization to emerge in human history. And I make that perhaps rather perilous claim in order to emphasize my belief that Hayek's attempt to explain the emergence of modern economies, or extended orders, in universal terms is historically off the mark.

Europe as a Free Civilization

I take the conventional view that modern Europe emerged from the medieval period in the form of an increasing number of individualists living urban (and soon literate) lives. European societies certainly did have distinctions of status (priest, noble, tenant, servant, etc.) but Europeans increasingly associated in terms of common interests and enterprises. What they valued in the rule of law, and in their form of monarchy, was the peace and protection that allowed them to pursue whatever these projects might be. Furthermore, in various areas, people had become accustomed to being consulted. That King John in the early thirteenth century had acted arbitrarily generated the Magna

Carta, which declared some liberties to be established custom and available to all men. In universities, philosophical exploration of Christian doctrine along with an interest in understanding nature could be, with some caution, increasingly explored. Italy, as Jacob Burckhardt famously remarked of the Renaissance period "swarmed with individuality," while historians studying English social life take it back to the twelfth century.

There is no single explanation of the remarkable changes that generated modern Europe. One obvious feature is that educated Europeans had available a number of distinct and separate forms of experience in which to respond to the world. They were of course Christians, which necessarily involved in the two Testaments quite different views of life and conduct. It was also important that Christianity distinguished the sacred from the secular worlds, and this distinction involved freedom from much religious regulation. The project of a Europe united under papal control such as had been adumbrated under Innocent III fared no better than many other projects that have sought (without success until very recent times) to subsume Western Europe under a single overriding power or authority. Here also were a set of people educated in the Latin tongue and thus familiar with a polytheistic religion as well as a republican political bias. This was thus a strikingly pluralistic world. A familiarity with classical Greek language, culture, and experience was by no means unknown. And one of the most powerful and familiar enterprises in which many of these people (in all European regimes) were involved was the growth of science. To be an educated European was thus, by the seventeenth century at least, to have available to reflection a variety of different worlds, languages, logics, and outlooks, and the practices in terms of which they were related to each other were conversational and philosophical. It has often been observed that all civilizations look back with reverence to inspiring ancestors, but here was a civilization that greatly admired earlier passages of human cultivation that were not those of their own ancestors.

The various liberties and forms of consultation widespread in later medieval life became self-conscious in early modern times as a self-identification in terms of liberty itself. The consequence, of course, was an extremely quarrelsome world in which conflict and civil war, especially on religious grounds, was widespread. Skepticism flourished no less than dogmatism, and after the settlement, Europe settled down into a set of states with varied religious arrangements, some Protestant and Catholic. States varied in the degree of freedom and toleration permitted. From early in the eighteenth century, England was widely regarded (especially by French writers such as Voltaire and Montesquieu) as notably free, and as gaining strength from this fact. But as time passed, all European states, with contingent variations, followed this pattern. Is there perhaps some basic feature that might allow us to characterize this peculiarity of free regimes?

Let me suggest that what had happened here, as the result of a vast number of historical contingencies, was the recognition of a basic human attitude to the world: namely, ambivalence. Such an attitude to the world results from the constant succession of appetites and aversions in any human response to the world, and in fact we all have a variety of responses to people, institutions, ideas, and virtually everything else that we encounter. This ambivalence is obviously potentially a source of conflict and disorder, and as we have seen, the characteristic feature of comprehensively just societies is to "solve" the "problem" of conflict by imposing a single attitude to society and the world, and to punish deviance severely. But the characteristic achievement of Western Europe was as a range of free states that an ever increasing variety of admirations and aversions were permitted. And it will be obvious that such conflict could only be accommodated if new forms of manners and courtesy facilitating civil peace emerged.

Curiously enough, one area in which such new courtesy emerged was from politics—and I say curiously because we know that the vulgar attitude to politics is one of grinding partisanship. Hayek makes an interesting observation in his discussion of his extended order by remarking that fitting in with a catallaxy is perhaps a game.[8] In political life, the notionally ideal absolutism was that the ruler made a decision (with or without advice) and declared a policy that everyone approved. Often, of course, the approval was in fact lacking, but only grumbling could protest. In Britain toward the end of the eighteenth century, the solution to a dangerous partisanship was to recognize the political life of the nation as a kind of game determined by periodic elections. This development has turned out to be a brilliant solution to the problems involved in changing governments, problems illustrated by civil war and reactionary repression in many places elsewhere. The invention of the concept of a "loyal opposition" exemplifies one case in which a dangerous ambivalence of modern life has been transposed into a more civil key in which, far from threatening disorder, it could also generate a more rational way of legislating and making public policy.

But what in this elaboration of freedom has become of what by general agreement is the central basis of all civilizations—justice? There are two features to be observed. The first is that these free societies have established systems of law supplying the rules subjects must follow as required for the enjoyment of a peaceful society. And the notional origin of this body of law was attributed not to some divine founder or religious plan, but to a contract agreed by individuals living outside government. It came, notionally, from below, and therefore must be understood, in a slightly remote sense, as a form of self-government. For the point about a free society is that individual subjects, obliged to conform to the civic law, largely govern themselves. That is one sense in which they may be described as free. And the second point to make is that while ideals of comprehensive justice—justice, that is to say, understood as a fixed and determinate outcome of the processes to which the subjects must conform—are a constant temptation in the politics of free states, they have never so far managed to eliminate the unpredictability of liberal democracy. New problems will, indeed, provoke new judgments of what is in the public interest, but a free society is an association of individualists pursuing their own enterprises, and how it will develop cannot be reliably predicted. A free society is not a fixed just ideal. But that does not, of course, dampen the widespread nostalgia among idealists and reformers for a better society that might be comprehensively just.

The Hayekian Problem

Hayek in later life was concerned with two problems. The first was to establish the irrefutable impossibility of rationalist constructivism alias central planning. The second was to explain why this irrefutability remained in doubt. My elaboration of recent developments in European states related to both problems. There is, I think, no doubt that the information available to planners of society depends entirely on a pricing system, and that without it, planning would be mere guesswork, as had happened in the Soviet example. It followed that central planning could not generate prosperity, and that its currency among governments in modern conditions would lead to massive depopulation. On the other hand, there is a strong somewhat puritanical strand of opinion in modern Western societies that takes the view that our pursuit of prosperity corrupts our morals and destroys the planet. Hayek is thus perfectly right about the unrealities of socialist planning. He cannot be politically conclusive because in politics much depends on the end advanced.

Hayek's broad explanation of the obdurate foolishness of the continuing nostalgia for anything as vacuous as "social justice" has recourse to the effect of evolution—the echoes of tribal rationality on the one hand, and the progressive evolution in rule-following leading to the emergence of the extended order. But evolution is a vague idea, and I suggest that my account of more or less rational grounds for still yearning for a planned society is more convincing.

Notes

1. Friedrich A. Hayek, "The Atavism of Social Justice," in *New Studies in Philosophy, Politics, Economics and the History of Ideas* (London and Henley: Routledge and Kegan Paul, 1978), 62.
2. Friedrich A. Hayek, *The Fatal Conceit: The Errors of Socialism*, ed. W. W. Bartley III (Chicago, IL: University of Chicago Press, 1988).
3. Ibid., 7.
4. Ibid., 134.
5. Friedrich A. Hayek, *Hayek on Hayek: An Autobiographical Dialogue*, ed. Stephen Kresge and Leif Wenar (Chicago, IL: University of Chicago Press, 1994), 181: "I think there is an intellectual reversion on the way, and there is a good chance it may come in timebefore the movement in the opposite direction becomes irreversible. I am more optimistic than I was twenty years ago, when nearly all the leaders of opinion wanted to move in the socialist direction. This has particularly changed in the younger generation. So, if the change comes in time, there still is hope."
6. Hayek, *Fatal Conceit*, 133.
7. Urich Witt, "The Theory of Societal Evolution," in *Hayek, Co-ordination and Evolution*, ed. Jack Birner and Rudy van Zijp (London: Routledge, 2002), 187.
8. Hayek, *Fatal Conceit*, 154.

CHAPTER FIVE

F. A. Hayek and the Early Foundations of Spontaneous Order

Emily Skarbek

> The short-sighted wisdom, of perhaps well-meaning people, may rob us of a felicity, that would flow spontaneously from the nature of every large society, if none were to divert or interrupt this stream.[1]
>
> I do not intend to pitch my claim on behalf of Mandeville higher than to say that he made Hume possible.[2]

As one of the most significant intellectuals of the twentieth century, F. A. Hayek's contributions in economics, political science, political theory, and psychology often overshadow his lifelong fascination with the origins and development of social theorizing, in particular his concern for the history of ideas in political economy. Throughout his intellectual history, Hayek credits the contributions of Scottish Enlightenment thinkers for their discovery of orderly processes that are of human action but not human design, and he maintains a strong interest in tracing the origin and decline of these ideas in political economy.[3] In particular, Bernard Mandeville is a key figure in Hayek's account of the early foundations of spontaneous order theorizing.

This chapter begins by examining Hayek's views on spontaneous order over the course of his career. I argue that the importance Hayek places on the early foundations of Mandeville and Smith is closely connected to both his unfinished project, *The Abuse and Decline of Reason*, and his increasingly evolutionary approach to understanding the relationship between rules and order. Then I detail the significance of Mandeville by way of two key relationships to Hayek's own contributions to spontaneous order theory. First, Mandeville had distinctive insights into the relationship between human nature and processes of spontaneous order. Second, Mandeville was central in creating conceptual space for positive theories of spontaneous order processes that recognized the limitations of rational constructivist interventions. This general applicability and way of understanding these processes were aided by his methodological individualist approach of giving conjectural historical accounts of these processes unfolding through time. These conjectural historical accounts can further be seen as early analytical narrative explanations of the principle that gives rise to such orders. I conclude with remarks concerning the relevance of these ideas to advancing modern research agendas in political economy.

The chapter's focus on Mandeville takes advantage of the fact that F. B. Kaye's commentary that accompanied his 1924 edition of *Fable of the Bees* was singled out by both Hayek and his friend Jacob Viner as the starting point to discuss the history of social evolutionary theorizing. One aspect of the controversy between Hayek and Viner, who for good reason Hayek believed to be the greatest authority on history of economic ideas, concerns Kaye's reading of Mandeville. Although their disagreement on evolutionary theorizing in Mandeville is well known,[4] it was prefigured by private correspondence. Moreover, Viner's 1961 review of *The Constitution of Liberty* asked (first) whether Hayek's evolutionary account escaped from the social Darwinism he had written against 20 years earlier and (second) why the role of government cannot itself be thought of in terms of an evolutionary process. Viner's questions to Hayek continue to be a matter of discussion.[5]

Hayek and the History of Spontaneous Order Theorizing

Beginning with his inaugural lecture at the London School of Economics in 1933, Hayek situates the current state of economics as a departure from a broader tradition of classical political economy. According to Hayek, social science had abandoned "analytical economics" by subscribing to the ideas of the German Historicists who advocated examining the causes of social phenomena not based on general principles but on the particular historical circumstances and exigencies unique to each case in question. Analyzing the social world without reference to individual action and general laws opened the door for ad hoc theories of social wholes and critiques of market processes independent of their composite parts. Failures of systems became the focus rather than theories of their operation, and this strengthened the temptation for planners to attempt to control the particular undesirable aspects of social processes.[6]

For Hayek, this "Trend in Economic Thinking" was a staunch departure from the Scottish Enlightenment project of a theoretically informed method of examining an interconnected system of social coordination. The classical approach centered on the idea that the orderly processes of the social world were often brought about by unintended consequences, and in many cases were the outcomes of what "in isolation might be regarded as some of the most objectionable features of the system."[7] Understanding these orderly features of life was possible by way of explicating the general mechanisms of their function.

In "Scientism and the Study of Society," a three-part article spanning 1942 to 1944, Hayek connected this trend in the scope of economic thought to the ill-suited adoption of methodological approaches that imitated the natural sciences, what Hayek termed "scientism."[8] Hayek thought the purview of social science was moving away from understanding the central processes of human progress.[9] To adequately study processes of human social coordination as articulated by the Scottish Enlightenment thinkers, Hayek argues, requires a methodological approach that is suitable to the objects of inquiry. Because the facts of the social sciences are the subjective interpretations of local contextual conditions and these data are not given, fixed, or stable over time, the methods of the natural sciences are not appropriate for social science. The fundamental nature of social science data restricts our ability to offer more than general "explanations of the principle" by which spontaneous orders operate.

In developing his arguments concerning the importance of context-specific local knowledge amid a wider debate on the viability of central planning,[10] Hayek came to place increasing importance on the role of institutions in creating the conditions for the utilization and transference of knowledge. In turn, Hayek began working on questions concerning the emergence of institutions through similar processes.

Hayek emphasizes the idea that the same mechanisms by which we understand successful plan coordination in markets can be applied to understanding the communicative function of rules that govern market activities. "Just as the existence of a common structure of thought is the condition of the possibility of our communicating with one another, of your understanding what I say, so is it also the basis on which we interpret complicated social structures as those we find in economic life or law, language, and in customs."[11]

To understand social order, Hayek begins with the idea that the data which individuals act upon are constructed from their own perceptions of the relevant facts on which they act. Individuals act based on their interpretations of the context and problems as they confront them. People attribute meaning to events because they "interpret the phenomena in light of our own thinking."[12] We rely on our interpretive understanding not only to supply meaning to our interactions but also to orient our action to those with whom we interact. Our understanding of ourselves and what it means to be human supply us with the mechanism by which we interpret and understand other social agents. Language is a mechanism to communicate with others, providing insight into human relations. For Hayek, to explain or "understand human action without access to this type of knowledge" would be impossible.[13]

For Hayek, the central question of social theorizing is how the diverse and often divergent interpretations of the world come to be coordinated with one another to achieve social cohesion. As Hayek states, the 1937 "Economics and Knowledge" marked the "decisive step in this development of my thinking" about the manner in which prices guide the behavior of agents in the market ex ante and "must be explained in determining what people ought to do—they're not determined by what people have done in the past."[14]

Adequately studying these complicated social structures is contingent on adopting a framework of thought that does not preclude the phenomena one wishes to investigate. Closely connected to Hayek's methodological critiques of the rise of formalism and positivism was his deep concern with the trend in social theorizing that had come to assume that man's reason was capable of designing systems superior to those complex, undesigned orders. These two particularly dangerous trends in the study of political economy led Hayek to want to understand the origins of spontaneous order theorizing and trajectory of thought that diverged from these origins.

In his 1945 lecture "Individualism: True and False," Hayek begins to unpack this question of the origins of spontaneous order theorizing by elaborating the distinction between the two general streams in economic thought.[15] The first is what he terms "individualism true," which he attributed to the British tradition beginning with John Locke and including Mandeville, David Hume, Josiah Tucker, Adam

Ferguson, Smith, Edmund Burke, as well as Alexis de Tocqueville and Lord Acton. The second are the French and Continental writers heavily influenced by Cartesian rationalism. The "individualism true" tradition sought to provide a positive theory of society based first and foremost on the understanding of "individual actions directed toward other people and guided by their expected behavior."[16] For Hayek, "there is no other way toward an understanding of social phenomena."[17] Hayek's most important and significant contribution is arguably his explanation of how the price mechanism captures the private and dispersed knowledge in an economy and utilizes that knowledge in such a way that leads to an efficient allocation of resources in society. Hayek's 1945 "The Use of Knowledge in Society" is the most well-known single expression of the idea that the economic problem facing societies is how to overcome the epistemic limitations of any one individual by spontaneous order of the price system.[18]

Beginning in the 1950s, Hayek's writing shows a movement from his arguments concerning the communicative function of the market price system to similar treatments of the knowledge transmission processes of spontaneous orders. Specifically, these arguments came to focus on the evolutionary mechanisms by which rules, morals, norms, and established practices emerge and operate in governing social order. Following an appointment to the Committee on Social Thought at the University of Chicago in 1950, Hayek published a portion of what he had originally intended to be part of a larger project on *The Abuse and Decline of Reason* under the title of *The Counter Revolution of Science*. This volume contained his "scientism" articles along with a fuller exposition of the problem of appropriate methodology of the social sciences.

The same year *The Counter Revolution of Science* appeared in print, Hayek also published *The Sensory Order*.[19] The latter dealt specifically with the human mind as an ordering mechanism displaying many of the same properties as other complex systems. Hayek's time at the Committee on Social Thought proved influential on his writings, and throughout the 1950s his work on spontaneous orders shows the influence of his increased interest in biologists, systems theorists, and cybernetics.[20]

Hayek's 1955 essay "Degrees of Explanation" is the decisive turning point in Hayek's thinking, advancing the ideas of his first efforts with The Abuse of Reason Project.[21] The methodological limitations to explanations of the principle were now the feature of complex (as opposed to simple) phenomena. Hayek could now attribute the properties and methodologies of complex spontaneous orders across the various sciences, whereas before he had distinguished the natural sciences from the social. As Bruce Caldwell shows, Hayek illustrates his ideas in "Degrees of Explanation" with examples from evolution—unifying his ideas of "explanation of the principle" with the evolutionary theories of variation and selection.[22]

There is private correspondence that prefigures public disputes. In early 1956, Hayek sent Viner a letter defending the concept of "explanations of the principle." This was likely a response to Viner's reading of Hayek's "Degrees of Explanation" piece, although the correspondence is incomplete. In the letter, Hayek addresses the nature of theory ex ante to inform a given problem. Hayek writes,

> I don't think it is possible to generalize about what will be essential for a given problem. Sometimes it may be sufficient to know only that if a and b move together in the same direction c will move in the opposite direction without even knowing the absolute signs, sometimes the signs will be the crux of the problem and sometimes even fairly precise quantitative data of the particular situation may be essential.[23]

Hayek is clearly emphasizing that it is the nature of the problem at hand and the specific context that will determine the best approach for the topic. Hayek continues by writing to Viner, "All I wanted to stress is that theoretical statement need not be unimportant although we may have not quantitative data whatever and incidentally give precise meaning to what is often inexactly referred to as 'merely qualitative' statements."[24]

Following this conceptual turn in Hayek's thought, it is not surprising that Hayek finds the evolutionary ideas regarding spontaneous order more interesting in the contributions of the early spontaneous order theorists. The 1960 *Constitution of Liberty* contains two chapters with direct treatments of evolutionary ideas.[25] Building on what he had first outlined in "Individualism: True and False," Hayek sought to detail the contributions of what he termed the "British Tradition." The legacy of the Scottish Enlightenment thinkers, writes Hayek, is "an interpretation of the growth of civilization that is still the indispensable foundation of the argument for liberty. They find the origin of institutions not in contrivance or design, but in the survival of the successful."[26]

Specifically, Hayek states that the "anti-rationalistic insight into historical happenings that Adam Smith shares with Hume, Adam

Ferguson, and others enabled them for the first time to comprehend how institutions and morals, language, and law, have evolved by a process of cumulative growth and that it is only with and within this framework that human reason has grown and can successfully operate."[27] Hayek made the switch from the natural–social science distinction he had developed within the context of his "Individualism: True and False" argument to a distinction between simple and complex evolutionary systems.

During the same year, Jacob Viner published "The History of Laissez-Faire," which downplayed the Smithian insights of interest to Hayek.[28] Viner challenged the evolutionary distinctions Hayek had been developing and suggested that Hayek's *The Road to Serfdom*—originally intended as the final component of The Abuse of Reason Project—was an arbitrarily selected point along the political economy spectrum.[29] Hayek also sent Viner an advanced copy of *The Constitution of Liberty* and Viner's review demonstrates that he was well aware of Hayek's more evolutionary take on the foundations of spontaneous order theorizing.[30] Hayek and Viner discussed both the greater issues surrounding the evolutionary perspectives on spontaneous orders as well as their interpretations and Mandeville.[31]

Throughout the 1960s while at the University of Freiburg, Hayek published a series of essays that expressed his evolutionary conception of rules and order. He revisited the work of Mandeville and Smith, publishing two essays dedicated to their insights amid his later work on the evolutionary nature of systems of rules.[32] In his "Lecture on a Master Mind: Dr. Bernard Mandeville," which he gave to the British Academy in 1966,[33] Hayek uses the occasion to address Viner's reading of Mandeville as non-evolutionary and anti-laissez faire.[34] Viner stressed Mandeville's frequent use of "the dexterous management by which the skillful politician might turn private vices into public benefits"[35] to imply that Mandeville advocated government intervention.[36] Hayek clarified his views on Mandeville and accepted the response offered by Nathan Rosenberg that the phrase Viner quoted is an unfortunately short-hand description that conceals the workings of an evolutionary process.[37] Hayek makes it explicit that he is not interested in Mandeville for his work in technical economics or his theory of ethics.

In response to Hayek's British academy lecture, Viner writes to Hayek. Viner indicates that he does not agree with Hayek's interpretation of Mandeville, that Hayek's views present a problematic interpretation. Viner nevertheless upholds his earlier views on Mandeville, stating that he has nothing substantive to change aside from an early error he attributes to following the Kaye edition. The letter is of interest however, because he indicated that he does in fact agree with Hayek about the evolutionary components in Mandeville. Viner thus recognizes some aspect of Mandeville's evolutionary contribution, particularly with respect to the way in which his thought stood outside of the accepted theology of the period, but does not afford it much weight. He remains unconvinced that these ideas are central to Mandeville's contribution and argues that Hayek and Kaye miss the spirit of Mandeville.[38] For Viner, whatever extent to which the evolutionary component in Mandeville is important, it does not prevent the deliberate design of interventions into spontaneous orders by political agents.

Hayek, however, attributes to Mandeville three distinct contributions that make him an important figure in the early foundations of spontaneous order theorizing. First, in circumscribing Mandeville's contribution, Hayek praises Mandeville for his psychological insight into human nature.[39] Second, Hayek credits Mandeville with originating the "breakthrough in modern thought of the twin ideas of evolution and of the spontaneous formation of order."[40] This breakthrough was a result of challenging the habits of thought that had persisted with the Greek dichotomy between "natural (*physei*) and that which is artificial or conventional (*thesei* or *nomo*)."[41] Third, Hayek clearly saw Mandeville's application of spontaneous order theorizing to new topics (those of both natural and social science) and broader social patterns as a distinguishing feature of his work in the history of ideas. As Hayek came to abandon his earlier natural/social science distinction for the study of systems in favor or a more evolutionary distinction between simple/complex orders, it is likely that he became more aware of the importance of Mandeville's contribution in this respect.

First, it is important to clarify that it is not Mandeville's economics or his notorious moral paradox that earn him significance for Hayek. In fact, Hayek believes that Mandeville did himself a disservice by starting with the contrast between the selfishness of motives and the general benefits that such privately motivated behavior produces. Reading Mandeville's *Private Vices, Publick Benefits* with a focus on the obvious moral paradox prevented, in Hayek's opinion, the appreciation of his more fundamental and general evolutionary contribution. Like Rosenberg, Hayek believed that Mandeville's central thesis was much deeper and more advanced in his later writings[42] and found in Mandeville the core building blocks of David Hume's views on mind and society.[43] In other words, Hayek saw in Mandeville a methodological individualist account of agents, "all of them very little differing from one another in natural parts and sagacity" producing an unintended order.[44] By sidestepping the ethical baggage of virtue and vice, Hayek focuses squarely on his positive contributions as a social theorist examining the mechanism by which particular orders emerge.

Hayek does, however, term Mandeville a "great student of human nature" but again, not for his characterization of selfish action. Hayek was impressed by Mandeville's psychological insights about the ways in which people tend to create "ex post rationalization of actions directed by emotions."[45] Hayek views Mandeville's insights into human psychology as remarkably modern and this is likely due to the connection with Hayek's own work on the emergent structure of the cognitive process in *The Sensory Order* and Hayek's ideas on the interpretive and subjective nature of economic phenomena.

Mandeville's psychology is thoroughly situated within the anti-rationalistic tradition in which Hayek grounds his theory of institutional evolution. Mandeville holds a philosophical position that believes that the rational faculties of man are determined by the mechanism through which it has its being. As such, these views reinforce Mandeville's idea that man's reason is directed toward discovering that which will further the agent's desires. This conception of the relationship between reason and action suggests that men will naturally act in accordance with what they perceive to be profitable behavior. Moreover, man's sociability comes about from both his insatiable wants and his frustrations with efforts to meet these wants. Man's rationality is therefore constrained by his practical limitations of local knowledge, time, and place. This anti-rationalistic, adaptive, and "ecologically rational" view of human agency in Mandeville is attractive to Hayek.[46]

As mentioned previously, Hayek's theory of the structure of the brain was influential in his thinking about the evolutionary conception of rules.[47] Hayek makes note of Mandeville's treatment of the structure and function of the brain[48] but does not draw out the precise connections. However, these connections are apparent in Mandeville's Fourth Dialogue. Here Mandeville discusses the structure of the human brain, and develops the idea that even if one could physically deconstruct and understand each of the component parts of the brain, "the best Naturalist must acknowledge . . . as to the mysterious Structure of the Brain itself, and the more abstruse Oeconomy of it, that he knows nothing."[49]

Mandeville suggests that operation of mind cannot be reducible to the physical operation of the parts, speaking of an "unconceivable Order" in which parts of the brain are "cluster'd together in a perplexing variety of Folds and Windings."[50] Here the "Senses deposite [sic] the vast Treasure of Images, constantly, as through their Organs they receive them... always, either searching for, or variously disposing the Images retain'd, and shooting through the infinite Meanders of that wonderful Substance, employ themselves, without ceasing, in that inexplicable Performance, the Contemplation."[51] This treatment of the complexity and spontaneous ordering of the mechanism was particularly attractive to Hayek to both his own conceptions of psychology in *The Sensory Order*, as well as his interpretive epistemology of social science. In fact, Hayek concludes his essay on Mandeville by directly pointing to the relationship between the two. He states that Mandeville and Hume were responsible for showing that "the sense of justice and probity on which the order in this sphere rested, was not originally implanted in man's mind but had, like that mind itself, grown in a process of gradual evolution which at least in principle we might learn to understand."[52]

To see the relationship between Hayek and Mandeville, consider Hayek's 1962 essay "Rules, Perception, and Intelligibility" where he interweaves his evolutionary ideas across a wide variety of fields, integrating ideas spanning biology, psychology, philosophy of mind, and methodology of the social sciences.[53] The essay preceded his piece on Mandeville and shows his early attempts to put his more evolutionary conceptions of order together with the idea that all animals, including humans, are rule-following creatures. The rules to which their behavior conforms are abstract, and in making use of these rules, individuals are unaware of their utilization. The two examples that Hayek uses to illustrate his point are the use of complex rules of grammar in language and the ability to recognize facial expressions and interpret emotions, both of which are examples Mandeville develops in Fourth Dialogue.[54]

Mandeville's evolutionary approach to understanding language transmission comes out of his later revisions of *The Fable*, where he offers a conjectural account of how children attain the skills of language and facial recognition. "The best Thing, therefore, we can do to Infants after the first Month, besides feeding and keeping them from Harm, is to make them take in Ideas, beginning by the two most useful Senses, the Sight and Hearing; and dispose them to set about this Labour of the Brain, and by our Example, encourage them to imitate us in Thinking."[55] The more adults play with and talk to infants in their early stages of development, the more capacity the child will have to mimic and adopt these traits.

Mandeville makes clear that these skills develop by habit and not because of constructed methods of learning. For instance, he suggests that to raise an infant, rather than "the Wisest Matron in the World, I would prefer an active young Wench, whose Tongue never stands still, that should run about, and never cease diverting and playing with it whilst it was awake; and where People can afford it, two or three of them, to relieve one another when they are tired."[56] For Mandeville, the "non-sensical Chat of Nurses" is "of inestimable Use" to infants because "[w]hat Infants should chiefly learn is the Performance itself, the Exercise of Thinking, and to contract a Habit of disposing, and with Ease and Agility managing the Images retain'd, to the purpose intended."[57]

As Hayek's theory of human social institutions became increasingly evolutionary, he argued that the rules conducive to human flourishing were never invented or designed. Institutions that have made the extended order of exchange possible emerged through a process of "winnowing and sifting, directed by the differential advantages gained by groups from practices adopted for some unknown and perhaps purely accidental reasons."[58] Informal and formal institutions led to patterns of behavior that made it possible for people to engage in greater degrees of complex coordination. Those patterns of behavior that promoted the division of labor and knowledge were adopted and successful institutions persisted and spread. The foundational rules governing "property, honesty, contract, exchange, trade, competition, gain, and privacy" were never "invented" but rather discovered over the course of many centuries of social evolution.[59]

Hayek's *Law, Legislation and Liberty* project contains further developments of what he had much earlier viewed as part of The Abuse of Reason Project. In Volume 1, Hayek introduces the distinction between *kosmos* and *taxis*, which develops the idea of the conceptual distinction for positive theories of spontaneous order that he found attractive in Mandeville.[60] Here Hayek's evolutionary treatments of spontaneous order theorizing come to full fruition—coming to perhaps their strongest forms in Hayek's essay on the three sources of human values: our genetic inheritance; those that are the product of rational thought; and finally culture, which "is neither natural nor artificial; neither genetically transmitted nor rationally designed."[61] Hayek brings the ideas full circle by suggesting that "mind and culture developed concurrently and not successively."[62] Finally, Hayek elaborates on this further in the *The Fatal Conceit* when discussing the extended order lying "between instinct and reason."[63]

By the end of his career, Hayek comes "to believe that both the aim of the market order, and therefore the object of explanation of the theory of it, is to cope with the inevitable ignorance of everybody of most of the particular facts which determine this order." By a process that men did not understand, their activities have produced an order much more extensive and comprehensive than anything they could have comprehended. However, "Even two hundred years after Adam Smith's *Wealth of Nations*, it is not yet fully understood that it is the great achievement of the market to have made possible a far-ranging division of labor, that it brings about a continuous adaptation of economic effect to millions of particular facts or events which in their totality are not known and cannot be known to anybody."[64]

Finally, what Hayek finds to be of direct relevance to his work on the limitations of our knowledge is Mandeville's investigation into the evolution of institutions over time. Mandeville argues, "that we often ascribe to the excellency of man's genius, and the depth of his penetration, what is in reality owing to the length of time, and the experience of many generations."[65] Developing this with direct reference to laws, Mandeville explains, "there are very few that are the work of one man, or of one generation; the greatest part of them are the product of the joint labor of several ages."[66] Hayek suggests that Mandeville's "new genetic or evolutionary view" was significant because of the applications he made to society at large and the extension of this thinking to new areas.[67]

Hayek concludes that Mandeville's argument is primarily concerned with showing how most of societies' institutions are not the result of design, but how "a most beautiful superstructure may be raised upon a rotten and despicable foundation"[68] and how "the order, oeconomy, and the very existence of civil society... is entirely built upon the variety of our wants... so that the whole superstructure is made up of the reciprocal services which men do to each other."[69]

Conclusion

The implications of this account have immediate relevance for contemporary economics and the practice of social science. First, embedded in this story of Hayek's intellectual trajectory is the idea that at any given period of time there may be competing notions of what constitutes advancement in the study of social order. Scientific progress may not be a simple linear ordering process where what is current, or at the forefront of science, is necessarily at the forefront of truth. If so, the role of the history of ideas becomes of pronounced importance in providing access to alternative ways of addressing pressing gaps in our current body of knowledge. By revisiting the work of Mandeville, Hayek orients his own thought concerning the knowledge properties of evolutionary spontaneous orders within the work of his theoretical predecessors.

Second, if the study of complex systems is fundamentally limited to explanations of the principle, then this warrants rethinking the place of conjectural histories and analytical narratives in contemporary social theory. For Hayek, Mandeville is an important character in the history of political economy because he widened the application of spontaneous order theorizing to areas of markets, law, morals, language, and culture. If the fundamental questions of social theory involve understanding the emergence and evolution of the institutions that give rise to an extensive process of division of labor and wealth creation, and the complex nature of the phenomena in question dictates the methods we employ in answering those questions, more room within the current debate may be allowed for these methods of understanding spontaneous order.[70]

Notes

1. Bernard Mandeville, *The Fable of the Bees or Private Vices, Publick Benefits*, vol. 2, ed. F. B. Kaye (Oxford: Clarendon Press, 1924), 353.
2. Friedrich A. Hayek, "Dr. Bernard Mandeville (1670–1733)," in *The Collected Works of F. A. Hayek*, vol. 3, ed. W. W. Bartley III and Stephen Kresge, *The Trend of Economic Thinking: Essays on Political Economists and Economic History* (Chicago, IL: University of Chicago Press, [1966] 1991), 95.
3. Friedrich A. Hayek, "The Results of Human Action but not of Human Design," in *Studies in Philosophy, Politics and Economics* (Chicago, IL: University of Chicago, 1967), 96–105.
4. The reprint of Hayek's essay on Mandeville in the *Collected Works* includes evidence that he continued to follow the scholarship in which his public discussion with Viner and Rosenberg were central issues. Hayek, "Dr. Bernard Mandeville," 100.
5. Jacob Viner, "Hayek on Freedom and Coercion," *Southern Economic Journal* 27, no. 3 (January 1961): 230–36. Hayek and Social Darwinism are discussed by Peart and Levy elsewhere in this present volume. Hayek and evolved rules are discussed by Gaus in this present volume. Viner's challenge to a listing of "appropriate" government functions is that on Hayekian grounds government policy is endogenous. Viner, "Hayek on Freedom and Coercion," 235: "It seems feasible

to me to apply Hayek's method of speculative history to government itself, and to treat it, with all its defects and such merits as Hayek may be willing to concede to it, as itself an institution which is in large degree a spontaneous growth, inherently decentralized, experimental, innovating, subject not only to tendencies for costly meddling but also to propensities for inertia and costly inaction."

6. Friedrich A. Hayek, "The Trend in Economic Thinking," in *The Collected Works of F. A. Hayek*, vol. 3, ed. W. W. Bartley III and Stephen Kresge, *The Trend of Economic Thinking: Essays on Political Economists and Economic History* (Chicago, IL: University of Chicago Press, [1933] 1991), 17–34.
7. Ibid., 26–27: "From the time of Hume and Adam Smith, the effect of every attempt to understand economic phenomena—that is to say, of every theoretical analysis—has been to show that, in large part, the coordination of individual efforts in society is not the product of deliberate planning, but has been brought about, and in many cases could only have been brought about, by means which nobody wanted or understood, and which in isolation might be regarded as some of the most objectionable features of the system. It showed that changes implied, and made necessary, by changes in our wishes, or in the available means, were brought about without anybody realising their necessity. In short, it showed that an immensely complicated mechanism existed, worked and solved problems, frequently by means which proved to be the only possible means by which the result could be accomplished, but which could not possibly be the result of deliberate regulation because nobody understood them. Even now, when we begin to understand their working, we discover again and again that necessary functions are discharged by spontaneous institutions. If we tried to run the system by deliberate regulation, we should have to invent such institutions, and yet at first we did not even understand them when we saw them."
8. Friedrich A. Hayek, "Scientism and the Study of Society" first appeared in three parts in the London School of Economics journal *Economica*. The original publications are 9, no. 35 (August 1942): 267–91; 10, no. 37 (February 1943): 34–63; 11, no. 41 (February 1944): 27–39. The standard edition in the future will be Friedrich A. Hayek, *The Collected Works of F. A. Hayek*, ed. Bruce Caldwell, vol. 13, *Studies in the Abuse and Decline of Reason: Texts and Documents* (Chicago, IL: University of Chicago Press, 2010).
9. Ibid.
10. Peter Boettke, Emily Schaeffer, and Nicholas Snow, "The Context of Context: The Evolution of Hayek's Epistemic Turn in Economics and Politics," *Advances in Austrian Economics* 14, no. 1 (2010): 69–86.
11. Hayek, *Studies in the Abuse of Reason*, 76.
12. Hayek, *The Sensory Order: An Inquiry into the Foundations of Theoretical Psychology* (Chicago, IL: University of Chicago Press, 1952), 135.
13. Ibid., 43–44.
14. Friedrich A. Hayek, *Hayek on Hayek*, ed. Stephen Kresge and Leif Wenar (London: Routledge, 1994), 68.
15. Friedrich A. Hayek, "Individualism: True and False," in *Individualism and Economic Order* (Chicago, IL: University of Chicago Press, [1945] 1948), 1–32.

16. Ibid., 5, 4: "The true individualism which I shall try to defend began its modern development with John Locke, and particularly with Bernard Mandeville and David Hume, and achieved full stature for the first time in the work of Josiah Tucker, Adam Ferguson, and Adam Smith and in that of their great contemporary, Edmund Burke—the man whom Smith described as the only person he ever knew who thought on economic subjects exactly as he did without any previous communication having passed between them."
17. Ibid., 6.
18. Friedrich A. Hayek, "The Use of Knowledge in Society," in *Individualism and Economic Order* (Chicago, IL: University of Chicago [1945] 1948), 77–91.
19. Hayek, *Sensory Order*; Friedrich A. Hayek, *The Counter-Revolution of Science* (Glencoe, IL: Free Press), 1952.
20. Hayek attended the Darwin Centennial Celebration at the University of Chicago. Papers on a variety of evolutionary topics had been circulated in the year leading up to the meeting in 1959. Curiously, Hayek did not himself contribute a paper but joined a panel on "The Evolution of the Mind." Bruce Caldwell, *Hayek's Challenge: An Intellectual Biography of F. A. Hayek* (Chicago, IL: University of Chicago Press, 2004), 303.
21. Friedrich A. Hayek, "Degrees of Explanation," in *Studies in Philosophy, Politics and Economics* (Chicago, IL: University of Chicago, 1967), 3–21.
22. Caldwell, *Hayek's Challenge*, 302–03.
23. See Hayek archives Box 56.
24. Ibid.
25. Friedrich A. Hayek, *The Collected Works of F. A. Hayek*, ed. Ronald Hamowy, vol. 17, *The Constitution of Liberty: The Definitive Edition* (Chicago, IL: University of Chicago Press, [1960] 2011).
26. Ibid., 112.
27. Hayek, *Constitution of Liberty*, 112.
28. Jacob Viner, "The Intellectual History of Laissez Faire," *Journal of Law and Economics* 3 (October 1960): 45–69.
29. The question of an evolved government is posed in Viner's "Hayek on Freedom and Coercion."
30. Ibid.
31. See also Hayek archives Box 56, file 21.
32. Friedrich A. Hayek, *New Studies in Philosophy, Politics, Economics and History of Ideas* (Chicago, IL: University of Chicago Press, 1978).
33. Hayek, "Bernard Mandeville," 79–100.
34. Ibid., 89. "I would not wish to dwell on this at any length, however, if it were not for the fact that Mandeville's long recognised position as an anticipator of Adam Smith's argument for economic liberty has recently been challenged by Professor Jacob Viner, than whom there is no greater authority on such matters. With all due respect, however, it seems to me that Professor Viner has been misled by a phrase which Mandeville repeatedly uses, namely his allusions to the 'dextrous management by which the skilful politician might turn private vices into public benefits'."

35. Mandeville, *Fable of the Bees*, vol. 1, 51, and 369; vol. 2, 319.
36. Jacob Viner, "Introduction," in Bernard Mandeville, *A Letter to Dion*, 1732 (Los Angeles, William Andrews Clark Memorial Library, University of California, 1953). Viner responds to F. B. Kaye's laissez-faire interpretation of Mandeville. Hayek explicitly credits Kaye for inspiring his evolutionary reading of Mandeville, Hayek, "Individualism: True or False," 9. Hayek is careful to note that outside the evolutionary developments Mandeville is a predictable mercantilist. Hayek, "Bernard Mandeville," 89. This would, of course, come as no surprise to a reader of Eli Heckscher, *Mercantilism*, trans. Mendel Shapiro, revised edition, ed. E. F. Soderlund (London: George Allen & Unwin, [1931] 1955), vol. 2, 164–67; 366–67.
37. Nathan Rosenberg, "Mandeville and Laissez-Faire," *Journal of the History of Ideas* 24, no. 2 (April–June 1963): 184–98.
38. Hayek sent Viner a copy of the British Academy lecture. In response, Viner writes that Hayek's lecture on Mandeville "presents some real puzzles of your making" and "as things stand now…I see nothing to withdraw, to amend, or to justify, in what I have written about Mandeville." The correspondence is cited in the notes to Hayek, "Berrnard Mandeville," 89.
39. Ibid., 80.
40. Hayek, "Bernard Mandeville," 81.
41. Ibid., 84.
42. Ibid.
43. Ibid.
44. Mandeville, *Fable of the Bees*, vol. 2, 141.
45. Hayek, "Bernard Mandeville," 80: "Professor Kaye has duly drawn attention to the more remarkable of Mandeville's psychological insights, especially to his modern conception of an *ex post* rationalization of actions directed by emotions."
46. See F. B. Kaye's "Introduction" in Bernard Mandeville, *Fable of the Bees*, ed. F. B. Kaye (Oxford: Clarendon Press, 1924), lxxxvi.
47. Hayek, *Sensory Order*.
48. Hayek, "Bernard Mandeville," 126.
49. Mandeville, *Fable of the Bees*, vol. 2, 165.
50. Ibid.
51. Ibid., 166.
52. Hayek, "Bernard Mandeville," 97.
53. Friedrich A. Hayek (ed.), "Rules, Perception and Intelligibility," in *Studies in Philosophy, Politics and Economics* (Chicago, IL: University of Chicago, 1967), 43–65.
54. Hayek employs this example in the "Scientism" and "The Facts of the Social Sciences" to explain that the principle by which we acquire these abilities operates by recognition of abstract patterns and unknowing obedience of rules.
55. Mandeville, *Fable of the Bees*, vol. 2, 169.
56. Ibid.
57. Ibid., 170.

58. Friedrich A. Hayek, *Law, Legislation, and Liberty*, vol. 3, *The Political order of a Free People* (Chicago, IL: University of Chicago Press, 1979), 155.
59. Friedrich A. Hayek, *The Collected Works of F. A. Hayek*, vol. 1, *The Fatal Conceit*, ed. W. W. Bartley, III (Chicago, IL: University of Chicago Press, 1988), 12.
60. Friedrich A. Hayek, *Law, Legislation and Liberty*, vol. 1, *Rules and Order* (Chicago, IL: University of Chicago Press, 1973), 37.
61. Hayek, *Political Order*, p. 155.
62. Ibid., 156.
63. Hayek, *Fatal Conceit*, 153.
64. Ibid., 19.
65. Mandeville, *Fable of the Bees*, vol. 2, 141.
66. Ibid., 142.
67. Hayek, "Bernard Mandeville," 92–93.
68. Ibid., 64.
69. Ibid., 329; quoted in Hayek, "Bernard Mandeville."
70. Email: emily.skarbek@kcl.ac.uk. Address: King's College London, Department of Political Economy, Strand Campus, WC2B 6NR, London, United Kingdom. Phone: +44(0207) 848–7339. The author thanks Marina Bianchi, Bruce Caldwell, Neil De Marchi, David Levy, David Skarbek, and participants at Duke University's Political Economy seminar for helpful comments. The generous support of the Center for the History of Political Economy during the 2011–12 academic year is gratefully acknowledged.

CHAPTER SIX

Hayek and the Nomothetes

CHRISTOPHER S. MARTIN

In both *The Constitution of Liberty*[1] and the later volumes of *Law, Legislation and Liberty*[2] Friedrich Hayek employed the political history of ancient Athens to illustrate his claims about democracy and liberty. The model national constitution Hayek provided in *Political Order of a Free People*—the third and last volume of *Law, Legislation and Liberty*—has found few admirers but many critics. Attacks from the latter group seem to have largely disqualified the constitution from ongoing serious discussion or consideration. It cannot, however, be dismissed as an unimportant element of Hayek's thought. He himself seemed to view it as the climax of what he believed would be his last major work, and describes the *Political Order* as "lead[ing] up to a proposal of basic alteration of the structure of democratic government" of which the constitution was an integral part.[3]

Criticism of Hayek's constitutional project, while probably fatal to the idea as originally presented, has nonetheless not fully appreciated his case for fundamental reform. Most hostile fire has been directed at Hayek's claim that a generality requirement for laws would protect freedom—an idea that explains many of the problematic features of the model constitution. But there was an additional and less recognized element of Hayek's case: an argument for insulating the law proper (carefully defined) from the dynamics of factional party politics. While the features of the model constitution inspired by this argument are also problematic, the problems may not be intrinsic to the concern itself. The design flaws could stem instead from Hayek's deep caution about democracy and consequent proposal for an awkwardly elected, almost oligarchic Upper

House in his constitution. Ironically, though Hayek justifies his caution about democracy by appeal to the historical experience of ancient Athens, it was Athens that inspired Hayek's central institutional innovation in the first place: the assignment of the tasks of lawmaking and governing to two distinct institutions. In explicit imitation of Athens Hayek calls the members of the former body, the Legislative Assembly, *nomothetae* (or nomothetes, in wieldier contemporary usage).[4]

Hayek's attitude toward independent Athens was therefore a complex one. He obviously admired some Athenian institutions but blamed the city's political failure on democratic excess. But the historical interpretation found in *Law, Legislation and Liberty* appears to be at variance with more recent classical scholarship. This is more than an obscure curiosity since Hayek's pessimistic reading of democracy led him to miss or ignore key features of Athenian practice. The nomothetes of Hayek's constitution resemble the Athenian ones only in their name and overall function; the originals operated in an institutional environment in many ways more responsive to his second case for fundamental reform than the convoluted system he in fact proposed. The Hayekian model constitution may, then, still be worthy of discussion only if Athenian institutions neglected by Hayek himself are again appreciated. Reaching that point requires, of course, a certain amount of background argument. This begins with a deeper assessment of Hayek's objectives for the model constitution and the institutional means he adopted to achieve them.

Rationales and Structure of the Model Constitution

The enterprise of the model constitution is most visibly inspired by Hayek's conception of freedom as developed both in the *Law, Legislation, and Liberty* volumes of the 1970s and in the earlier *Constitution of Liberty*. In the latter work, Hayek attempted to define liberty as the absence of coercion and coercion, in turn, as a situation in which another human will manipulates a person's possible choices to induce them to act as the coercer desires.[5] Accordingly, freedom was linked closely with the idea of generally applicable laws:

> When we obey laws, in the sense of general abstract rules laid down irrespective of their application to us, we are not subject to another man's will and are therefore free...Because the rule is laid down in ignorance of the particular case and no man's will decides the coercion used to enforce it, the law is not arbitrary.

> This, however, is true only if by "law" we mean the general rules that apply equally to everybody.[6]

Hayek shortly later states even more clearly that "freedom can never mean more than that [men's actions] are restricted only by general rules."[7] Using this relatively flexible definition of freedom enabled him to make a wide range of state activities compatible with a free society. Health and safety regulations, a social security system, a social minimum, and support for education were all in principle compatible with the rule of law and hence with freedom. The legal framework could be altered to improve market outcomes (perhaps with some priority on reforms beneficial to the poor) although explicit redistribution, price controls, and other discretionary measures failed the generality test and so were forbidden.[8]

Hayek recognized that the state must still be allowed some power to coerce, both to prevent individuals from coercing one another and to obtain resources for collective action. He therefore restricted the objective of his theory to depriving this "threat of coercion...of most of its harmful and objectionable character."[9] Generality of the coercive laws would promote this objective, as would predictability. Citizens could often avoid coercion by abstaining from prohibited actions. When the state had to compel the performance of specific duties—Hayek cites mandatory jury service—pressure could at least be applied through some mechanism (such as a random lottery) independent of the arbitrary will of any specific individual. Even the evils of taxation and military conscription could be mitigated if predictably and impersonally applied in this way; Hayek believed that such a method would "depriv[e] them largely of the evil nature of coercion."[10]

This set of claims about generality and freedom are what I identify as Hayek's first rationale for constitutional reform, and their influence clearly determines the very demanding task Hayek sets for the Constitutional Court in his proposed system. This Court would be guided by a Basic Clause in the written constitution that would define a just law; this clause, in other words, would ensure that the only laws that could pass judicial review would coerce individuals (if at all) by predictable and common rules rather than by the arbitrary will of officials. In Hayek's tentative description of the clause, legislation could be just in this way only if it were

> intended to apply to an indefinite number of unknown future instances, to serve the formation and preservation of an abstract

> order whose concrete contents were unforeseeable, but not the achievement of particular concrete purposes, and finally to exclude all provisions intended or known to affect principally particular identifiable individuals or groups.[11]

Thanks in part to this clause, the model constitution possessed a three-layered structure of authority. The constitution itself formed the top layer, since it not only described the structure of the government but also restricted the scope of laws. In this respect, though not in the content of the restriction, it of course resembles many modern democratic constitutions. The distinguishing feature of the Hayekian constitution, though, is the presence of two rather than one layers of authority below the constitution itself. The middle layer is the law in a specially defined sense, what Hayek says is "what political theorists have long regarded simply as *the law*, the lawyer's law, or the *nomos* of the ancient Greeks and the *ius* of the Romans."[12] This *nomos* consists of the "general rules of just conduct" that emerge primarily from the efforts of judges to resolve disputes.[13] These are the only rules permitted by the Hayekian constitution, in normal circumstances, to authorize the coercion of specific individuals. Even then, such coercion can only be exercised for the purpose of "defin[ing] and protect[ing]" each individual's sphere or domain of freedom, or (in the case of tax collection) financing the services rendered by government.[14]

Comprising the third layer of authority in the model constitution are what Hayek variously describes as enactments, statutes, or *thesis* after the Greek for "set" law.[15] Whereas a judge guided by the background *nomos* waits for disputes to come to him, sovereigns must actively pursue specific goals. In a very primitive or simple form of government, a ruler might be able to do this by issuing personal commands to his henchmen. In a government of any greater complexity, however, even an autocrat would find it necessary to issue rules prescribing the operation of the apparatus of government itself. Such rules would include (e.g.) budgets, the scope of authority of different departments, and procedures for specific tasks as well as (perhaps) direct commands to pursue particular goals.[16] But such rules for the operation of government could conceivably operate within the broader framework of the *nomos*. The government would interact with society on the same legal terms as any other organization would, with the sole but important exception that it received taxpayer money. Statute or *thesis* would "regulate the powers of the agents of government over the ...resources entrusted to them" without conferring any special ability to command ordinary citizens who were not employees of the government.[17] In this conception, *nomos* and *thesis* control, respectively, the distinct categories of government action famously described by John Stuart Mill as authoritative and unauthoritative interference—a connection Hayek explicitly makes in *The Constitution of Liberty.*[18] In effect, Hayek has adopted Mill's typology of government action while imposing a generality requirement on the *nomos* or set of authoritative rules. The two categories could also be seen as reflecting a distinction between a ruler's will and the limits on the exercise of his will imposed by the subject's view of his just authority, a framework that Hayek noticed in David Hume.[19]

But though this generality requirement is Hayek's most obvious rationale for constitutional reform, it does not stand alone. The *Law, Legislation and Liberty* volumes contain a related but distinct line of reasoning about what the American framers would have called factions. Hayek feared that the pursuit of partial rather than general interests through the manipulation of the *nomos*, the coercively enforceable rules of just conduct, was a primary threat to freedom in a democracy. This concern flows logically from Hayek's definition of freedom as the absence of arbitrary coercion, or equivalently his stipulation that coercion must be applied only by general rules. If only the law proper can coerce, then the application of law for any reason other than the general good will unjustly disadvantage particular groups or individuals and therefore violate their freedom. But such abuse of the law is almost inevitable if legislation emerges from the chaotic arena of party politics. By its very nature, the bargaining process that gives rise to factional (party) programs and resulting legislative compromises rarely or never reflects the preferences even of any single individual, much less the common opinion of the community as a whole. Voters or their representatives must almost always be content with selecting an imperfect choice. This (Hayek argues) is unavoidable when decisions about the allocation of resources must be made, when there is no possible answer that could fully satisfy everyone. But party bargaining over the content of the *nomos* has the toxic result that the resulting enforceable rules of just conduct reflect no one's considered judgment; instead of determining the general opinion of what was just, lawmaking became a matter of issuing "special advantages to a sufficient number of groups to obtain a majority support."[20] The political majority is guided not by what they believe is right but what is necessary in the bargaining game of politics.[21] Politics becomes a trap:

> Though as individuals we have learnt to accept that in pursuing our aims we are limited by established rules of just conduct, when

> we vote as members of a body that has power to alter these rules, we often do not feel similarly restrained…[voters will often] claim for themselves benefits of a kind which they know are being granted to others, but which they also know cannot be granted universally and which they would therefore perhaps prefer not to see granted to anybody at all…majorities will approve measures of a kind which, if they were asked to vote on the principle, they would probably prohibit once and for all.[22]

Such a situation resembles the classic prisoner's dilemma. Everyone would prefer a world without special privileges to the existing world, but each individual would prefer a world in which he or she *alone* gets special privilege even more. The result of course is that *everyone* seeks special privileges, resulting in wasteful and irrational policy. The Hayekian constitutional project aims to provide an escape from this trap by removing law from the factional arena. The escape can only work if a political space is created that allows binding votes on questions of principle rather than evanescent factional compromises.

The model constitution purports to create such a space through a dramatic institutional innovation. Hayek proposed to separate the power to revise the higher *nomos*, the rules of just conduct, from the power of controlling the organization of government.[23] The two functions could be analytically separated even if legislatures in modern democracies tended to lump them both together as "lawmaking." The latter function would be entrusted to a popularly elected lower house, a Governmental Assembly, which in Hayek's description resembles a parliament of the British model. This Assembly, Hayek expected, would be dominated by parties just as contemporary legislatures are. Under its direction would be all the personnel and resources entrusted to government, including the power to prescribe the total amount of revenue to be collected and its disposition—though not the *manner* of its collection.[24] Critically, however, this Governmental Assembly or lower house would have to operate within the framework of the rules of just conduct established by the upper house or Legislative Assembly. It could issue no direct commands to private individuals that were not implied "directly and necessarily" by the general laws not under its control.[25] Although these laws could be interpreted and evolved by common-law judges, they could be directly altered in Hayek's scheme only by the Legislative Assembly, which would thus have ultimate control over "all enforceable rules of conduct" including the rules for the apportionment of the tax burden.[26] For this powerful body, Hayek devised an unusual method of election, reflecting his hope that the same voters who choose Governmental Assembly representatives based on their [self] "interest" could be encouraged to choose the legislators of the upper house based on more permanent reflections about "what kind of action is right or wrong—not as an instrument for the achievement of particular ends but as a permanent rule and irrespective of the effect on particular individuals or groups."[27] The Legislative Assembly members or *nomothetae* would stand from and be elected by not the electorate at large by the small cohort of voters reaching the age of 45 years in a given calendar year; Hayek suggests that even this restrictive method of election could be made indirect by adopting "regionally appointed delegates" who would "elec[t] the [nomothetic] representative from their midst."[28] The successful nomothetes would serve a single term of 15 years, be removable only for gross misconduct, and be guaranteed light duties and a pension for the remainder of their lives. They would thus achieve an almost judge-like insulation from both partisan and financial motivations.

Obviously, the workability of this system depended, as Hayek himself openly recognized, on the feasibility of distinguishing between the "enforceable rules of just conduct" in the purview of the Legislative Assembly and the more quotidian decisions of the Governmental Assembly.[29] Otherwise, one assembly could easily reject the decision of the other as lying outside its proper sphere of authority. Adjudication of such boundary disputes was another task of the Constitutional Court in addition to its role as guarantor of the justice of the laws proper.[30] The relationship between the two houses was made even more delicate by Hayek's provision for a state of emergency. If the state were threatened so seriously by invasion or natural disaster that commands to specific people were necessary for its survival—or as Hayek put it, if "the spontaneous order...must for a time be converted into an organization," then the Legislative Assembly could temporarily enable the majority government based in the lower house to wield extraordinary power.[31]

Criticism of the Model Constitution

Despite the ingenuity and novelty of Hayek's proposals, reaction to the model constitution has been either muted or negative. Often, if the model constitution is mentioned at all, it is not discussed on its merits but rather used to illustrate tensions in Hayek's political and social thought more broadly. Bruce Caldwell's intellectual biography of Hayek, for instance, discusses the apparent puzzle of Hayek the opponent of "rationalist constructivism" apparently engaging in the rationalist construction of social rules.[32] Chandran Kukathas similarly sees the model constitution mainly as a puzzling example of conflict between "the conservative elements in Hayek, which deny the power of reason successfully to reconstruct human institutions ... and the more rationalist Hayek."[33] But the criticism targeted at the model constitution's actual feasibility falls instead into two broad categories corresponding to Hayek's two rationales for reform: first the desirability and power of the legal generality requirement, and second the potential of his constitutional design to free the law from factional influence. Both areas of criticism appear fatal to Hayek's project as originally presented, but the relatively weaker second line of attack offers some hope that its objectives might be at least partially rescued.

As the more prominent feature of his thought, Hayek's attempt to link freedom with the requirement of legal generality has been severely censured—first after its initial statement in *The Constitution of Liberty*[34] but continuing into the seventies concurrently with Hayek's revised statements in *Law, Legislation and Liberty.*[35] As John Gray later summarizes the objection, the rule of law on its own would seem to

> permit highly oppressive policies and legislation ... Hayek's rule of law will protect individual liberty only if it already incorporates strong moral rights to freedoms of various sorts: the Kantian test of universalizability, taken by itself, is almost without substance, in that highly oppressive laws will survive it, so long as legislators are ingenious enough to avoid mentioning particular groups or named individuals in the framing of the law itself.[36]

Put somewhat more concretely, the test of legal generality does nothing to guarantee freedom in the commonly understood sense. A general rule could command everyone to wear a particular kind of hat or perform forced labor. The economist Daniel Klein has pointed out that the law "one may install bathtubs only if one has obtained a state-granted plumber's license" seems to be general; as a result Klein views Hayek's definition of liberty to be a "jumble of platitudes and convolutions."[37] Put in terms of the actual operation of the model constitution, Hayek's own student Ronald Hamowy argued that the generality test would either be ignored or render the Legislative Assembly virtually powerless. It would be hard to imagine a law anyone might be interested in passing that would *not* attempt to "[achieve] particular concrete purposes" or include "provisions intended or known to affect principally particular identifiable individuals or groups"[38] and therefore be struck down under the constitution's Basic Clause. But if the Hayekian Legislative Assembly could therefore not legislate, the Governmental Assembly could usurp its functions through the constitution's devolution of authority clause—therefore rendering the whole complex machinery worthless.[39]

Hayek himself was not unaware of difficulties with the general rules concept. Even in *The Constitution of Liberty* he had acknowledged that there was no clear-cut distinction between general laws and specific commands, and that in fact "laws shade gradually into commands as their content becomes more specific."[40] And in *Rules and Order* he explicitly took up the charge that "even rules that are perfectly general and abstract might still be serious and unnecessary restrictions of individual liberty."[41] It was in an attempt to meet this charge that he famously implied that laws could only affect "actions towards others," since only disputes that could conceivably come before a judge were the rightful subject of law. Hayek believed that this maneuver would protect private and voluntary activity from the intrusion of the law—unless, he added somewhat dismissively, it were believed that supernatural powers would punish entire groups for the "sins of individuals."[42] But this is an enormous weakness, as Chandran Kukathas recognized; a fanatic could easily define as conduct toward others someone's refusal to adopt his preferred beliefs.[43] Kukathas concludes that Hayek's entire attempt to define liberty fails, since he fails to substantively defend the protected domains of individual liberty.[44] John Gray's own ultimate verdict is somewhat more favorable; reconsidering his earlier objection to Hayek's reasoning about generality, he read into the criterion of universalizability a richer set of features much more favorable to Hayek's thesis. These included the requirements of consistency between similar cases, impartiality between agents, and "moral neutrality" or refusal to impose our own preferences on others.[45] But this partial rehabilitation of Hayekian ideas about law does not earn more than a cursory mention of the mechanics of the model constitution itself.[46]

The second line of criticism against the model constitution, focusing on its actual institutional arrangements, corresponds roughly to Hayek's reasoning about factions. The essential question here is whether the institutional arrangements that Hayek proposes would succeed in insulating the law from political jockeying. Criticisms here are potent but thinner on the ground than in the case of the generality requirement. Ronald Hamowy believed that the Governmental Assembly's control of the direction (if not the collection techniques) of tax funds would easily allow it to manipulate social outcomes, cherry-pick the laws it wished to enforce, and if need be choke the Legislative Assembly into submission.[47] Norman Barry questioned the purity of motive of the nomothetes themselves; it was certainly possible that their assembly itself could become politicized and exploit the inadequacy of the generality requirement to "make perverted rules of just conduct on behalf of particular interests."[48] Furthermore, the very features that Hayek introduced in an attempt to insulate the legislators from factional politics—their long tenure and freedom from ever again facing voters—seem just as likely to turn them into a self-serving elite as a band of disinterested solons. If the fundamental *nomos* is supposed to represent general opinion about what is just, placing it under the control of an unaccountable body renewing itself with glacial slowness seems a curious way to proceed, and at least one unlikely to command much popular legitimacy. And besides lagging behind new ideas, without proportional representation, the Legislative Assembly would seem likely to systematically exclude disliked minorities from *any* participation at all in the shaping of the fundamental law; another feature likely to lead to subtle (or not so subtle) warping of the *nomos* for particular group objectives.

Hayek does make an intriguing suggestion in *The Constitution of Liberty* that seems to offer a means to guard against oppression of minorities of any kind. He points out that there are many legitimate laws that could, for defensible and even benevolent reasons, differentially affect only part of the population such as the blind or women. The same could be observed (though Hayek does not explicitly make this connection) about any other functionally distinguished subgroup such as Klein's plumbers or a despised religious or ethnic subgroup. Differential treatment of course also opens the possibility of abuse, and the formal requirement of generality would be unable to detect either possibility. Hayek instead suggests a political procedure as a solution. The law would need to command majority support both among the group to be differentially affected and the balance of the population. He observes that if "only those inside the group favor the distinction, it is clearly privilege; while if only those outside favor it, it is discrimination."[49] Only laws supported by a majority in both categories could be presumed, though not guaranteed, to be just. This solution, highly elegant in principle, nevertheless does not appear later in the model constitution. Reflection on the practical difficulties involved probably deterred Hayek from including it. Actually implementing such a test would require two national voting rolls, one containing the group to be affected and the second the balance of the population. Even if the authority charged with making this identification were completely disinterested, it would have to overcome an immense logistical challenge even to identify the members of the first group; the goal of preventing discrimination would probably be thwarted if voter self-classification were allowed. There surely also would be many cases in which even to define the relevant affected subgroup would be impossible, since many imaginable laws affect multiple subgroups to different degrees.

The double majority test is nevertheless interesting as a conceptual ideal. It suggests a route for Hayek to achieve rough-and-ready legal generality not through a formal test but through a political procedure. The powerful criticism of the generality requirement seems to indicate that such a strategy is really the only viable one for the model constitution, although Hayek's nomothetic assembly as designed fails to implement it. But here the Athenian roots of the model constitution enter the picture. Hayek's clumsily undemocratic Legislative Assembly stems from a misreading of history and, more importantly, neglects the elements of Athenian practice most responsive to his own priorities in constitutional design.

The Athenian Roots of the Model Constitution

Appeals to the precedent of ancient Athenian practice are found throughout the model constitution and its supporting architecture in *The Political Order* and the earlier *The Constitution of Liberty*. It was probably the principal inspiration for Hayek's key idea to give legislative responsibility to "body distinct from the body ... entrusted with the task of government" since he notes that the Athenians attempted "something like this" by "allowing only the *nomothetae*, a distinct body, to change the fundamental *nomos*."[50] Hayek does credit John Stuart Mill and Philip Hunton (a seventeenth-century political pamphleteer) with similar ideas, but these are clearly less important than the Athenian example. The only relevance of Hunton's 1643 *Treatise of Monarchy* seems to be that it describes as "nomotheticall" one of the "degrees" of the power of the magistrate along with the "Architectonicall and Gubernative" and the "executive."[51] No further explanation of these somewhat cryptic categories appears. John Stuart Mill's *Considerations on Representative Government*[52] is a more plausible if still incomplete anticipation. In any case Mill, too, cites Athenian precedent by arguing that

> The necessity of some provision corresponding to this [Mill's proposed Commission of Legislation] was felt even in the Athenian Democracy, where ... the popular Ecclesia could pass Psephisms (mostly decrees on single matters of policy), but laws, so called,

> could only be made or altered by a different and less numerous body, renewed annually, called the Nomothetae.[53]

Moreover, the justification and role of Mill's Commission of Legislation is quite different from Hayek's Legislative Assembly. Parliament, Mill argues, is ill-suited to provide the expertise and time needed to properly draft legislation. Even when it employs experts to draft legislation, their careful design work is often ruined by clumsy or self-serving amendments. It would be preferable for a dedicated body of legal experts to draft laws for a straight up or down vote by Parliament. Mill's Commission lacks the power of Hayek's Legislative Assembly to pass laws on its own, and could not in fact "refus[e] its instrumentality to any legislation which the country desired" as represented by Parliament's direction to draft a law on a given matter.[54] The basic idea of a separate body focusing on lawmaking is of course visible, and arguably Mill's plan to populate the Commission by royal appointment (with Commission alumni becoming life peers) resembles the heavy insulation of Hayek's nomothetes from popular election.[55] But the division of labor between two institutions, one concerned with rules of just conduct and one with daily government, is clearly of Athenian inspiration.

The parallels between the Athenian and Hayekian conceptions of law are very close, and Hayek chose the Greek *nomos* above several other possibilities as his preferred shorthand for the "rules of just conduct," which needed to be "distinguished from other commands called law."[56] In contrast to the very elaborate definition of a true law suggested in Hayek's Basic Clause, however, the Athenians themselves defined a law more simply as "a decision in the affairs of the polis taken by the majority without limit of duration," according to Plato's *Definitions*.[57] What Hayek in the same place refers to as the "commands…binding those who are members of the organization of government" similarly is a close but not exact parallel of the Greek concept of *psephisma* though Hayek does not use this word to describe the commands of his Governmental Assembly.[58] For the Athenians, *psephisma* were passed by majorities in the popular Assembly and were "decision[s] in the affairs of the polis limited in duration"; the Hayekian Governmental Assembly is described as being the "complete master in organizing the apparatus of government, and deciding about the use of material and personal resources entrusted to the government" within the rules of just conduct.[59] The close parallels between the Athenian and Hayekian concepts are perhaps easier to illustrate through the table of examples (Table 6.1) based on Mogens Hansen's *Athenian Democracy*.[60]

Table 6.1 Laws versus decrees at Athens

Scope	*Duration*	
	Temporary	*Permanent*
General	*Decree* Launch 40 triremes (war galleys) and impose a one-time property tax to pay for them.	*Law* Authorize prosecution of anyone who attempts to overthrow the democracy, betray the armed forces. or speak to the assembly after taking bribes.
Individual	*Decree* Honor the orator Demosthenes with a golden crown to be bestowed at a festival.	*Decree* Bestow Athenian citizenship on a friendly ruler, Dionysius of Syracuse.

Beyond the imposition of the one-time tax (which in the Hayekian constitution would be province of the Legislative Assembly), the decree–law distinction exactly parallels the jurisdictional boundary between the Governmental and Legislative Assemblies. There was even an Athenian analog to the Basic Clause regulating legislation itself. Called the Law of Definition by classical scholars, according to one ancient report it read:

> No decree passed by the Council or the people [the Assembly] may have higher validity than a law. No law may be passed that applies only to a single person. The same law shall apply to all Athenians, unless otherwise decided [in the assembly][61] with a quorum of 6,000, by secret ballot.[62]

Only in their financial arrangements do the Athenian and the Hayekian constitutions differ in which powers are placed in the realm of law and which are retained at the level of decrees. Hayek recommended that the methods of raising revenue be fixed by legislation, so that the tax impact of governmental decisions to increase spending would be clearly known. Beyond this, however, the Governmental Assembly had full power to allocate spending.[63] The Athenians after 403 BCE however used a "rule of division" or *merismos*—which was a law rather than a decree—to allocate revenue from ongoing taxes. Although the Assembly could move funds between government boards, it could not decree permanent expenditures in excess of the total budget without legislation. For a temporary expense, however, it could pass a one-time property tax or *eisphora*.[64] The Athenian Assembly therefore had more ability to raise funds than the Governmental Assembly, but generally less flexibility in allocating funds.

Despite the close parallels between the model constitution and many Athenian institutions, Hayek's attitude toward the ancient city was by no means uncritical. While he found much to admire in some of its political practice, he also saw it as a case study in the dangers of excessive democracy. These seemingly contradictory influences could coexist for Hayek because he read the history of independent Athens as one of constitutional decline. The very first page of *The Political Order* in fact features a passage from Xenophon that frames Hayek's argument that democracies have a "glorious first period" followed by democratic excess. Xenophon here dramatically describes a disastrous incident late in the Peloponnesian War, in which the Athenian Assembly (in the heat of passion, and in contravention of established trial procedure) decided to execute several victorious military leaders whom a storm had prevented from rescuing sailors drowning after a battle.

> But the great number [of the Athenian Assembly] cried out that it was monstrous if the people were to be prevented from doing whatever they wished...Then the Prytanes, stricken with fear, agreed to put the question...all of them except Socrates, the son of Sophroniscus, and he said that in no case would he act except in accordance to the law.[65]

Hayek continues that early in a democracy a higher law (*nomos*) is respected, but that subsequently, the masses demand the right to decide anything by majority vote and destroy it. He explicitly says that this happened to Athens toward the end of the Peloponnesian War, which is of course consistent with the Xenophon's description of the Trial of the Generals.[66] The account resembles the one given in *The Constitution of Liberty*, in which Hayek says that the decline of the concept of isonomy or rule of law "probably represents the first instance of a cycle that civilizations seem to repeat." After the wise rule of Solon at Athens in the sixth century, and the continued appeal of the ideal of the rule of law in the mid-fifth century, "democratic government soon came to disregard that very equality before the law from which it had derived its justification."[67] Hayek even refers to the "degenerate democracy of Plato's time" (i.e., the later fifth and fourth centuries BCE) as one in which individual liberty in the modern sense probably did not exist, in contrast to the Athens at the time of Pericles and later of the Sicilian expedition (!) when Thucydides described Athens as the "freest of free countries" in which everyone had "unfettered discretion in it...to live as they pleased."[68] In *The Political Order* Hayek advances a similar interpretation by quoting the famous mid-fourth-century orator, Demosthenes, to the effect that "our laws are no better than so many decrees; nay, you will find that the laws which have to be observed in drafting the decrees are later than the decrees themselves."[69]

But Hayek's historical narrative is confused. His implied story is that Solon established the laws of Athens (which obeyed the principle of *isonomia* or rule of law), that the constrained democracy flourished, but then that the ascendancy of radical majoritarianism undermined and eventually destroyed the Athenian empire. However, more than 50 years passed between the incident described by Xenophon (406 BCE) and the time of Demosthenes's quote about decrees and laws, which occurred in 355 or 356 BCE.[70] Hayek's omission suggests that nothing important occurred in that half-century, only a continuation of majoritarian misgovernment. In his endnotes, he quotes Lord Acton's statement that "in this way the emancipated people of Athens became a tyrant."[71] But the very next paragraph in Acton's book hints that something of note happened in that 50-year lacuna:

> The Athenians, wearied and despondent, confessed the true cause of their ruin. They understood that for liberty, justice, and equal laws, it is as necessary that democracy should restrain itself as it had been that they should restrain the oligarchy...the laws...were reduced to a code; and no act of the sovereign assembly was valid with which they might be found to disagree...Between the sacred lines of the Constitution which were to remain inviolate, and the decrees which met from time to time the needs and notions of the day, a broad distinction was drawn.[72]

Whether due to time pressure, or Acton's at best half-true statement that "the repentance of the Athenians came too late to save the Republic,"[73] Hayek either did not know about or did not want to complicate his discussion by including what happened in those missing 50 years. If he had, he would have had to confront the fact that the distinction between laws and democratically passed decrees on which he so relied in the model constitution arose not in the mists of an oligarchic past but as part of a self-consciously democratic reform, and that it was implemented not by elites but by ordinary people. Perhaps even more importantly, he would have noticed that the Athenian nomothetes were selected and operated very differently from the elite Legal Commissioners of Mill's imagination, or Hayek's own. Although supporting these points requires repeating some familiar history as well as relying completely on classical specialists for more difficult topics (particularly Mogens Herman Hansen's magisterial *Athenian Democracy in the Age of Demosthenes*), the insights for Hayek's constitutional project justify the (brief) excursion into the Athenian past.

While Hayek views Athenian constitutional history as on a downward trajectory after the legendary lawgiver Solon, a sounder interpretation is one of uneven but discernible movement *toward* the ideals that Hayek would later adopt as his own. It is only honest, as part of this argument, to deny any pretense to a *precise* evaluation of the complex historical and etymological issues surrounding the evolution of the concept of law at Athens (and the exact timing of its changing relationship to popular sovereignty over the course of the sixth through fourth centuries). A more approximate evaluation is acceptable only because Hayek himself painted with such a broad brush, painting a downward arrow from Solon's time to the ruin of Athens. It is admittedly true, as Hayek said, that the Athenians at the time of Solon (and his predecessor Draco) possessed a concept of higher law called *thesmos.* This term carried a sense of a custom "laid down" even though it described the provisions of the criminal and civil codes altered by Draco and Solon.[74] But there is no reason to think that the concept of *thesmos* exclusively possessed the properties that Hayek admired in law, or that it was superior to the concept of *nomos*, which eventually replaced it. Solon did however enact many policies that Hayek (presumably) would have approved. In 594, he freed tenants from their semifeudal obligations to the aristocrats, abolished debt slavery, and redeemed anyone previously enslaved. According to the *Athenaion Politeia* (whose traditional attribution to Aristotle is contested)[75] he also resisted demands from the poor to redistribute land. In fact, later archons (key magistrates in the Athenian state) had to swear upon entering office that "whatever a person possessed before he entered upon his archonship he will have and possess until the end of his term."[76] But although Solon codified the laws, his efforts covered only what might roughly be described as private or civil law; he did not codify the constitutional procedures of the state.[77] Although there may have been a popular Assembly in his day, its powers were probably so limited[78] as to make a distinction between democratic passed decrees and fundamental laws questionable. Athens later underwent a turbulent period of rule by the tyrant Pisistratus and his sons, and it was only in 510 that the disgruntled aristocrat Cleisthenes (having expelled the Pisistratidae) "won the support of the common people by promising to give the state into their hands."[79] Cleisthenes is widely viewed as the real founder of Athenian democracy, establishing or empowering many of its key institutions around 507 BCE; and at around this time this concept of *nomos* began to replace *thesmos* to describe a "statute."[80]

These institutions, the core of the new democratic order, comprised the *ecclesia* or popular Assembly; the *boule* or council; and the *dikasteria* or law courts.[81] The division of labor between these roughly approximated the familiar legislative, executive, and judicial functions, although with an unusual level of involvement by ordinary citizens. The Assembly's role in passing decrees or *psephisma* has already been seen, although well into the fifth century no distinction was made between these and a *nomos*; the historian Xenophon used both terms within a few sentences of one another to describe the same measure. *Nomos* itself seems to have first been used to describe the laws of Cleisthenes, and evolved in meaning from "distribution," to "custom" and finally to "law" proper.[82]

The *boule* or Council is of limited relevance for Hayekian themes, but this is not true of the *dikasteria* or People's Court, actually a collection of courts staffed from a pool of 6,000 citizen jurors. To serve, an Athenian citizen had to be at least 30 years old, to volunteer at the beginning of a year, and to be among the 6,000 selected by sortition (the lot) from the total pool of volunteers. If chosen, he and all the other jurors marched to a hill outside Athens and took the "Heliastic Oath" binding himself by Zeus, Apollo, and Demeter to listen to all parties and to cast his vote impartially and in accordance with the laws.[83] The fourth-century orator Demosthenes also reported that the oath included the following strictures:

> I will not allow private debts to be cancelled, nor lands nor houses belonging to Athenian citizens to be redistributed. I will not restore exiles or persons under sentence of death. I will not expel, nor suffer another to expel, persons here resident in contravention of the statutes and decrees of the Athenian People or of the Council.[84]

Once sworn, the juryman was eligible to serve in individual trials. Although after 403 this required a separate, daily selection by lot, in the fifth century, a jury was apparently filled on a first-come, first-served basis. The juries were massive by modern standards; for small civil suits

201 citizens, for public prosecutions 501, and for extremely important political cases from 1,001 up to 2,501.[85] Although bound by their oath, Athenian juries were otherwise very powerful; though a magistrate presided over each court, they had no directive powers and the jury decided both law and fact.[86]

Equipped with their new political institutions, in 490, the Athenians famously defeated the first Persian invasion at the battle of Marathon. This victory was won principally by the middle-class men able to afford the heavy weapons and armor of a hoplite, but the much larger Persian follow-up invasion in 480 was thwarted principally by an Athenian fleet rowed by lower-class, propertyless *thetes*. As Athens subsequently became a maritime empire, the influence of the lower classes correspondingly rose. In the new balance of power, a series of popular leaders made the constitution ever more democratic. In 462, the reformer Ephialtes succeeded in stripping the old, aristocratic Areopagus council of most of its oversight of the laws and of political trials; the popular institutions of Council, Assembly, and People's Courts divided the new powers among themselves. Although Ephialtes himself was murdered, his younger ally Pericles continued his work as "leader of the people"; he instituted pay for citizens serving as jurors and members of the Council. It now became possible, and even desirable, for many poorer citizens to participate in government.[87] Through the force of his oratory and personality, Pericles dominated the Athenian democratic state for over 30 years, leading it to the height of its power and grandeur. In the last years of his life, however, he infamously led the city into a conflict that would destroy both its empire and, briefly, the democracy itself.

Beginning in 431, the rivalry between Athens and Sparta for the leadership of Greece erupted into open war. Although the elite Spartan army could pillage Attica at will, the Athenians ruled the waves with their experienced navy and supplied all their needs from overseas. The first ten years of the war ended with no clear advantage to either side; Athenian momentum was checked by a plague that swept through their crowded city, carrying off Pericles and thousands of others. Finally, a Spartan disaster at the island of Sphacteria and a corresponding Athenian one at Amphipolis led the exhausted opponents to conclude a "Fifty Years Peace." Although warfare never really stopped, the peace gave the Athenians enough breathing space to recover their strength. Unfortunately, with Pericles gone, strategic decisions in the Assembly became erratic under the influence of lesser men—the popular orators known, at least by scornful oligarchs, as the "demagogues," and whom

Hayek (and Lord Acton) perhaps had most saliently in mind in their evaluation of Athenian democracy. Perhaps an even worse influence on the polity, though, was the brilliant but utterly unreliable aristocrat Alcibiades. In 415, he managed to convince the Athenians to launch a daring and nakedly aggressive expedition against Syracuse, a large and wealthy Sicilian city friendly to Sparta. Their massive expeditionary force achieved initial success, but through a series of missteps the Athenians not only failed to capture Syracuse but were in fact trapped in Sicily by a naval defeat. In a staggering disaster, their entire army of tens of thousands of men was either slaughtered or captured by the vengeful Syracusans in 413.[88]

With Athens dramatically weakened, the war with Sparta resumed in earnest. At home, the democracy was discredited by the disaster, and for a confused period in 411, a group of pro-Spartan oligarchs used violence, assassination, and finally a coup to seize control of the city and overthrew the democratic constitution. They failed, however, to win over the large Athenian military force stationed at Samos in the Aegean. This group served as the nucleus for the overthrow of the extremist oligarchs and their replacement by a more moderate constitution within four months of the initial coup. In the spring of 410, however, with the morale of the prodemocratic lower classes boosted by an Athenian naval victory at Cyzicus, the radical democracy was fully restored.[89] Instead of reconciliation with their opponents, however, the demagogues who led the democratic party sought vengeance. They persecuted anyone with even a tenuous connection to the brief oligarchic regime, even the moderates who had turned against it. The prosecutions took on overtones of class war, as conviction meant forfeiture of property to the state. Bribery could either free the truly guilty or ensure the conviction of innocent men who merely happened to be rich.[90] In foreign affairs, the demagogues were comparably belligerent and unwise, refusing several opportunities to make peace with Sparta after Athenian victories.

This is the period of reckless litigation and belligerence that Hayek and Lord Acton had in mind when they condemned the Athenians as having destroyed themselves through unlimited democracy. As alluded to briefly earlier, the passage from Xenophon that opened Hayek's *Political Order of a Free People* describes a particularly infamous incident, the "Trial of the Generals."[91] In 406 BCE, the Athenians, who were now fighting a Spartan fleet strengthened by subsidies from the Persian Empire, had by straining every nerve just won an unexpected naval victory at Arginusae in the eastern Aegean. However, during the battle several Athenian ships had been sunk. As the surviving crewmembers struggled in the water, a storm blew up preventing the remaining ships from rescuing their comrades. The loss by drowning of so many men infuriated the Athenian popular assembly, despite their joy at the victory. They used a special procedure, *eisangelia*, to put the commanders of the fleet on trial for their lives in the assembly for failing to rescue the drowning sailors. Socrates, who by chance was a member of the prytaneis (the group of presiding officers of the Council and assembly, chosen by lot) and several others attempted to prevent the question being put to the assembly, but they were overruled by colleagues intimidated by the crowd. The six Athenian naval commanders were found guilty and put to death. Shortly afterward, under the influence of the demagogue Cleophon, the Athenians refused yet another peace offer from Sparta. Their reckless and arbitrary conduct had its predictable result: Athenian luck ran out at the naval disaster of Aegospotami. After refusing yet another Spartan peace offer, the city itself was besieged in 404 BCE and forced to surrender.[92]

Unfortunately for the Athenians, their sufferings continued after the trauma of a siege in which many perished from starvation. Under coercive pressure from the victorious Spartans led by the pro-oligarch Lysander, the assembly was forced to appoint a committee of 30 commissioners to revise the constitution and draft a new code of laws. This group of 30, known to history as the Thirty Tyrants, assembled a force of 300 policemen and invited 700 Spartans to garrison the city. The financial upkeep of these forces both required and enabled the Thirty to look for new sources of revenue, and they embarked on a campaign to execute their opponents and confiscate their property. After disarming all citizens who were not supporters of the oligarchy, the Thirty instituted a reign of terror, executing without trial both their personal enemies and citizens whose property they coveted. At one point, they judicially murdered 30 resident aliens (metics), each member of the Thirty taking the property of a murdered man; many farmers in the Athenian countryside were likewise expropriated, their property going to the Thirty or their oligarchic friends.[93] It seemed a grim end to the Athenian democratic experiment. But even in the last disastrous years of the war, however, a remarkable intellectual transformation was gathering momentum that contradicts the Hayekian narrative of inevitable democratic decline.

For most of the fifth century the Athenians made no distinction between "laws" and "decrees" and they did not even have an established written canon for what the laws actually were. The disadvantages of this position became apparent during the crisis of 411–410, in which the democracy was violently overthrown and then restored. Both the democrats and the oligarchs argued that they were defending the "ancestral constitution" established by Draco and Solon, but without codification there was no means of determining which side was right. Indeed, Draco and Solon may not have prescribed any laws about the form of government at all, legislating only on civil and criminal matters. To remedy matters, as soon as the democracy was restored in 410 it appointed a "Codification Board" to collect all existing laws and inscribe them on the wall of a portico in the Athenian marketplace.[94] The work dragged on for six years, until interrupted by the Thirty who characteristically removed the laws published to date from the marketplace.[95]

This returns the narrative to the political situation at Athens in the winter of 404–403. Persecuted and expropriated by the Thirty, many democrats had fled to the neighboring city of Thebes. A small band under the former general Thrasybulus mounted a desperate invasion of Attica, and through good luck and courage managed to besiege the Thirty and their supporters in Athens. At this point a Spartan relief army arrived. Instead of dooming the rebellion, however, its commander Pausanias laid the foundation for social peace. He did not interfere with the restoration of democracy, but imposed an oath known as "the reconciliation" or "the covenant" on the warring parties. It proclaimed a general amnesty for actions during the civil war, excepting only the Thirty themselves and their closest associates who were allowed to depart into exile. All property seized during the turmoil was restored to its original owners, but sales (many, presumably, made under duress) were allowed to stand unless the original owner wished to repurchase his property at the sale price. The new leaders of the democracy—Thrasybulus, Anytos, and Archinos—endorsed and defended the amnesty for former oligarchs despite their personal losses in the civil strife.[96] Within a year of total defeat, and within three years of the demagogic excess of the Trial of the Generals, the restored Athenian democracy seemed to have transformed its approach to public life.

The new approach was reflected in a wave of legal and constitutional reform. To accompany the general amnesty, the restored assembly ordered that "whole of the laws should be revised," in the meantime leaving the laws of Solon and Draco in force. The Assembly established two legislative boards (*nomothetai*) of 500 citizens apiece to carry out the task: one elected by the Council to collect laws for consideration, and the second to "test" them for acceptance into the revised body of law. These laws, for the first time, included not just "private" law but constitutional procedures as well, including new procedures for legislation itself.[97] The restored fourth-century democracy now clearly distinguished between "laws" and "decrees" and employed the Law of Definition mentioned earlier; and its sophisticated legislative procedures both contradict Hayek's democratic pessimism and contrast strongly with Hayek's elite-reliant approach to lawmaking in the model constitution. There were three distinct approaches to changing the *nomoi*. In the first procedure, each year the assembled citizens gave an up or down vote on each existing law. If a law failed this vote, any citizen could propose an alternative. The Assembly then appointed five men to defend the existing law before a board of *nomothetae*, selected by lot from the usual pool of volunteer citizen jurors, who decided between the arguments of the defenders and the reformers just like a trial. The judgment of the *nomothetae* was final; surviving laws bear the prefix "it was decided by the nomothetae" as opposed to mere decrees which say "it was decided by the people."[98]

The two other methods of changing the laws differed only in the path they took to the *nomothetae*. Individual citizens could propose a change in a law, as long as they met several conditions: They were required to offer a new law in place of the old one, their new proposal had to be universal in application, it had to be be posted publicly, and any conflicting law was required to be repealed by the new resolution. A majority of the Assembly could then direct a body of *nomothetae* to gather and decide the issue. Similarly, a group of senior magistrates known as the *thesmothetae* were charged with annually scrutinizing the laws for any contradictions and redundancies. The orator Aeschines described their mission as including "making an annual revision of the laws in the presence of the people…in order to determine whether any law stands written which contradicts another law, or an invalid law stands among the valid, or whether more laws than one stand written to govern each action."[99] If such problematic laws were found, the Assembly convened *nomothetae* to settle the issue as in the previous methods.

Obviously, the whole superstructure of *nomothesia* would have been worthless had there been no mechanism to enforce the distinction between decrees and laws. Likewise, the procedural and generality rules would have been empty without some type of judicial review of laws themselves. The Athenians possessed robust solutions to both problems. The first was addressed by the institution of *graphē paranomon* or "prosecution for proposing an unlawful decree." Under this procedure, any citizen could accuse the proposer of a decree either on the grounds that it was undesirable or that it was unconstitutional (that it conflicted with a law). The issue was decided not in the Assembly but in an ordinary People's Court of at least 501 members; while the debate was in progress, enforcement of the decree was suspended. If the challenger won his case, the decree was both vacated and the proposer fined (sometimes heavily). As a deterrent to unconstitutional activity, citizens prosecuted successfully three times under *graphē paranomon* suffered *atimia*, complete political disenfranchisement and virtual outlawry.

Fortunately for politicians, there was a statute of limitations of one year on such prosecutions; after that, only the decree itself was repealed. Yet even with this limitation, and the incomplete legal records that have survived, there is evidence of 39 *graphē paranomon* prosecutions between the second restoration of democracy and the subjugation of the city by the Macedonians in 322 BCE. The true number is almost certainly much higher.[100]

The second enforcement tool arose after the reforms of 403. The Athenians now introduced a separate procedure for judicial review of the *nomoi* themselves, the *graphē nomon me epitedeion theinai*. Penalties for the proposer were similar, in at least one case actually including death.[101] Although fewer examples of this procedure survive than of the *graphē paranomon*, some are extant. In his oration *Against Timocrates*, Demosthenes argued that a new law was invalid because it contradicted an existing one, had not been properly publicized beforehand, and violated other procedures ensuring proper consideration.[102] His oration *Against Leptines* made similar procedural charges, and in the *Aristocrates* case he had implied that the generality norm operated fully on the laws as well on the decrees:

> LAW: And it shall not be lawful to propose a *statute* [i.e., a nomos] directed against an individual, unless the same apply to all Athenians…a decree for the special benefit of Charidemus, such as is not applicable to all the rest of you…[is evidently] in defiance of this statute also; of course *what it is unlawful to put into a statute* cannot legitimately be put into a decree.[103] [emphasis added]

Although Hayek uses Demosthenes's rhetoric in the *Leptines* case to claim that Athens did not respect the distinction between laws and decrees,[104] other surviving speeches by Attic orators and Demosthenes himself praise the system of law and imply that it operated relatively well.[105] Even in the *Leptines* case the *nomothetae*, not the Assembly, had actually passed the law in question, though not according to the exact constitutional procedures. Besides, Demosthenes was making a prosecutorial speech and could be expected to exaggerate for rhetorical effect.[106] At the very least, the language used by the orators implies that the Athenian jurors were familiar with the law–decree distinction and generality norms. That this cultural transformation arose so quickly *after* military and political disaster belies Hayek's pessimistic assessment of Athenian democracy. While the causes of his pessimism may be difficult to recover at this date, the *effects* are easier to see; a missed opportunity to mine the later Athenian traditions for tools helpful to his constitutional project.

Sortition and the Nomothetes

The most salient of these traditions that Hayek overlooked was the use of sortition, or the lot. Sortition's role in the selection of Athenian state offices has been analyzed before in modern times, notably by David Levy,[107] who develops a claim in the ancient *Rhetoric to Alexander* that justified "appointment by lot" in a democracy for "the less important and the majority of the offices (for thus faction will be avoided)" while the more important offices, such as generalships, could still be filled by election—a similar procedure, interestingly, as was recommended by Rousseau in *The Social Contract*.[108] Levy concludes that selection of minor offices by lot, in a direct democracy, has unobvious advantages. While it may sometimes choose poor officeholders, the damage from this will be limited in a lower office. As a benefit however the randomly chosen candidates will on average reflect the will of the median voter, and spare the more productive in society from wasteful debate over the policies of the dog-catcher.[109] But there is another benefit connected with the logic of party or factional competition in a direct democracy. Parties, it could well happen, could be tightly disciplined because of kinship, common interest, or perhaps even the threat of violence. As a result, each faction could be modeled as choosing its preference on a given issue internally, and then voting as a bloc in the larger polity. In a city–state split nearly evenly between 501 Blues and 499 Greens, the Blue party's policy preference aligns with the Blue median voter, who is quite far from the preferences of the Green median. But this means that the mysterious death of three or more Blue voters would swing policy outcomes drastically, not slightly toward Green's preferences as in the independent voting case, but dramatically: all the way from the Blue median to the Green median. There is, consequently, a massive incentive within such a system for political violence. Levy points out that the use of sortition for some political decisions greatly reduces these incentives; with many citizens, the expected policy gain for eliminating a political opponent approaches zero.

To see this, we can again consider a state with two rival parties X and Y. In any area of dispute between the two sides there will be a spectrum of possible outcomes serving each group's interests to a greater or lesser degree. Members of X might routinely lose their lawsuits against Ys, and Ys might capture more rents from the political process; alternatively perhaps Xs might be able to use the legal system to expropriate their political enemies or even judicially murder them. These are not entirely far-fetched cases given the already discussed historical episodes such as the Trial of the Generals and the reign of murder and expropriation perpetrated by the Thirty Tyrants. Very abstractly then, the decision of the political system in any given issue area could be characterized by an imagined variable, θ, whose value reflects the degree of bias toward the preference of one or the other of the factions. In issue areas with where impartial policy is possible (for instance, the provision of fair trials to all in criminal cases regardless of status) a value of θ, $\theta^\star$, could be imagined that reflects an ideal of equality before the law. This value may or may not reflect the preference of the median citizen, of course, which will instead depend both on the relative strength of factions and beliefs about justice.

Political institutions will, however, affect how close policy comes to $\theta^\star$ or the median preference, if different. The two-party situation discussed earlier could easily be associated with a bimodal voter preference distribution such as that envisioned by Levy. Voters have preferences along the abscissa for some crude approximation of "preferred bias"—at any given point in time, they have an idea of where they want θ to be. But the Xs and Ys are highly partisan, and so the modal preferences of each are quite far from each other. Most members of each faction gaze at each other across a vast gulf, at the trough of which are the few partisans of impartiality. They would, nevertheless, converge on an outcome close to the median if they all voted independently by the usual logic of median preference. If the factions impose voting discipline on their followers however, and internal factional decision making is in effect, then each group will take a position corresponding to its own median voter—either θ_y or θ_x (Figure 6.1). The dynamic Levy describes will prevail: The actual outcome will swing wildly between θ_y and θ_x based on which faction holds an overall majority, and something close to the impartial outcome $\theta^\star$ will never be observed.

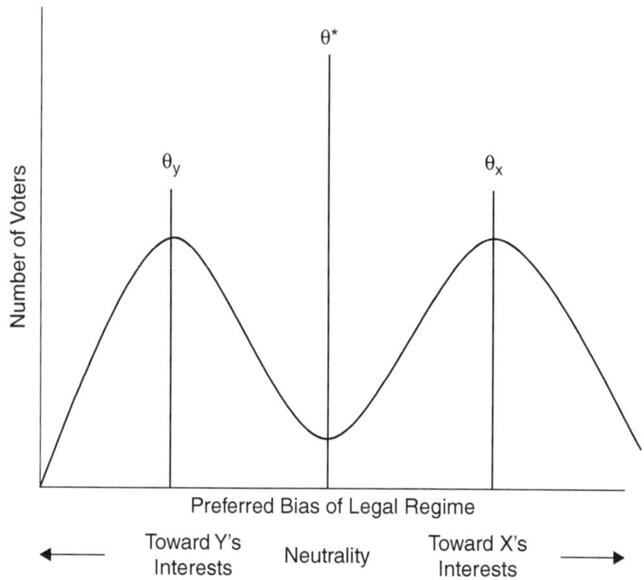

Figure 6.1 A state riven by factions.

Internal factional discipline will be most likely to be achieved when voters can be swayed by fear, shame, peer pressure, mass enthusiasm, or dynamics such as logrolling or package deals. It would seem more likely when votes are public; a private vote gives little scope for deals, intimidation, or shaming. A packed rally-type setting would be best, to allow political leaders to work up the crowd, and perhaps give an edge of fear to those standing out against a popular measure (or perhaps standing *within* the mass of its supporters). This is an obvious description of the Athenian Assembly, and it is known that "snowball" effects sometimes happened there. In the disastrous debate on the Sicilian Expedition, for example, Thucydides reports that "[t]he result of this excessive enthusiasm of the majority was that the few who actually were opposed to the expedition were afraid of being thought unpatriotic if they voted against it, and therefore kept quiet."[110] It isn't, perhaps, a stretch to see the extreme decisions of the radical democracy (such as the refusal of peace terms with Sparta late in the war) as products of exactly this kind of factional dynamic.

The significance of the Athenian constitutional procedures, the *nomothetai*, the *graphē paranomon*, and the *graphē nomon me epitedeion theinai* now becomes apparent. Each in their way was a safeguard against factional dynamics in the Assembly. The *graphē*, it will be recalled, were adjudicated in an ordinary court—a court, that is, which was large (at least 500 persons), assembled the day of the proceedings, selected by lot, and in which the minimum age was 30 years rather than the 18 or 20 years for the Assembly. Removed from the excitement of the Assembly, the jurors had a full day to consider the law or decree in question, whereas in the Assembly they might have been voting on many issues.[111] Most critically, votes in the People's Courts that heard *graphēs* were secret. Discussion among the jurors during vote-casting was prohibited, and each man held two slightly different bronze discs, one representing a vote for the accuser and one for the defendant. Ballots were cast into one of two urns, a bronze one for the vote intended to be valid and another for the discard. Since the bronze disks could be concealed in the hand, voting was very effectively anonymous and therefore independent.[112] The importance of this was clearly recognized at the time. The orator Lysias, for example, decried the departures from ordinary procedure used by the Thirty to try some imprisoned democratic partisans 404:

> The Thirty were seated on the benches which are now the seats of the presiding magistrates; two tables were set before the Thirty, and the vote had to be deposited, not in urns, but openly on these tables,—the condemning vote on the further one [i.e., a vote for acquittal]—so what possible chance of escape had any of them?[113]

Although the example is for a criminal trial, the *graphē* procedure—if followed properly—would yield the same nearly independent voting when a decree was being challenged. Secrecy would prevent the voters from being intimidated; bribery or logrolling would be almost impossible to implement because of the large number of voters, and the fact that they were only selected the actual morning of the case.

The power of this procedure to allow an escape from expediency into principle now becomes clear. To recall, a *graphē paranomon* challenge could be made on the grounds of either illegality or mere undesirability. *Graphē paranomon* effectively allowed, therefore, a second vote on any act of the Assembly in the realm of independent voting rather than in the realm of factional politics. To return to the idea of θ outcomes, we can imagine a situation in which Faction X slightly outnumbers Faction Y. In the Assembly, thanks to factional discipline, a decree implementing a θ_x policy carries the day despite being far from the preferences of the median voter. When subsequently challenged by a *graphē paranomon*, however, the large number of jurors called to hear the case makes it statistically likely that they will reflect the voter preference distribution of the wider polity. Since their votes are (nearly) independent, the voting outcome in the jury will probably lie only slightly to the right of $\theta^{\star}$. Since this is quite distant from the Assembly policy of θ_x, the decree will be defeated (Figure 6.2). The *graphē* procedure will therefore block extreme legislation. Even more than that, it will probably prevent extreme legislation from being proposed in the first place since (as we have seen) substantial penalties attached to a politician who made too many proposals subsequently overturned in court. Since politicians will understand this, they will have less incentive to engage in factional politics in the first place. The existence of the citizen jury procedures stabilizes the entire polity.

This is of course an extreme idealization of how Athenian politics actually worked, distant in many cases from messy historical reality. The level of abstractness, however, allows connections with Hayek's similarly top-level view of the problems of modern democracy. It is

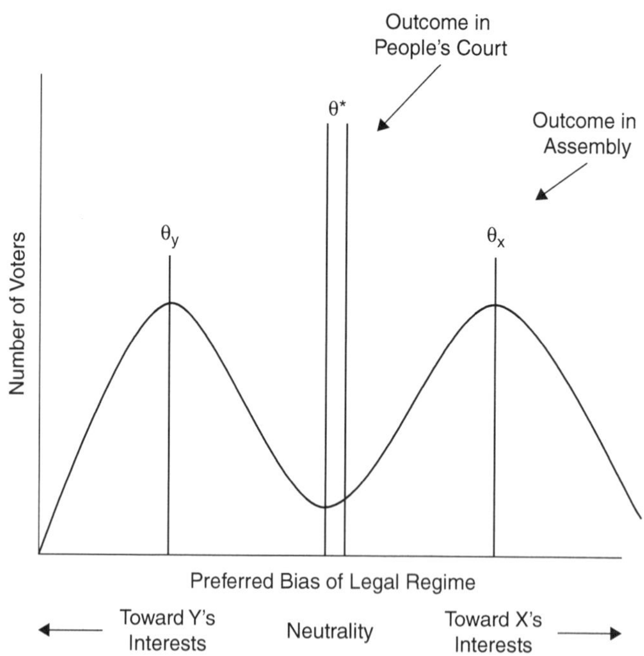

Figure 6.2 Policy outcomes in the Assembly and the People's Court: Faction X > faction Y.

not impossible to see in the confrontation between the Xs and Ys, with their internal party discipline, the interplay of parties in a modern parliamentary system or the polarization produced by the American system of primaries in Congressional races. This was, after all, the problem that Hayek confronted and attempted to resolve via a standing nomothetic body with a jurisdiction policed by a Constitutional Court. The integrity of this system can only be defended if the Constitutional Court finds, and enforces, a logical interpretation of Hayek's Basic Clause that can separate the jurisdiction of his two legislative bodies. Critics of the model constitution have made a strong case that the court will likely fail in this project. In the Athenian constitution, by contrast, the functions of the Legislative Assembly and the Constitutional Court are in effect combined. Any citizen can propose or challenge a law, but only the decision of the nomothetes can give effect to such a proposal or challenge. The additional and logically problematic step in the Hayekian construct, by which the Constitutional Court draws the line between two houses, is done away with. The appropriate scope of decrees is simply decided by the nomothetes since the Law of Definition states that no decree can be superior to a law. It would be as if Hayek's Constitutional Court (or the Supreme Court, in the American system) simply set the law directly. This would be objectionably undemocratic, but the problem is avoided in the Athenian system since the nomothetes statistically represent the people. All of their decisions reflect the current constitutional understanding of the mass of the population, who even if they underappreciate the finer points of justice and jurisprudence will at least be motivated to seek their own interest. This interest would seem to dovetail with Hayek's own formulation of welfare economics, which assesses societies by their ability to provide the "best chance for any member selected at random successfully to use his knowledge for his purposes."[114] It is hard to resist the Gordian-knot approach to improving the well-being of the average citizen by putting authority in the hands of many citizens selected at random.

Athenian history would seem to provide another useful precept for the Hayekian project through the contrast between the Athenian Law of Definition—which demands only that laws be of general application—and Hayek's requirement that laws serve no concrete purpose or be intended to affect certain known individuals. The definitional contortions are meant to prevent the Legislative Assembly from either conferring a privilege on an affected group or imposing a disability. If this is an impossible task to achieve using a logical rule alone, it may be best to concede that discrimination or privilege can only be recognized by disinterested human judgment about a specific enactment. This is the solution that Hayek seemed to be groping toward with the double majority test of the *Constitution of Liberty*. Since this test itself seems impossible to implement for practical reasons, the next best alternative may well be to appeal to the constitutional judgment of the people as a whole. Sortition and large numbers prevent factional dynamics to a large extent, and so randomly selected constitutional juries seem to promise a partial fulfillment of the Hayekian constitutional dream.

Conclusion

Hayek viewed his constitution-making as a quest to find "intellectual emergency equipment" that could serve as an alternative to dysfunctional majoritarian politics.[115] Although Hayek most obviously wanted to tame democracy with a robust version of the rule of law, he was also attracted to the related but not identical project of reducing the power of political factions. It has been argued here that this second aspect of his project would have benefited from more appreciation of the later Athenian constitution and its use of randomly chosen juries to decide constitutional questions. While it would be foolish to make definitive categorical claims about vast literatures, this particular *combination* of a Hayekian concern for generality and the Athenian application of the lot at least does not seem to have received sufficient attention despite the voluminous discussion on either topic taken individually. The Athenian model suggests an underexploited line of approach to the problems of democracy: Perhaps Madison was wrong when he suggested in *Federalist* Ten that "a pure democracy…can admit of no cure for the mischiefs of faction."[116] The institution of the nomothetic court suggests that an enlightened people can indeed create, as Publius again put it in *Federalist* 63, "a safeguard against the tyranny of their own passions."[117] It may of course seem unlikely that the practices of a city-state of 300,000 can be applied in a nation of tens or hundreds of millions. In the age of networked computing, however, size and distance are probably less significant obstacles to experiment than established constitutional traditions and the unmanageable volume and complexity of existing law. Hayek himself introduced his speculations with the disclaimer that he did not intend his model constitution for countries with long-standing constitutional traditions. He thought, however, that articulating constitutional principles both made them clearer and could conceivably be of use to emerging democracies without long-standing political traditions.[118] It is also not inconceivable that subnational governments, organizations, or even virtual worlds might choose to experiment with constitutional forms Hayekian in spirit but also reflective of Athenian constitutional juries. Since the maladies of democracy that motivated Hayek's model constitution have not noticeably improved in the decades since he wrote, the need to search for "intellectual emergency equipment" is, unfortunately, as strong as ever.[119]

Notes

1. Friedrich A. Hayek, *The Collected Works of F. A. Hayek*, vol. 16, *The Constitution of Liberty: The Definitive Edition*, ed. Ronald Hamowy (Chicago, IL: University of Chicago Press, 2011).
2. Friedrich A. Hayek, *Law, Legislation, and Liberty*, vol. 1, *Rules and Order* (Chicago, IL: University of Chicago Press, 1983); vol. 2, *The Mirage of Social Justice* (Chicago, IL: University of Chicago Press, 1978); vol. 3, *The Political Order of a Free People* (Chicago, IL: University of Chicago Press, 1979).
3. Hayek, *Political Order,* xiii.
4. Ibid., 111–14.
5. Hayek, *Constitution of Liberty*, 200.
6. Ibid., 221–22.
7. Ibid., 223.
8. Ibid., 330–41.
9. Ibid., 209–11.
10. Ibid., 210.
11. Hayek, *Political Order,* 109.
12. Hayek, *Rules and Order*, 94.
13. Hayek, *Political Order*, 111.
14. Ibid., 109–11.
15. Hayek, *Rules and Order,* 124, 126.
16. Ibid., 124–27.
17. Ibid., 125.
18. John Stuart Mill, *Principles of Political Economy: With Some of Their Applications to Social Philosophy*, ed. W. J. Ashley (London: Longmans, Green, and Company, 1909), 942; Hayek, *Constitution of Liberty*, 332.
19. Norman P. Barry, *Hayek's Social and Economic Philosophy* (London and Basingstoke. Macmillan, 1979), 94; Hayek, *Rules and Order,* 92.
20. Hayek, *Political Order,* 29.
21. Ibid., 12–19.
22. Ibid., 18–19.
23. Ibid., 105–06.
24. Ibid., 120, 126.
25. Ibid., 119.

26. Ibid., 114, 126.
27. Ibid., 112.
28. Ibid., 114.
29. Ibid., 119–20.
30. Ibid., 119–21.
31. Ibid., 124–25.
32. Bruce Caldwell, *Hayek's Challenge: An Intellectual Biography of F. A. Hayek* (Chicago, IL: University of Chicago Press, 2003), 358–59.
33. Chandran Kukathas, *Hayek and Modern Liberalism* (Oxford: Clarendon Press, 1989), 189.
34. Lord Robbins, "Hayek on Liberty," *Economica* 28, no. 109 (February 1961): 66; Ronald Hamowy, "Hayek's Conception of Freedom: A Critique," *The New Individualist Review* 1, no. 1 (April 1961), http://oll.libertyfund.org/title/2136/195251 (accessed on May 2, 2013); J. C. Rees, "Hayek on Liberty," *Philosophy* 38, no. 146 (1963): 346–60.
35. Ronald Hamowy, "Law and the Liberal Society: F. A. Hayek's Constitution of Liberty," *Journal of Libertarian Studies* 2, no. 4 (1978): 287–97; Barry, *Hayek's Social and Economic Philosophy*; J. Raz, "The Rule of Law and Its Virtue," in *Liberty and the Rule of Law*, ed. Robert L. Cunningham (College Station: Texas A&M University Press, 1979); John N. Gray, "F. A. Hayek on Liberty and Tradition," *The Journal of Libertarian Studies* 4, no. 2 (Spring 1980): 119–37; Ronald Hamowy, "The Hayekian Model of Government in an Open Society," *The Journal of Libertarian Studies* 6, no. 2 (1982): 137–43.
36. John Gray, *Hayek on Liberty*, 3rd edn. (London and New York: Routledge, 1998), 59.
37. Daniel B. Klein, "Mere Libertarianism: Blending Hayek and Rothbard," *Reason Papers* 27 (Fall 2004): 9–10.
38. Hayek, *Political Order*, 109.
39. Ibid., 116; Hamowy, "Hayekian Model."
40. Hayek, *Constitution of Liberty*, 218.
41. Hayek, *Rules and Order*, 101.
42. Ibid.
43. Kukathas, *Hayek and Modern Liberalism*, 159–60.
44. Ibid., 163.
45. Gray, *Hayek on Liberty*, 61–62.
46. Ibid., 67, 69.
47. Hamowy, "Hayekian Model."
48. Barry, *Social and Economic Philosophy*, 192–94.
49. Hayek, *Constitution of Liberty*, 222–23.
50. Hayek, *Political Order*, 111.
51. Philip Hunton, *A Treatise of Monarchy*, ed. Ian Gardner (London: Thoemmes Press, 2000), 16.
52. John Stuart Mill, *Considerations on Representative Government*, 2nd edn. (London: Parker, Son, and Bourn, 1861).
53. Ibid., 101–02.

54. Ibid., 97–101.
55. Ibid., 101–02.
56. Hayek, *Mirage of Social Justice*, 34.
57. Mogens Herman Hansen, *The Athenian Democracy in the Age of Demosthenes: Structure, Principles, and Ideology* (Oxford, UK: B. Blackwell, 1991), 171.
58. Hayek, *Constitution of Liberty*, 242, 242n; Hayek, *Political Order*, 2.
59. Hansen, *Athenian Democracy*, 171; *Hayek, Political Order*, 119.
60. Hansen, *Athenian Democracy*, 112 and 171.
61. The exception to the generality rule after the "unless" covers the infamous institution of ostracism, which allowed a citizen thought to be dangerous to political stability (suspected, for instance, of seeking to be a tyrant) to be exiled from the city for ten years. Such exiles were not otherwise harmed, however, and even allowed to retain their property in their absence.
62. Andocides, "On the Mysteries," in *Minor Attic Orators: Antiphon, Andocides*, trans. Kenneth J. Maidment and J. O. Burtt (Cambridge, MA: Harvard University Press, 1982).
63. Hayek, *Political Order*, 125–26.
64. Hansen, *Athenian Democracy*, 263.
65. Hayek, *Political Order*, 1; Xenophon, "Hellenica," in *Xenophon in Seven Volumes*, trans. Carleton Brownson, vol. 1 (Cambridge, MA: Harvard University Press, 1918), vii, 12–16, http://data.perseus.org/citations/urn:cts:greekLit:tlg0032.tlg001.perseus-eng1 (accessed May 2, 2013).
66. Hayek, *Political Order*, 2.
67. Hayek, *Constitution of Liberty*, 241.
68. Ibid., 238.
69. Hayek, *Political Order*, 2.
70. William C. West, "The Decrees of Demosthenes' 'Against Leptines'," *Zeitschrift* Für Papyrologie Und Epigraphik 107 (1995): 237–47.
71. Hayek, *Political Order*, 178.
72. John Emerich Edward Dalberg Acton, *The History of Freedom: And Other Essays* (London: Macmillan, 1907), 12–13.
73. Ibid., 13.
74. Hansen, *Athenian Democracy*, 161.
75. Peter J. Rhodes, *A Commentary on the Aristotelian "Athēnaiōn* Politeia" (Oxford: Oxford University Press, 1993), 62–63.
76. Aristotle, *Constitution of Athens*, trans. Kurt von Fritz and Ernst Kapp (New York: Hafner Publishing Co., 1950), sec. 78 (11.2) and 132 (56.2).
77. Hansen, *Athenian Democracy*, 29–33.
78. Martin Ostwald, *Nomos and the Beginnings of the Athenian Democracy* (Oxford: Clarendon Press, 1969), 156–57.
79. Aristotle, *Constitution of Athens*, sec. 89 (20.1–2).
80. Hansen, *Athenian Democracy*, 33–34; Ostwald, *Nomos*, 4.
81. Charles Hignett, *A History of the Athenian Constitution* (Oxford: Clarendon Press, 1952), 215.
82. Hansen, *Athenian Democracy*, 161.

83. Ibid., 178–82.
84. Demosthenes, "Against Timocrates," in *Demosthenes with an English Translation*, trans. A. T. Murray (Cambridge, MA: Harvard University Press), 24.149, http://data.perseus.org/citations/urn:cts:greekLit:tlg0014.tlg024.perseus-eng1 (accessed May 8, 2010).
85. Hansen, *Athenian Democracy*, 183–87.
86. Hignett, *Athenian Constitution*, 223.
87. Hansen, *Athenian Democracy*, 38.
88. John V. A. Fine, *The Ancient Greeks: A Critical History* (Cambridge, MA: Harvard University Press, 1983), 496–98.
89. Hignett, *Athenian Constitution*, 270–80.
90. Ibid., 281.
91. Hayek, *Political Order*, 1; Xenophon, "Hellenica," vii, 12–16.
92. Hignett, *Athenian Constitution*, 234; Xenophon, "Hellenica," I, vii, 12–16.
93. Ibid., 290.
94. Hansen, *Athenian Democracy*, 162–63.
95. Christopher W. Blackwell, "Nomothesia (Legislation)," in *Demos: Classical Athenian Democracy*, ed. Christopher W. Blackwell, *The Stoa: A Consortium for Electronic Publishing in the Humanities*, 2003, http://www.stoa.org/projects/demos/article_legislation?page=1&greekEncoding=UnicodeC (accessed May 2, 2013).
96. Hignett, *Athenian Constitution*, 290–96.
97. Hansen, *Athenian Democracy*, 163–69.
98. Ibid., 166; Blackwell, "Nomothesia."
99. Aeschines, "Against Ctesiphon," in *Aeschines with an English Translation*, trans. Charles Darwin Adams (Cambridge, MA: Harvard University Press, 1919), 3.38, http://www.perseus.tufts.edu/hopper/text?doc=Perseus%3Atext%3A1999.01.0002%3Aspeech%3D3%3Asection%3D39 (accessed May 2, 2013).
100. Hansen, *Athenian Democracy*, 206–9.
101. Ibid., 212.
102. Demosthenes, "Against Timocrates," 24.33.
103. Demosthenes, "Against Aristocrates," in *Demosthenes with an English Translation*, trans. C. A. Vince (Cambridge, MA: Harvard University Press, 1926), 23.86, http://www.perseus.tufts.edu/hopper/text?doc=Perseus%3Atext%3A1999.01.0074%3Aspeech%3D23%3Asection%3D96 (accessed May 2, 2013).
104. Hayek, *Political Order*, 2, 178.
105. Consider for example this passage from Aeschines's Timarchus (177–78): "Why do you suppose it is, fellow citizens, that the existing laws are good, but that the decrees of the city are inferior to them, and that the verdicts rendered in the courts are sometimes open to censure? I will explain to you the reason. It is because you enact the laws with no other object than justice, not moved by unrighteous gain, or by either partiality or animosity, looking solely to what is just and for the common good."
106. Hansen, *Athenian Democracy*, 176–77.
107. David M. Levy, "The Statistical Basis of Athenian-American Constitutional Theory," *The Journal of Legal Studies* 18, no. 1 (January 1989): 79–103.

108. Ibid., 81–82; Jean-Jacques Rousseau, *The Social Contract: & Discourses* (London: J. M. Dent & Sons, Ltd., 1920), 95–96.
109. Levy, "Statistical Basis," 90–93.
110. Thucydides, *History of the Peloponnesian War* (New York: Penguin, 1972), VI.24, 425; P. J. Rhodes, "Sessions of Nomothetai in Fourth-Century Athens," *The Classical Quarterly* 53, no. 1 (2003): 125.
111. Hansen, *Athenian Democracy*, 210.
112. David L. Stockton, *The Classical Athenian Democracy* (Oxford: Oxford University Press, 1990), 73; *Constitution of Athens* 68.2–4.
113. Lysias, "Against Agoratus," in *Lysias with an English Translation*, trans. W. R. M. Lamb (Cambridge, MA: Harvard University Press, 1930), 13.37, http://data.perseus.org/citations/urn:cts:greekLit:tlg0540.tlg013.perseus-eng1 (accessed May 2, 2013).
114. Friedrich A. Hayek, "The Principles of a Liberal Social Order," in *Studies in Philosophy, Politics and Economics* (Chicago, IL: University of Chicago Press, 1967), 163.
115. Hayek, *Political Order*, 152.
116. Jacob Ernest Cooke, *The Federalist* (Middletown, CT: Wesleyan University Press, 1961), 61.
117. Ibid., 425.
118. Hayek, *Political Order*, 107–08.
119. The author wishes to thank the organizers and attendees of the "Hayek and the Modern World" conference at the University of Richmond in April 2013 for very helpful comments on this chapter, and particularly the conference organizers Sandra Peart, David Levy, Terry Price, and Gary McDowell.

PART III

Hayek and Policy Making

CHAPTER SEVEN

The Control of Engagement Order: Attlee's Road to Serfdom?

ANDREW FARRANT AND NICOLA TYNAN

F. A. Hayek's ideas have repeatedly reared their head in political debate and commentary over the past 70 years. For example, Hayek's arguments in *The Road to Serfdom* are widely thought to have influenced the caustic tenor of Winston Churchill's infamous "Gestapo" election broadcast of June 4, 1945.[1] According to Churchill, any "Socialist Government" that sought to conduct "the entire life and industry of the country ... would have to fall back on some form of Gestapo ... [and] would gather all the power to the supreme party and the party leaders, rising like stately pinnacles above their vast bureaucracies of Civil servants—no longer servants and no longer civil."[2] Unsurprisingly, the average voter viewed Churchill's charges with much dismay. As Lord Moran (Churchill's personal physician) noted in his diary, the Gestapo jibe had "not gone down with anybody ... No one agreed with the line that Winston had taken."[3] Similarly, *The Recorder* (a rabidly pro-Churchill popular newspaper) reported that many voters who heard "Mr. Churchill's broadcast ... [were much] surprised by his statement that Socialism must inevitably lead to totalitarianism." As *The Recorder* went on to note, however, "the fact has already been well proved. Last year appeared a book 'The Road to Serfdom.' It was recognized as one of the most important books of our generation."[4]

Accordingly, when Clement Attlee—leader of the Labour Party—gave his own radio broadcast on the evening of June 5 he had ample reason to note that Churchill's Gestapo jibe—Churchill's "theoretical stuff"—was scarcely more than a "secondhand version of the academic views of an Austrian professor—Friedrich August von Hayek—who is very popular just now with the Conservative Party."[5]

Attlee's charge had much credence. Indeed, Hayek's arguments had been readily taken up by a wide variety of Conservative Party figures when *The Road to Serfdom* was initially published in March 1944. For example, Ralph Assheton—appointed Conservative Party Chairman by Churchill in October 1944—sent 50 copies of Hayek's book to various parliamentary colleagues.[6] Similarly, Kenneth Pickthorn—Conservative Member of Parliament (MP) for Cambridge University—sent a copy of *The Road to Serfdom* to William Barkley of the *Daily Express*, urging Barkley to "interpret" Hayek's argument "for the three million *Daily Express* readers." Accordingly, Barkley provided a lengthy account of Hayek's thesis—Hayek's book "is causing a stir"—and noted that Hayek had persuasively shown why socialism would inevitably lead "to totalitarianism and Fascism and Nazism."[7]

As we note in this chapter, Hayek's arguments were similarly taken up by those who were eager to lambast Clement Attlee's postwar Labour Government. For example, the highly colorful Conservative Parliamentarian Sir Waldron Smithers frequently invoked *The Road to Serfdom* during parliamentary debates and was particularly assiduous in his efforts to heighten awareness of Hayek's ideas within the Conservative Party during the mid-late 1940s and early 1950s.[8] Indeed, Hayek had himself urged Smithers to try and bring Hayek's ideas to the attention of Winston Churchill in mid-October 1944.[9] Although Smithers sent Churchill a copy of *The Road to Serfdom* and an accompanying note suggesting that Churchill could pick up the gist of Hayek's thesis by reading the introductory chapter, Smithers had himself been urging Churchill to heed Hayek's message for several months. Indeed, Smithers had written to Churchill on behalf of the newly created Fighting Fund for Freedom in August 1944 to solicit Churchill's assistance in publicizing their cause.[10] As the Fund noted in a two-page statement that Smithers sent to Churchill: "Something must be done now to arrest the race down the road to the totalitarian State... The mortal danger is fully explained in Dr. Hayek's epoch-making book, 'The Road to Serfdom', dedicated to 'the Socialists of all Parties'."[11] Although we lack clear-cut evidence to signify that Churchill read Hayek's book, the tenor of the "Gestapo" broadcast rather suggests that Churchill had some familiarity with Hayek's message. Indeed, Hayek himself later noted that Churchill was clearly familiar with the argument of his book.[12]

As might be expected, Sir Waldron Smithers was a scathing critic of Attlee's Government. Indeed, Smithers argued that the introduction of the Control of Engagement Order (purportedly akin to "forced labour") in the autumn of 1947 provided ample proof that Hayek's 1944 fears were far from groundless. As Smithers tartly noted in late October 1947, Attlee's Government had taken yet "another step down the totalitarian road. The dictator Bill that was passed in August [a caustic allusion to the Supplies and Services (Extended Purposes) Act, 1947] and the proposals in the Gracious Speech, especially those in ... [the] section about the direction of labour, are all further steps down the road to serfdom."[13] According to Smithers, "the insane Socialist policy put forward at the General Election in 1945 ... [had] proved a delusion." Accordingly he urged his parliamentary colleagues to carefully read "'The Road to Serfdom' by Professor Hayek ... one of the most remarkable books ever written."[14]

Hayek and Smithers shared much the same negative view of the Attlee years. According to Hayek, the Control of Engagement Order amply illustrated the way in which the purportedly "inherent logic" of Attlee's interventionist policy had driven an initially "unwilling socialist government" into adopting "the kind of coercion it disliked."[15] As Smithers similarly told his parliamentary colleagues in December 1947, any attempt to "direct labour or money or goods from Whitehall" would assuredly "set in motion forces" that Attlee and company had not anticipated "and over which they have no control ... [they] released ... all the bricklayers from the Army, but they forgot to release the brickmakers." Accordingly, there was a dearth of "bricks to be laid" and the Government inevitably found itself directing "men into various industries."[16]

Although Hayek's message in *The Road to Serfdom* may have fallen on somewhat deaf ears in the mid–late 1940s, there can be little doubt that Hayek's views became increasingly influential within the Conservative Party during the late 1960s and early 1970s.[17] Indeed, Hayek's ideas—for example, Hayek's analysis of the baneful consequences of inflationary monetary policy—arguably came to influence macroeconomic policy at the highest level when Margaret Thatcher initially came to power in May 1979.[18] Although Margaret Thatcher noted that she did not really appreciate many of Hayek's arguments in defense of a free society—for example, Hayek's analysis of the rule of law—until the mid-1970s, she also noted that she carefully read *The Road to Serfdom* in the 1940s and found herself much persuaded by the logic of Hayek's thesis.[19] Margaret Thatcher (she was named Margaret Roberts at the time) fought her first election campaign when she contested Dartford in February 1950.[20] Although unsuccessful in her initial attempt to become an MP, John Campbell has noted that "Hayek may well have been in... [Margaret Roberts's] mind as she painted the election as a choice between two ways of life—'one which leads inevitably to slavery and the other to freedom'... 'In 1940 it was not the cry of nationalization that made this country rise up and fight totalitarianism. It was the cry of freedom and liberty'."[21] Accordingly, it is scarcely surprising that the young Miss Roberts would adopt a highly negative view of the Control of Engagement Order. Indeed, as we show later in this chapter, Miss Roberts's objections to the direction of labor were at the center of her somewhat heated autumn 1949 exchange with Norman Dodds (her opponent in the 1950 election). For now, however, it is necessary to take a closer look at the nature and purview of the Control of Engagement Order and the rationale that underlay its introduction in the autumn of 1947.

Paradise or Purgatory: The Control of Engagement Order?

In early August 1947, Herbert Morrison (Attlee's Lord President of the Council) moved the second reading of the Supplies and Services (Extended Purposes) Bill. As Morrison told Parliament, the Bill would merely "enable the use of the powers conferred by still existing Defence Regulations to be directed more particularly to increasing production and redressing the balance of trade."[22] Winston Churchill was manifestly less than persuaded by Morrison's reasoning, however, and argued that the Supplies and Services Bill was nothing more than "a blank cheque for totalitarian government."[23] Peter Thorneycroft (Conservative MP for Monmouth) adopted a similar tack and argued that Attlee had "no mandate whatever for the policy he is now seeking to pursue. He was elected in 1945 to introduce a paradise and not a purgatory. If he thinks these measures are necessary and wants to direct labour and wants the all-out Socialist totalitarian system for which the hon. Member for East Coventry [Richard Crossman] was arguing, let him have the courage to get up and say so, and let him take his case before the people of this country and argue it there."[24] Thorneycroft's suggestion that Attlee wanted to "direct labour" was an allusion to Attlee's earlier announcement of the way in which the Government planned to alleviate the severe labor shortages (manpower shortages in the parlance of 1947) that were plaguing a variety of 'essential' industries (primarily industries that produced for export to dollar markets). As Attlee himself had explained two days earlier, "We propose to re-impose the control over the engagement of labour which was almost universal during the war, but has since been removed from all industries except coalmining, building [various relatively minor yet somewhat labyrinthine controls that are beyond our scope in this chapter] and agriculture. This will enable all workers, leaving one job and entering another to be guided into that class of work in which they can best assist towards overcoming our economic difficulties [for example, the ever-burgeoning balance of payments deficit and the massive capital flight that had been seemingly initiated by the injudicious restoration of sterling convertibility in mid-July]. Control of engagement only controls the movement of those falling out of employment. To find necessary manpower for essential employment, it may be necessary to take steps to limit employment on less essential work."[25]

Thorneycroft would have none of Attlee's reasoning, however, and charged that "the only countries which have tried that system of allocation [the full-blown socialist planning purportedly advocated by Crossman] and direction of manpower, and have tried it in peacetime, have found that the ultimate sanction is the machine gun. The Government... [has] got to choose whether they are to have that system, or whether they are to have a system which goes back to the prices system... There is no halfway house between the machine-gun system and the prices mechanism system."[26]

Despite Thorneycroft's acerbity, the Supplies and Services (Extended Purposes) Act, 1947, received the Royal Assent on August 13, 1947.[27] The Attlee Government's Control of Engagement Order—subsequently made under Defence Regulation 58A in mid-September 1947—came into effect on October 6, 1947. Under the Control of Engagement Order, men between the ages of 18 and 50 years and women between the ages of 18 and 40 years were legally required to visit an official Employment Exchange (or approved equivalent) whenever they wanted to acquire employment or change job. As George Isaacs (Attlee's Minister of Labour) explained to Parliament in early November, any person visiting a Ministry of Labour and National Service Employment Exchange would be "offered on an average, four different jobs of an essential character," and any worker who repeatedly refused to take "essential work" (whether because they preferred to take "inessential" work or to remain unemployed) could ultimately be directed to take a suitable vacancy in a first-preference industry (e.g., textile bleaching and wire rope manufacture).[28]

Although any worker who was subject to direction was legally required to stay in his new job for a minimum of six months, he usually had an opportunity to appeal to his Local Appeal Board.[29] As Ness Edwards—Labour MP for Caerphilly and Parliamentary Undersecretary to George Isaacs—had explained during a heated November 3, 1947, parliamentary debate over the Order, no legal penalty whatsoever could be imposed "upon a man for refusing to take up any job offered to him by the Ministry of Labour. The penalty arises only if he is directed, and the purpose of giving the direction enables the man to exercise his appeal rights."[30]

The penalties for refusing to obey a Ministry of Labour direction (or for breaching the Control of Engagement Order more generally—for example, taking a job without the permission of the Ministry of Labour)—included "a fine up to £100 or imprisonment for anything up to three months, or both fine and imprisonment."[31]

Attlee's Totalitarian Planning?

As noted earlier, Hayek frequently maintained that British experience under the Attlee Government provided much evidence to illustrate the veracity of his 1944 thesis.[32] Indeed, Hayek argued that the Weimar "Social Democrats in the comparable period of the 1920's, under equally or more difficult economic conditions, never approached as closely to totalitarian planning as [had] the British Labour government."[33] As Hayek explained in the 1956 preface to the first American paperback edition of *The Road to Serfdom*, the Attlee Government—making much of the purportedly "essential distinction between totalitarian and democratic planning," and similarly trumpeting its steadfast commitment to "conduct its economic planning in a manner which preserves the maximum possible freedom of choice to the individual citizen"[34]—had "found itself...forced to put the conscription of labor back on the statute book."[35]

Hayek's negative assessment of the Order was shared by Milton Friedman. According to Friedman, "Fully enforced and carried through, the law [the Control of Engagement Order] would have involved centralized allocation of individuals to occupations."[36] In contrast, Evan Durbin (Labour MP for Edmonton and a former colleague of Hayek at the London School of Economics [LSE]) explained that the wartime "powers to direct labour and to keep men and women in particular jobs were progressively abandoned in 1946 and, despite the restoration of a very mild and temporary version of them in 1947, it remains true to say that, broadly speaking, labour is now uncontrolled—apart from military service."[37]

While Friedman and Hayek argued that the Control of Engagement Order had much similarity to a regime of wholesale industrial "conscription," Durbin's measured 1948 assessment of the Order ("very mild") is far closer to the mark. For instance, the Order did not "apply to every sort of work ... you do not have to obtain the following kinds of work through an Employment Exchange:—agriculture, coalmining, dock work ... fishing, employment without pay ... and employment in a managerial, professional, administrative or executive capacity."[38] Similarly, the Order did not apply to part-time employment (part-time work was officially defined as 30 hours or less per week) or to women who had household responsibilities (e.g., women with children aged 15 years or under living with them).

Rather tellingly, the Ministry of Labour—noting that it would provide a "card of introduction" to any worker interested in a particular first-preference vacancy—itself explained that "it's the firm that finally decides whether to engage you."[39]

The Dodds–Roberts Exchange and Attlee's "Direction of Labour Order"?

The Dodds–Roberts exchange over the direction of labor was initiated in late August 1949 when Norman Dodds (the sitting Labour MP for Dartford and Margaret Roberts's opponent in the February 1950 election) wrote to the *Dartford Chronicle* to challenge Miss Roberts's charge that the Control of Engagement Order assured that when "people of her generation ... were ready to go along the road to their careers" they faced "more restrictions than any other generation had had to face in this country."[40] Although Dodds very much doubted that any young person in 1949 enjoyed far fewer opportunities for career advancement than would have proven the case for their early–mid-1930s counterpart, he was primarily "concerned" by her "amazing reference to the Direction of Labour Order. If Miss Roberts is correct ... I have been completely misinformed about this seemingly devastating Order." Accordingly, he invited Miss Roberts to provide additional information about the Control of Engagement Order—particularly the circumstances under which the Ministry of Labour had the power to direct an individual to take essential work—and to provide figures for the total number of "persons" directed to take essential work by the Ministry of Labour.[41]

Miss Roberts responded at length in early September: The Control of Engagement Order—initially intended to remain in force until January 1, 1949—came into effect in early October 1947.[42] The Order—the Attlee "Government's plan for direction of labour"—"was issued by the Minister of Labour . . . acting in exercise of his powers of legislation by decree, conferred on him under the Supplies and Services (Extended Purposes) Act, 1947." Accordingly, the Control of Engagement Order—as with delegated legislation more generally—was not "subject to amendment by Parliament."[43]

Although Parliament was unable to amend delegated legislation, it could Pray (move a motion) to annul particular instances of such legislation. Indeed, Miss Roberts noted that a Prayer to annul the Control of Engagement Order—"a Socialist motion to annul it"—had been moved in early November 1947: "The motion was unfortunately lost . . . [and] Mr. Dodds was one of those who voted for the *retention* of the Order."[44] The Prayer to annul the Order had been initially moved by the veteran Labour MP Rhys Davies (Westhoughton) who warned "that, unless Parliament puts a stop to these totalitarian tendencies, there will be a goodly number of our working class folk sent to prison."[45] When the House finally divided—the debate over the Prayer having lasted a mere six-and-a-half hours—there were 144 Ayes and 252 Noes. The Ayes included such prominent figures as Harold Macmillan, Brendan Bracken, Quintin Hogg, Rab Butler, Peter Thorneycroft, Frank Byers (Liberal MP for Dorset Northern), and Clement Davies (leader of the Liberal Party), while Aneurin Bevan, James Callaghan, Richard Crossman, Barbara Castle, Woodrow Wyatt, Herbert Morrison, and Hugh Gaitskell were among the 252 MPs who voted against Davies's Prayer to annul the Order.

Unsurprisingly, Sir Waldron Smithers, Sir Ernest Graham-Little, and J. G. Braithwaite—all three of whom were among the 26 signatories to the two-page statement that Smithers had sent to Churchill on behalf of the Fighting Fund for Freedom (FFF) in August 1944—voted to annul the Order.[46] Although Smithers (the initial Chairman of the Fund) was seemingly no longer involved in the Fund's activities by September 1947, the Fund was greatly perturbed by the way in which "During the month of August 1947 the British people travelled much further down the Totalitarian Road."[47] Indeed, the Fund was particularly steadfast in its opposition to the direction of labor (Figures 7.1–7.3).[48]

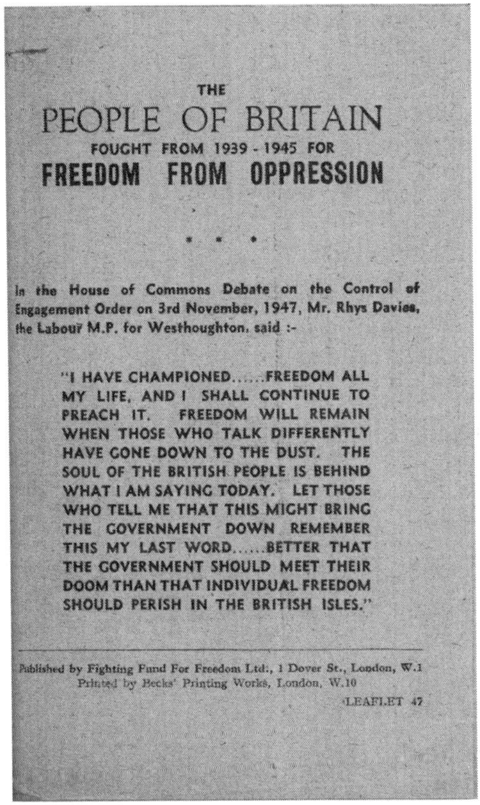

THE
PEOPLE OF BRITAIN
FOUGHT FROM 1939 - 1945 FOR
FREEDOM FROM OPPRESSION

* * *

In the House of Commons Debate on the Control of Engagement Order on 3rd November, 1947, Mr. Rhys Davies, the Labour M.P. for Westhoughton, said :-

"I HAVE CHAMPIONED......FREEDOM ALL MY LIFE, AND I SHALL CONTINUE TO PREACH IT. FREEDOM WILL REMAIN WHEN THOSE WHO TALK DIFFERENTLY HAVE GONE DOWN TO THE DUST. THE SOUL OF THE BRITISH PEOPLE IS BEHIND WHAT I AM SAYING TODAY. LET THOSE WHO TELL ME THAT THIS MIGHT BRING THE GOVERNMENT DOWN REMEMBER THIS MY LAST WORD......BETTER THAT THE GOVERNMENT SHOULD MEET THEIR DOOM THAN THAT INDIVIDUAL FREEDOM SHOULD PERISH IN THE BRITISH ISLES."

Published by Fighting Fund For Freedom Ltd., 1 Dover St., London, W.1
Printed by Becks' Printing Works, London, W.10
LEAFLET 47

Figure 7.1 FFF Leaflet 47-Rhys Davies Prayer to Annul.

Explaining the Official Figures: Direction of Labor or Control of Engagement?

Although Hayek argued that the Attlee Government had "found itself...forced to put the conscription of labor [the Control of Engagement Order] back on the statute book," he acknowledged that the power to direct labor "was in fact never used." As Hayek noted, however, "if it is known that the authorities have power to coerce, few will wait for actual coercion."[49] Unsurprisingly, the nub of Hayek's argument was a regularly invoked staple in the litany of objections that Conservative Parliamentarians leveled against the Control of Engagement Order in the late 1940s: As John Boyd-Carpenter

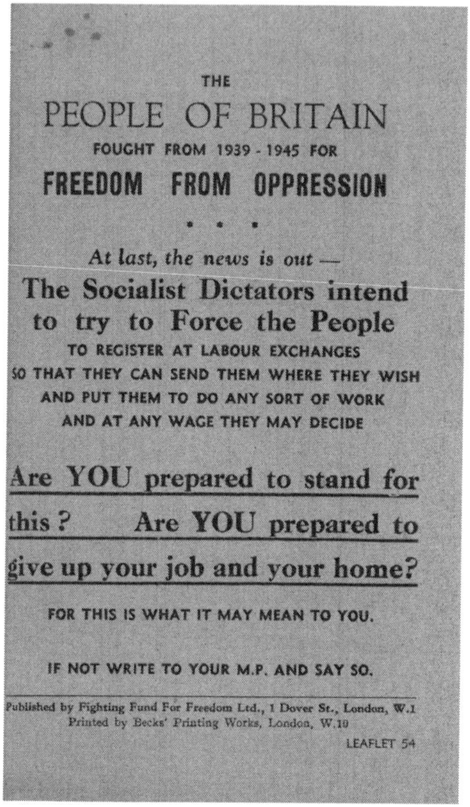

Figure 7.2 FFF Leaflet 54-Dictators and Register at Labour Exchange.

(Conservative MP for Kingston-upon-Thames) had argued in June 1949, many "persons are, in fact—though not in law—directed."[50] Indeed, Miss Roberts had herself made much the same argument in her initial reply to Norman Dodds. As she put it, while a "sum total of 95" persons had been "formally directed by the Order…the figures considered alone are misleading…they relate only to the formal directions which the Ministry [of Labour] issues as a last resort. The majority of people, when threatened with direction, 'go quietly,' but it is the existence of these powers which causes them to go."[51]

On the face of it, Miss Roberts's logic is eminently plausible. Nevertheless, Norman Dodds was not to be drawn by any charge that the "small number of cases in which compulsion has had to be applied" painted an inadequate "picture of the amount of control exercised" by

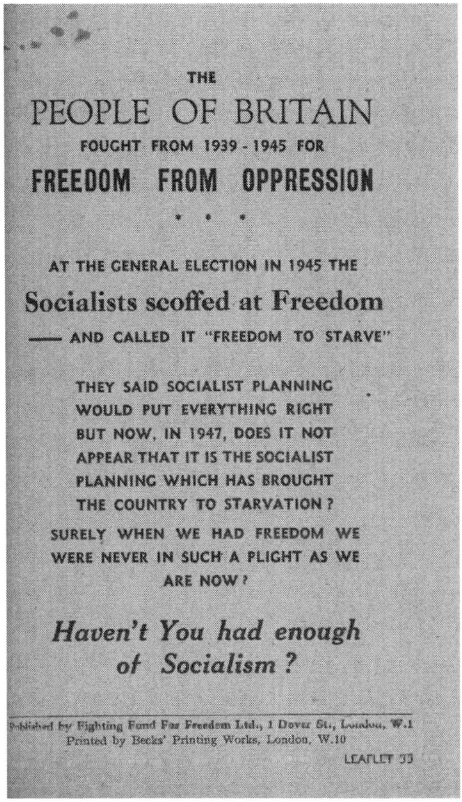

Figure 7.3 FFF Leaflet 55-Scoffed at Freedom.

the Control of Engagement Order.[52] Instead, he noted that her figure for the number of persons directed "by the Order" was wide of the mark: "Mr. Isaacs... informs me that up to July 31, 1949, the official figures are 19 men and 10 women... the persons directed were all unemployed... [and] had turned down offers of employment."[53]

At this juncture, it is necessary to take note of a somewhat arcane legal technicality that had initially reared its head during the parliamentary debate over Rhys Davies's Prayer to annul the Order. As Ness Edwards explained, "No person can be directed under this Order. He can only be directed under [Defence] Regulation 58A... the Control of Engagement Order does not confer on my right hon. Friend [George Isaacs] the authority to direct any person... There is a difference between direction and the control of engagement."[54] Accordingly, it is important to note that while the Control of Engagement Order per se came into effect in early October 1947, the Ministry of Labour already enjoyed the legal authority to direct any worker employed in coalmining or agriculture to remain in their job. Indeed, as had been the case during the war years, these particular industries were surrounded by a legal "'ring fence,' inside which workers already in the industry were to be retained."[55] As Clement Attlee had himself acknowledged in Parliament in early August 1947, while the final vestiges of the wartime and early postwar Control of Engagement Orders (e.g., the Control of Engagement Order, 1945, the Control of Engagement [Amendment] Order, 1945, and the Control of Engagement [No. 3] Order, 1946) had been progressively "removed from all industries," this was manifestly not the case in a ring-fenced industry such as "coalmining... [or] agriculture."[56]

As we now explain, however, Miss Roberts's tally of 95 workers purportedly directed "by the Order" was mistaken. In particular, her tally had wrongly included 66 directions that required men who were usually employed in a ring-fenced industry to remain in their jobs.[57] Indeed, in early 1948 the Ministry of Labour had taken many pains to stress that any worker who was between the ages of 18 and 50 years inclusive and normally employed in coalmining and agriculture had "remained throughout the year [1947] subject to the Control of Engagement Orders."[58] Consequently, they could not leave their industry without official approval and were "subject, if necessary, to the issue of directions under Regulation 58A to secure compliance with the Orders... The position was not substantially altered by the Control of Engagement Order, 1947, under which the 'ring fence' round the... [industries] remained."[59] Accordingly, the Ministry of Labour reported that the "number of directions issued under the new arrangements [the COE] was negligible."[60] Indeed, a sum total of 233 persons were directed under Defence Regulation 58A in the final three months of 1947. A mere 15 of these particular directions, however, were directions to take essential work "under the new arrangements."[61] Much the same was the case in 1948: "14 persons... were directed to employment during the year under the arrangements instituted in [October] 1947."[62]

Indeed, whenever George Isaacs responded to parliamentary questions about the total number of directions that were made because a person had explicitly refused to take essential work, he would frequently note that the official figures necessarily excluded directions "issued to workers normally employed in agriculture and coalmining requiring them to remain within their industry."[63] Indeed, shortly after the Control of Engagement Order came into effect, Isaacs had told Parliament that a sum total of "One hundred and one directions were issued during the four weeks ended 29th October... 91 in respect of coalmining and agriculture, which were already covered by a Control of Engagement Order before 6th October... [but] only 10 directions were issued as a direct consequence of the new Order during this period."[64]

Although the Control of Engagement Order was not revoked until March 13, 1950, the overwhelming majority of the 697 directions that were issued under the purview of Regulation 58A over the lifetime of the Order were directions that required persons who were usually engaged in a ring-fenced industry to remain in their industry: As George Isaacs explained to Parliament in May 1950, "29 persons were directed to take new employment [in a first preference industry] and 668 persons were directed to remain in coalmining or agricultural employment."[65]

The Control of Engagement Order: Attlee's "Dead Letter" or Attlee's "Live Wire"?

As we noted earlier, Norman Dodds had somewhat skirted Miss Roberts's charge that the threat of direction per se had much de facto potency. Indeed, Dodds concluded his September 9 letter by invoking the views of the journalist A. J. Cummings—a great "champion of the Liberal cause" (and well-known columnist for *The News Chronicle*)—who had said that "'we remain a free people... healthily suspicious of all forms of compulsion however benevolently inspired.'" According to Cummings, "[i]t was that healthy instinct which caused the Labour Government's measures for the direction of labour to become a dead letter."[66] Miss Roberts's response appeared a week later and she vehemently rejected any claim that the Control of Engagement Order was a "'dead letter'" ("I do not concur with this view"). As she tartly noted, why would a "'dead letter'... [be] extended for a further year?" Furthermore, she wondered whether Dodds would "be prepared to move its annulment forthwith?" As she explained, "If he refuses, then, on the 'dead letter reasoning' set out in his own correspondence, it can only mean one of two things—either he wants to keep this control for control's sake or he agrees with me that the Order is not a 'dead letter,' but a live wire."[67]

Norman Dodds's response to Miss Roberts's jibes appeared in the September 23, 1949, edition of the *Dartford Chronicle*: The Order was manifestly a "dead letter"—the Government would only direct a person to take a specific first-preference vacancy when they "cannot find employment and consistently... [refused] the offer of work"—but Dodds (having already twice voted against a Prayer to annul the Order) would not support any "move to annul the Order." Moreover, Dodds charged that "If the Tory Party came to power much more effective methods would, as in the past, be used to 'inspire' a section of the workers."[68] Accordingly, he urged Miss Roberts to attend one of his public meetings and learn "first hand" about what had transpired on "Tyneside and Wearside between the two wars."[69]

Howsoever one might view Norman Dodds's somewhat dogged defense of the Control of Engagement Order, he assuredly hit the mark when he alluded to the "labour discipline" effect that was induced by the mass unemployment that had blighted the North-East of England throughout the interwar years (Dodds had himself been born in Gateshead). For example, in 1933, the unemployment rate in Jarrow (a town in Tyne and Wear) reached a staggering 77 percent.[70] Indeed, the tenor of Dodds's argument about "direction" by involuntary unemployment was similarly invoked by many Labour MPs during parliamentary exchanges over the Control of Engagement Order. For instance, during the December 1949 debate over the third and final Prayer to annul the Order, William Blyton (Labour MP for Houghton-le-Spring) acidly observed that "direction in peace time has always been the lot of the unemployed under the [Conservative] Administrations formed and supported by hon. Gentlemen opposite." Indeed, Blyton accusingly noted that "in the years between the wars the coalfields of Kent and Yorkshire were filled with men directed from the north-east [Houghton-le-Spring was in Tyne and Wear]," and he thus charged that it rather "ill" became the Conservative "Opposition to talk about freedom."[71]

As it was, the Dodds–Roberts exchange over the Order came to a close with the publication of Miss Roberts's reply on September 30, 1949. Unsurprisingly, Miss Roberts sharply castigated Mr. Dodds for blithely ignoring her arguments—he "crashed on with his thesis that...the Order was a 'dead letter'"—and for repeatedly attempting to "skate round my point." As she tartly noted, Dodds had revealed his "real attitude...when I challenged him to try and remove the Order." As she explained, "most people 'went quietly' when threatened with direction." Hence, the Control of Engagement Order—far from being a "dead letter"—was "very much *alive* as a threat which in itself is sufficient to control large sections of the population in the event of their wanting to change jobs." As she acidly noted, "Mr. Dodds"—wanting to "retain" the Order—had "indirectly admitted the truth" of her point.[72]

While any adequate consideration of the evidence is clearly beyond our scope here, the Ministry of Labour did appear to implicitly cede much of the tenor of Miss Roberts's logic. Indeed, the Ministry of Labour, noting that the vast majority of workers seeking to change employment had generally proven "willing to accept the suggestions of Local Offices as regards taking 'essential work'" heavily stressed that the Ministry had sought to rely in "the first instance on persuasion rather than to use the power of direction under Defence Regulation 58A."[73] The Ministry of Labour made the same argument in early 1949 when it vaunted its "slight" use of the power of compulsion as providing much "evidence of the success of the policy of relying upon persuasion in the first instance [during 1948]... [with any recourse to] the power of direction... only [proving necessary] in the rare cases where persuasion failed."[74] As John Boyd-Carpenter was to acidly note during the debate over the third and final Prayer to annul the Control of Engagement Order, however, the Ministry of Labour appeared to invoke the "word 'persuasion'... [in much the same] sense in which it is used in many totalitarian countries... the same sense in which the Jews were persuaded voluntarily to hand over their property in Nazi Germany—the polite request masking the power behind the request."[75]

Although Margaret Roberts was unsuccessful in her initial two attempts to gain a seat in Parliament (she was defeated by Norman Dodds in February 1950 and October 1951), the Attlee Government finally abolished the ring-fences surrounding agriculture and coalmining on January 1, 1950. Indeed, the Control of Engagement Order was itself revoked in early March 1950. As the Labour MP Cecil Poole noted, George Isaacs merited much praise for having announced the revocation of the Order "after the election rather than before it."[76] As it was, however, Attlee's initial working majority of 146 parliamentary seats—136 seats at the time of the election—had itself been whittled down to a mere five seats at the February 1950 election, and the Labour Government would meet its eventual electoral defeat at the hands of Churchill and the Conservatives in October 1951.

Conclusion: The Socialists of All Parties?

Although Hayek deemed the Attlee years to provide much evidence illustrating the veracity of his thesis in *The Road to Serfdom* he was himself "unable to examine the effect of... [Attlee's] policies in detail" and hence invoked the "summary judgments of other observers who may be less suspect of preconceived opinions."[77] In particular, Hayek invoked Ivor Thomas's *The Socialist Tragedy*.[78] Thomas was elected to Parliament in February 1942 (he "won" the Keighley byelection—he was unopposed—under the wartime electoral truce) and his book provided a damning assessment of the Attlee Government. Indeed, Thomas—having resigned the Labour whip in October 1948 and joined the Conservative Party in early 1949—charged that the Control of Engagement Order provided ample evidence that Britain was inadvertently heading toward the full-blown totalitarian state.[79] Accordingly, he made much of J. Rhys Davies's Prayer to annul the Order. Although Thomas noted that Davies had told the House that if "honourable members... [can] convince me that we cannot have as much individual freedom in a socialist society as we could get under capitalism, I am opposed to a planned socialist state,"[80] he neglected to tell the reader that he had himself voted against Davies's Prayer!

Although Sir Waldron Smithers—urging his readers to carefully "study Dr. Hayek's book, The Road to Serfdom"[81]—was adamant that Attlee and company had dragged Britain "much farther down the Totalitarian Road than we realise,"[82] we leave it to the reader to decide whether Friedman and Hayek ("conscription of labour") or Durbin ("very mild") had the more accurate grasp of the nature and purview of the Control of Engagement Order. For purposes of comparison, however, we note that 23,517 workers in England and Wales had—as of late February 1944—been prosecuted for noncompliance (e.g., refusal to obey a direction) with the provisions of the wartime Essential Work Orders (initially made under the authority of Regulation 58A in March 1941): 1,807 workers were subsequently sent to prison.[83] By stark contrast, a sum total of 302 directions were made under the purview of Regulation 58A in 1948. As noted earlier, however, a mere 14 of these particular directions were directions to take new employment. Moreover, the Ministry of Labour noted that the vast majority of the markedly few alleged infringements of the Order that came to its notice were related to the activities of private employment agencies.[84] Due to lack of evidence, however, only one such case of noncompliance resulted in successful prosecution.[85] In contrast, a total of 78 men were prosecuted in 1948 for refusing to submit to the medical examination that was required under the National Service Acts: 74 of these men were later convicted and 37 of them were fined or sent to prison. Twelve of these men were prosecuted a second time, however, and the ten who still refused to comply with a Court Order to undergo the examination were themselves subsequently fined or sent to prison.[86]

As we noted earlier, Smithers was highly critical of what he viewed as a particularly dangerous turn toward collectivism within the Conservative Party in the years after its 1945 election defeat. Indeed, Smithers was immensely fond of noting that "Dr. Hayek dedicated his book, 'The Road to Serfdom,' to 'the Socialists of all parties'."[87] Consequently, it is scarcely surprising that Smithers[88] would roundly object to the Conservative Government's Notification of Vacancies Order (initially introduced in late January 1952 and not revoked until early May 1956). The Order came into force on February 25, 1952, and had some prima facie similarity to the Attlee Government's Control of Engagement Order. As with the 1947 Order, the Notification of Vacancies Order made it illegal for any full-time worker to obtain or change their employment through any means other than a Ministry of Labour and National Service Employment Exchange or an officially approved equivalent (e.g., a trade union). Similarly, any worker who visited an Employment Exchange would find himself entreated to take a job that was designated as a "First Preference" vacancy. These vacancies were primarily in industries that had defense contracts or produced goods for export.[89] According to the 1952 Order, employers could only legally engage workers through a Ministry of Labour Employment Exchange (or approved equivalent) and employers could be prosecuted for any violations of the Order. The 1952 Order, however, did not provide Ministry of Labour officials with the power to invoke Defence Regulation 58A and compel a worker to take a particular First Preference vacancy.

As noted earlier, the Control of Engagement Order came into effect on October 6, 1947. Ironically enough, however, the Attlee Government's Control of Engagement Order had much similarity to the Control of Engagement Order, 1945, made by Churchill's Coalition Government on May 22, 1945. The Coalition Government broke up the following day—Labour left the Coalition—and the Order was slated to come into effect on June 4, 1945: This, of course, was the very same day upon which Churchill would make his "Gestapo" election broadcast![90]

Notes

1. Friedrich A. Hayek, *The Road to Serfdom* (Chicago, IL: University of Chicago Press, [1944] 1994).
2. "The General Election—The Rt. Hon. Winston S. Churchill's broadcast of June 4," *The Listener* (June 7, 1945): 629.

3. Lord Moran, *Churchill, Taken from the Diaries of Lord Moran* (Boston, MA: Houghton Mifflin, 1966), 271.
4. *The Recorder*, June 9, 1945. Hayek was himself reputedly very pleased that Churchill had taken up his ideas. Richard Cockett, *Thinking the Unthinkable* (London: Fontana Press, 1995), 95.
5. Clement Attlee, *Purpose and Policy: Selected Speeches* (London: Hutchinson, 1947), 7.
6. Cockett, *Unthinkable*, 92. Indeed, the evidence shows that Attlee—having obtained a copy of Hayek's book due to Assheton's largesse—had himself read *The Road to Serfdom* (Andrew Farrant, *Hayek and the 1945 Election*, Working Paper, 2013).
7. *Daily Express*, April 25, 1944.
8. As one contemporary put it, Smithers—"an extreme Tory out of a vanished age"—had an apparently healthy appetite for the "consoling effect of alcohol" (John Boyd-Carpenter, *Way of Life: The Memoirs of John Boyd-Carpenter* [London: Sidgwick & Jackson, 1980], 79). Also see Andrew Farrant and Nicola Tynan, "Sir Waldron Smithers and the Muddle of the Tory Middle," *Economic Affairs* 32, no. 2, (2012).
9. Smithers subsequently published the provocatively titled *Socialism Offers Slavery* (Sir Waldron Smithers, *Socialism Offers Slavery* [London: Heath Cranton, 1945]) and noted that his book was intended to buttress Hayek's thesis "in simple language...[and] facts" (7). Smithers had met "Professor Hayek" and had been authorized to "say that...[Hayek had] read the sections of this book which deal with *The Road to Serfdom*, and confirms that I represent his views correctly" (7).
10. The Fund hoped to raise £1,000,000 to be spent in defense of "liberty and freedom." By late 1945, the Fund had grown "from a small group of friends meeting in a borrowed room to an organisation with its own suite of offices, a staff of 12, a mailing list of 50,000 to 60,000, and subscriptions coming in from all over the country" (*British Journal of Nursing* 93 [June 1945]: 67).
11. The statement berated Churchill's Coalition Government for introducing "Bill after Bill...which involves compulsion and loss of personal freedom" (Andrew Farrant and Nicola Tynan, "Sir Waldron Smithers and the Long Walk to Finchley," *Economic Affairs* 32, no. 1 [2012]: 44). As Smithers noted in a December 1944 letter to the *British Medical Journal*, "the 'Fighting Fund for Freedom'...[is] doing all...[it] can to educate the voters of this country against the mortal danger of State control, of which an outstanding example is the medical White Paper recently issued by the Government" (Sir Waldron Smithers, "Tuberculosis in Kent," *The British Medical Journal* 2, no. 4381 [December 23, 1944]: 835). Although Smithers wrote to Churchill on behalf of the Fund on several occasions it is rather unclear whether Churchill himself paid much attention to Smithers's missives. Indeed, Churchill's Private Secretary (John Peck) told Churchill that Smithers and company opposed many policies that were in the public interest (Farrant and Tynan, "Long Walk to Finchley," 44).
12. Friedrich A. Hayek, *Hayek on Hayek: An Autobiographical Dialogue*, ed. Stephen Kresge and Leif Wenar (Chicago, IL: University of Chicago Press, 1994), 107.
13. 443 Parl. Deb., H. C. (5th ser.) [1947] 440.

14. 443 Parl. Deb., H. C. (5th ser.) [1947] 434.
15. Friedrich A. Hayek, "Preface [to the 1956 paperback edition]" in *The Road to Serfdom* (Chicago: University of Chicago Press, [1944] 1994), xxvii–xlvi. (Hereafter cited as "1956 Preface.") When the Labour Government came to power in 1945 it was "committed to honouring the objectives of both the 1944 White Paper on Employment Policy and the Beveridge Report on the Social Services. All this was to be realized by a rather nebulous economic policy which they referred to as 'democratic planning'. It can best be described as a mixture of physical controls, nationalization and exhortation, laced with a dash of Keynesianism and a liberal dose of wishful thinking" (Sir Edwin Plowden, *An Industrialist in The Treasury* [London: Andre Deutsch, 1989], 4). Plowden became the Government's Chief Planning Officer in spring 1947. Although R. W. ("Otto") Clarke (the inventor of what became the *Financial Times* Ordinary Share Index and an important Treasury Civil Servant) was an advocate of planning, he described the Attlee Government's attempt to "plan"' as "bricks without straw... there was no known plan and no known means of implementing a plan even if there had been a plan" (Clarke's diary quoted by David Hubback, "Sir Richard Clarke—1910–1975," *Public Policy and Administration* 3, no. 1 [1988]: 27).
16. 445 Parl. Deb., H. C. (5th ser.) [1947] 479.
17. Cockett, *Unthinkable.*
18. Ibid.
19. Margaret Thatcher, *The Path to Power* (New York: Harper Collins, 1995), 50–51.
20. According to Saint (Tony Saint, "How a TV dramatist made even the BBC—and other Lefties—cheer for Margaret Thatcher," *Daily Mail*, June 7, 2008, http://www.dailymail.co.uk/femail/article-1024877/How-TV-dramatist-BBC – assorted-Lefties – cheer-Margaret-Thatcher.html (accessed April 24, 2013), Smithers did his utmost to stymie Margaret Roberts's initial attempt to become a Member of Parliament. As Saint explains, Smithers was outraged by the Dartford Conservative Association's adoption of Miss Roberts to contest the seat in the 1950 General Election and wondered why Dartford had been unable to get "a local businessman to stand?" (Ibid.) According to the evidence, however, Smithers had written to Conservative Central Office in early 1949 to report that other Tories—taking much umbrage at Dartford's adoption of a "young girl of 23, Miss Margaret Robertson [sic]"—had asked Smithers why Dartford "Could... not have got some prominent businessman?" (Smithers quoted in John Campbell, *Margaret Thatcher—Volume One: The Grocer's Daughter* [London: Random House, 2000], 72–73). Indeed, Smithers had never met Miss Roberts and had no knowledge of her views. Accordingly, he asked Central Office for guidance and was subsequently assured that "Dartford had made an excellent choice" (ibid., 73). We imagine that Smithers would have viewed Miss Roberts's subsequent campaign speeches with enthusiastic approval: As Smithers's son would later note, "my father... would have been a great Thatcher supporter" (D. W. Smithers, *Not a Moment to Lose* [Cambridge: The Memoir Club, 1989], 4).

21. Campbell, *Margaret Thatcher*, 80.
22. 441 Parl. Deb., H. C. (5th ser.) [1947] 1794.
23. 441 Parl. Deb., H. C. (5th ser.) [1947] 1805.
24. 441 Parl. Deb., H. C. (5th ser.) [1947] 1834. Crossman had insisted that the gravity of the economic situation—for example, the ever-burgeoning balance of payments deficit—necessitated that Attlee's Government "either go forward to full Socialist planning or back to a pool of unemployed—one way or the other." 441 Parl. Deb., H. C. (5th ser.) [1947] 1820.
25. 441 Parl. Deb., H. C. (5th ser.) [1947] 1500.
26. 441 Parl. Deb., H. C. (5th ser.) [1947] 1829. Hayek had similarly argued that it was markedly "difficult to stop planning just where we wish." Hayek, *Road to Serfdom*, 117.
27. 441 Parl. Deb., H. C. (5th ser.) [1947] 2481.
28. 441 Parl. Deb., H. C. (5th ser.) [1947] 1362.
29. The right of appeal had been instituted under the wartime Essential Work Orders.
30. 443 Parl. Deb., H. C. (5th ser.) [1947] 1446.
31. Ministry of Labour and National Service, *Control of Engagement Order QUIZ: How Does the Order Affect me?* 1947: 2. The Order also made it illegal for an employer to engage workers covered by the Order unless they engaged them through a Ministry of Labour Employment Exchange. Any employer who was convicted of breaching the Order was similarly liable to the penalties noted above. *QUIZ* (1947): 3.
32. "This experience has strengthened my concern... [and] taught the reality of the difficulties I pointed out to many for whom an abstract argument would never have carried conviction" Hayek, "1956 Preface," xxxvii.
33. Ibid., xlii.
34. *Economic Survey for 1947* quoted by Hayek, "1956 Preface," xxxviii.
35. Ibid.
36. Milton Friedman, *Capitalism and Freedom* (Chicago, IL: University of Chicago Press, 1962), 11.
37. E. F. M. Durbin, "The Economic Problems Facing the Labour Government," in *Socialism: The British Way*, ed. D. Munro (London: Essential Books, 1948), 9.
38. *QUIZ*, 2.
39. Ibid., 3.
40. Margaret Roberts quoted by Norman Dodds, *Dartford Chronicle*, August 26, 1949.
41. Dodds, *Dartford Chronicle*, August 26, 1949.
42. As Miss Roberts noted, the Order was extended "to January 1, 1950, by Statutory Instrument No. 2608, 1948" (Margaret Roberts, *Dartford Chronicle*, September 2, 1949).
43. Margaret Roberts, *Dartford Chronicle*, September 2, 1949. As George Isaacs had explained to Parliament, "The Order is made under the Defence (General) Regulations, 1939, as having effect by virtue of the Supplies and Services (Transitional Powers) Act, 1945, as extended by the Supplies and Services

(Extended Purposes) Act, 1947. That sounds a pretty awful rigmarole, but it is the authority under which we work." 443 Parl. Deb., H. C. (5th ser.) [1947] 1359.

44. Margaret Roberts, *Dartford Chronicle*, September 2, 1949. Norman Dodds had also voted against a Prayer to annul the Order that was introduced by John Boyd-Carpenter in early December 1948. The Prayer sought to annul the Control of Engagement (Amendment) Order, 1948. The latter had been made on December 1 and extended the Control of Engagement Order for an additional year.
45. 443 Parl. Deb., H. C. (5th ser.) [1947] 1343. H. H. Wilson notes that Davies "permitted his name to be placed on a pamphlet written by the Aims of Industry attacking the Control of Engagement order" (H. H. Wilson, "Techniques of Pressure: Anti-Nationalization Propaganda in Britain," *The Public Opinion Quarterly* 15, no. 2 [1951]: 230). We have been unable to obtain a copy of Davies's seven-page *Bond or Free. Mr. J. Rhys Davies, M.P., Here Re-states the Supreme Issue of Personal Liberty Menaced by the Control of Engagement Order, 1947, etc.* (London: Nigel Cragoe, 1948).
46. Farrant and Tynan, "Long Walk to Finchley," 44.
47. Fighting Fund for Freedom, *Report No. 15*, September 1947: 1. Mark Pitchford, *The Conservative Party and the Extreme Right: 1945–75* (Manchester: Manchester University Press, 2011), 27, 221–22 notes that Smithers's involvement in the FFF ended in late 1945. The Fund had become involved in a manifestly unsavory October 1945 campaign against Jewish refugees that had been organized by Charles Challen, Conservative MP for Hampstead (ibid., 15). Also see G. Macklin, *Very Deeply Dyed in Black: Sir Oswald Mosley and the Resurrection of British Fascism after 1945* (London: I. B. Tauris, 2007), 40. It is noteworthy that the Fund's *Report No. 3* (Fighting Fund for Freedom, *Report No. 3*, September 1946) describes Sir Ernest Graham-Little as a Member of its Executive Committee (1) whereas Smithers himself is merely invoked as an MP who opposes Ministry of Food regulations governing the production of flour and is not mentioned in connection with the Fund per se (2). Similarly, the Fund's *Report No. 53* (Fighting Fund for Freedom, *Report No. 53*, January 1951) notes that Earl Stanhope—one of the original signatories to the statement that Smithers sent to Churchill in 1944—had stood down as Chairman of the Fund. Stanhope had initially agreed to become Chairman "for a few weeks" (presumably after Smithers left the Fund) in January 1946 (1).
48. A detailed consideration of the Registration for Employment Order (introduced in December 1947) is beyond the scope of this chapter.
49. Hayek, "1956 Preface," xxxviii.
50. John Boyd-Carpenter, *The Times* (June 21, 1949): 5.
51. Margaret Roberts, *Dartford Chronicle*, September 2, 1949.
52. Ibid.
53. Norman Dodds, *Dartford Chronicle*, September 9, 1949.
54. 443 Parl. Deb., H. C. (5th ser.) [1947] 1446. Under Defence Regulation 58A, the "Minister of Labour and National Service or any National Service

Officer... [can] direct any person in Great Britain to perform such services in the United Kingdom or in any British ship... as may be specified by or described in the direction, being services which that person is... capable of performing" (Defence Regulation 58A quoted by John Boyd-Carpenter, "The Political Abuse of the Defence Regulations," *The New English Review* 13, no. 1 [July 1946]: 11).

55. H. M. D. Parker, *Manpower: A Study of War-time Policy and Administration* (London: Her Majesty's Stationary Office, 1957): 222. Agricultural workers could freely take a job in coalmining without obtaining official approval prior to the reintroduction of the Control of Engagement Order on October 6, 1947, while coalminers could only leave their industry with official approval. After October 6, 1947, any worker engaged in a ring-fenced industry—whether coalmining or agriculture—could only change jobs without official approval if he stayed within his particular industry (e.g., any miner could take employment at a different mine).
56. 441 Parl. Deb., H. C. (5th ser.) [1947] 1500.
57. Ministry of Labour, Operation of the Control of Engagements Order, Report 23.
58. Ministry of Labour and National Service—Report for the Year 1947: 63.
59. Ibid.
60. Ibid., 35.
61. Ibid., 36.
62. Ministry of Labour and National Service—Report for the Year 1948: 21.
63. 457 Parl. Deb., H. C. (5th ser.) [1948] 1027.
64. 444 Parl. Deb., H. C. (5th ser.) [1947] 1768.
65. 475 Parl. Deb., H. C. (5th ser.) [1950] 187W.
66. Cummings quoted by Dodds, *Dartford Chronicle*, September 9, 1949.
67. Margaret Roberts, *Dartford Chronicle*, September 16, 1949. The jibe that Dodds may favor controls for their own sake is squarely in keeping with Churchill's June 1945 charge that Attlee's socialists displayed a "hunger for controls of every kind" and viewed state control and regulation as if they were "delectable foods instead of war-time inflictions and monstrosities" ("The General Election," *The Listener* [June 7, 1945]: 629).
68. Samuel Bowles and Herbert Gintis, "Contested Exchange: New Microfoundations for the Political Economy of Capitalism," *Politics and Society* 18, no. 2 (1990): 165–222 and C. Shapiro and J. E. Stiglitz, "Equilibrium Unemployment as a Worker Discipline Device," *American Economic Review* 74, no. 3 (1984): 433–44, provide the microeconomic logic implicitly underlying Dodds's allusion to the way in which involuntary unemployment disciplines labor.
69. Norman Dodds, *Dartford Chronicle*, September 23, 1949.
70. G. McCrone, *Regional Policy in Britain* (London: Allen & Unwin, 1969), 91. Also see, A. Glynn and A. Booth, *Modern Britain: An Economic and Social History* (London: Routledge, 1996), 91. We thank Graham Brownlow for directing us (no pun intended) to the sources we note.
71. 470 Parl. Deb., H. C. (5th ser.) [1949] 2838. The December 1949 Prayer to annul the Order had been initially moved by Sir David Maxwell Fyfe (Conservative

MP for Liverpool West Derby and one of the prosecutors at the Nuremberg Trials).

72. Margaret Roberts, *Dartford Chronicle*, September 30, 1949.
73. Ministry of Labour and National Service—Report for the Year 1947: 35, 49.
74. Ministry of Labour and National Service—Report for the Year 1948: 21.
75. 470 Parl. Deb., H. C. (5th ser.) [1949] 2864.
76. 472 Parl. Deb., H. C. (5th ser.) [1950] 471.
77. Hayek, "1956 Preface," xliii.
78. Ivor Thomas, *The Socialist Tragedy* (London: Latimer House Limited, 1949).
79. Thomas, *The Socialist Tragedy*, 131–37.
80. Davies quoted in Thomas, *The Socialist Tragedy* (1949): 134–35.
81. Waldron Smithers, *Principles and Politics* (Bromley: Kentish Times Limited, 1951), 2.
82. Ibid., 14.
83. Labour Research Department, *EWO: Questions and Answers* (London: Labour Research Department, 1944), 19–20.
84. Ministry of Labour and National Service—Report for the Year 1948: 18.
85. The employer of Sarah Alterkovsky was successfully prosecuted in October 1948 for its failure to engage her through an official Ministry of Labour employment exchange or approved equivalent. Alterkovsky, however, was not punished for her employer's actions (459 Parl. Deb., H. C. [5th ser.] [1948] 239).
86. Ministry of Labour and National Service—Report for the Year 1948: 12.
87. Smithers, *Principles and Politics*, 2.
88. 521 Parl. Deb., H. C. (5th ser.) [1953] 259W.
89. Walter Monckton, "Manpower Problems," *Tory Challenge*, July 1952: 1.
90. We thank John Blundell for helpful comments on an earlier draft. We also thank David M. Levy and Malinda Triller for their invaluable assistance with the graphics reproduced in this chapter.

CHAPTER EIGHT

Hayekian Perspectives on Canada's Economic and Social Reforms of the 1990s

Jason Clemens and Niels Veldhuis

The years between 1987 and 2000 were a period of profound change in Canada.[1] Due to the scope and depth of the changes and reforms enacted in that period, the Canada that existed in 1987 did not exist, in many meaningful ways, by the end of the 1990s. Those changes are assessed in light of a number of principles espoused by F. A. Hayek, which help to understand not only the reforms but also the reasons for their success.

The chapter begins with a brief discussion of several Hayekian principles that were used to assess and understand the reforms enacted in Canada. The second section of the chapter details the broad changes implemented in Canada during the 1990s by the federal and many provincial governments. The third and fourth sections outline specific areas of government activity in more detail. Specifically, section three looks at welfare reform in Canada with some commentary based on contrasts with the United States, which also enacted welfare reform during the same period. The fourth section compares and contrasts the delivery and regulation of kindergarten-to-grade-12 (K–12) education in Canada and the United States. This is followed by a brief conclusion and commentary.[2]

Hayekian Ideas and Canadian Reforms

The risk of undertaking a discussion that aims to understand government reforms in the context of Hayekian ideas, particularly when it is presented in such esteemed company, is that rather than assess the reforms undertaken in Canada from a Hayekian perspective, the Canadian reforms are forced into a Hayekian framework. There is an additional risk of stretching the bounds of explanation for why such dramatic and historic reforms were undertaken in Canada.

Our aim is to avoid both risks by acknowledging, first, that Hayek's teachings and writings played no direct role that we are aware of in the design or implementation of Canada's reforms in the 1990s and, second, that it is highly unlikely Hayek had a direct influence on any but a handful of the major players who crafted and introduced the reforms.

Benefits of Decentralization

That being said, it is the intention of the authors to show a distinct Hayekian flavor to some of the reforms introduced in Canada, particularly with respect to devolvement of responsibilities from the federal government to the provinces, localities, and in some cases, individuals themselves.

In several of his writings, including *Law, Legislation and Liberty*, Hayek discusses the efficacy and benefits of decentralizing programs to regional or local authorities.

> Most service activities now rendered by central government could be devolved to regional or local authorities which would possess the power to raise taxes at a rate they could determine but which they could levy or apportion only according to general rules laid down by a central legislature.[3]

Later in this section, Hayek further discusses the benefits of decentralized service and program provision through the lens of competition on the part of government for citizens. Specifically, he states:

> the transformation of local and even regional governments into quasi-commercial corporations competing for citizens. They would have to offer a combination of advantages and costs which made life within their territory at least as attractive as elsewhere within the reach of its potential citizens.[4]

Similarly, in *The Constitution of Liberty*, Hayek argues that:

> There are strong reasons why action by local authorities generally offers the next-best solution where private initiative cannot be

> relied upon to provide certain services and where some sort of collective action is therefore needed; for it has many of the advantages of private enterprise and fewer of the dangers of coercive action of government. Competition between local authorities or between larger units within an area where there is freedom of movement provides in a large measure that opportunity for experimentation with alternative methods which will secure most of the advantages of free growth.[5]

Hayek clearly favored devolving responsibility for service provision and programs to lower levels of government from the federal or national level, where such programs would not or could not be delivered by the market. In particular, Hayek stresses the role of competition between subnational jurisdictions both with respect to the delivery of services as well as their cost (i.e., taxes).

Before discussing the second Hayekian concept applicable to our analysis, namely, the nature of knowledge and information, it is worthwhile to further explore Hayek's importance in connecting decentralized service provision by government and experimentation.

Hayek clearly argues that a key benefit of decentralized provision of services and programs by lower levels of governments is the positive incentive and ability to experiment. That is, by decentralizing, central governments enable lower levels of government to innovate and customize service, and program provision to meet the needs of their citizens.

Not only does this offer the potential to better match the needs of citizens with the programs and services delivered by government, but it also allows learning from doing. Simply put, as lower levels of government experiment with different service models, other governments are able to observe their successes and failures, and hopefully adjust their own services and programs accordingly.

In addition, the connection of service provision with taxation levels between competing jurisdictions imposes a competitive discipline on subnational levels of government. If services are provided at too generous a level, which implies higher tax rates in some dimension, then jurisdictions will face a two-fold response. First, the higher marginal tax rates required to extract the taxes necessary for the programs will discourage the very activities required to generate the income for the programs—namely, work effort, savings, investment, and entrepreneurship. And, second, individuals benefitting from such programs in other jurisdictions may well decide to relocate, putting yet more pressure on the spending demands of the government. Put differently, the competitive pressures discussed by Hayek impose a limited discipline on subnational governments that would not be present if the program were centralized, which provides an added benefit to the experimentation discussed previously.

Information and Responding to Change

The second Hayekian concept applicable to this analysis is the ability to respond to change, and the availability of information necessary to make informed decisions about such change. Hayek himself characterized the centrality of change in economic decisions: it is "worth stressing that economic problems arise always and only in consequence of change."[6]

One of Hayek's most prominent works, his 1945 *American Economic Review* article "The Use of Knowledge in Society," speaks to this very issue. While a full analysis of this watershed article is beyond the scope of this chapter, its key insight into the nature of knowledge and information is worth noting. Hayek argues that any single individual lacks the information and knowledge of time and place to make accurate, or even proximate, decisions about the best use of resources. The nature of knowledge and information demands a decentralized approach to decision making and a reliance on the price system as a conveyor of information. Indeed, one of the most powerful insights of the article is Hayek's description and explanation regarding how individual actors can make decisions based on prices as if they had vast amounts of information, because of the power of the price system to convey information. Hayek put it succinctly in the article this way: "We need decentralization because only thus can we insure that the knowledge of the particular circumstances of time and place will be promptly used."[7]

One has to be cautious not to extend Hayek's knowledge and information argument too far with respect to government, since a critical aspect of Hayek's knowledge argument is the role and importance of prices in conveying information. However, the combination of Hayek's advocacy for decentralized provision of services by government, the benefits of competition between governments, the incentive and ability to experiment, and the nature of information all combine to form a fairly strong Hayekian principle regarding the efficacy of decentralized governance.

What follows are two analyses of Canadian service provision. The first relates to social welfare, and highlights both the absolute reforms enacted in Canada during the 1990s as well as a relative analysis comparing the reforms to those implemented in the United States at the same time. The second example is the provision of K–12 education based on a comparison of Canada and the United States. Both case studies provide stark examples of the benefits of decentralized service provision as advocated by Hayek.

Background on the Canadian Reforms of the 1990s

The negotiation and implementation of the Free Trade Agreement (FTA) with the United States in the late 1980s marked the beginning of a period of enormous change for Canada. The opening of trade and introduction of greater competition via the FTA set the foundation for much larger, and more profound, fiscal changes in the 1990s.

The decade began with pronounced financial pressures on the federal and provincial governments in Canada, pressures that had been mounting for the previous decade or so. From 1992 to 1993, deficits were present in every budget: the federal government's deficit as a share of gross domestic product (GDP) was 5.6 percent, and the provinces ranged from a low of 1.7 percent in British Columbia to 4.4 percent in neighboring Alberta (Figure 8.1). Ontario's deficit of 4.3 percent of

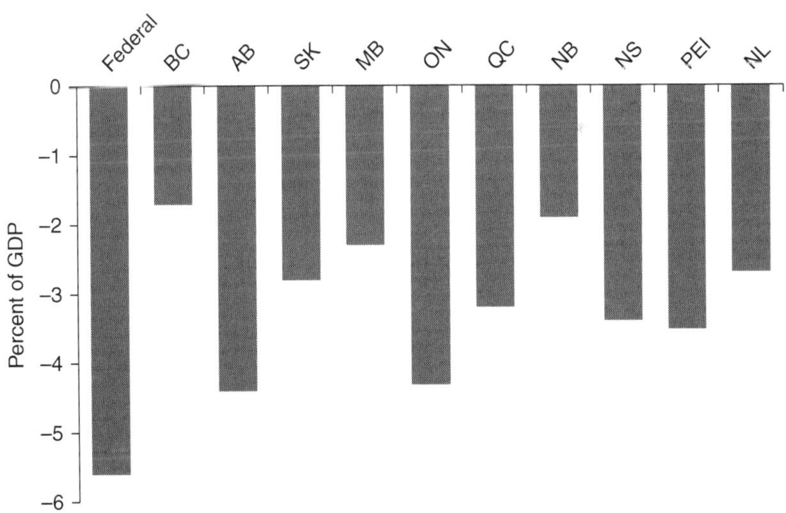

Figure 8.1 Federal and provincial deficits as a share of gross domestic product (GDP) (1992–93).

Source: TD Economics (2012). *Government Budget Balances and Net Debt* (as of November 12, 2012). Toronto, ON: TD Bank Financial Group. Accessed on January 15, 2013.

GDP and Alberta's deficit of 4.4 percent of GDP were of particular concern given those provinces' prominence in the Canadian economy.

As a result of well over a decade of consistent deficits, government debt in Canada was growing to worrying levels. Federal net debt reached almost 70 percent in 1992–93, with provincial net debt ranging from a low of 12.1 percent in British Columbia to 44.7 percent in Newfoundland and Labrador (Figure 8.2).[8]

In 1993, Canada maintained the second highest level of net liabilities (debt) among the G-7 countries, with only Italy having a higher level of debt.[9] International financial markets, commentators, and many domestic politicians were increasingly worried about the country's finances.[10] A prominent piece in the *Wall Street Journal* (WSJ) in 1995 characterized Canada as having "become an honorary member of the Third World in the unmanageability of its debt problem."[11]

While the WSJ editorial focused on the federal government, there was already movement to fundamentally deal with deficits and debt at the provincial level. Political leadership first emerged in the Prairie province of Saskatchewan under a left-leaning, union-dominated New Democratic Party (NDP). The Saskatchewan NDP began cutting spending and raising taxes in 1991 to deal honestly with their

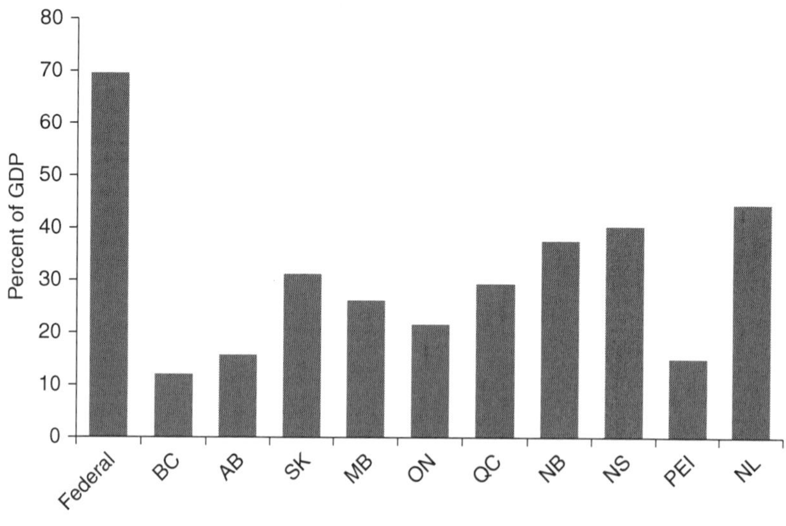

Figure 8.2 Federal and provincial net debt as a share of GDP (1992–93).

Source: TD Economics (2012). *Government Budget Balances and Net Debt* (as of November 12, 2012). Toronto, ON: TD Bank Financial Group. Accessed on January 15, 2013.

budget deficit. By 1994–95, the province had balanced its budget and was beginning to pay down its accumulated debt. The actions by the NDP in Saskatchewan, particularly given their political and ideological predispositions, set the stage for action by other provinces and the federal government.

Federal Reforms

Table 8.1 summarizes some of the dramatic reductions in nominal program spending by Canadian governments during this period of reform. The federal government, for instance, reduced program spending from C$123.2 billion in 1994–95 to C$111.3 billion in 1996–97, a reduction of 9.7 percent in nominal terms. The spending cuts required real reductions in departmental budgets across the entire government, with many departments experiencing reductions in spending of well over one-third over a three-year period: regional agencies (subsidies) were cut by 49 percent, transportation was reduced by 51 percent, agriculture was reduced by 40 percent, and spending on human resource development was cut by 35 percent.[12]

The reduction in federal program spending is illustrated in Figure 8.3 to highlight the fact that actual program spending by the federal government was cut as opposed to the often-discussed reduction in the

Table 8.1 Summary of Canadian government program spending changes (in Canadian dollars)

	Peak Program Spending ($)	*Trough Program Spending ($)*	*Percentage Change*	*Start Year–End Year*
Federal Government	123.2	111.3	9.7%	1994–95 to 1996–97
Newfoundland and Labrador	3.0	2.9	3.5%	1992–93 to 1993–34
Prince Edward Island	0.7	0.7	5.0%	1994–95 to 1995–96
Nova Scotia	3.9	3.8	3.0%	1992–93 to 1994–95
New Brunswick	3.7	3.7	0.9%	1992–93 to 1993–94
Quebec	36.2	33.0	8.8%	1994–95 to 1997–98
Ontario	58.2	56.0	3.8%	1995–96 to 1998–99
Manitoba	4.9	4.8	3.1%	1992–93 to 1993–94
Saskatchewan	4.5	4.1	8.9%	1990–91 to 1993–94
Alberta	16.2	12.7	21.6%	1992–93 to 1995–96
British Columbia	19.6	19.3	1.5%	1996–97 to 1997–98

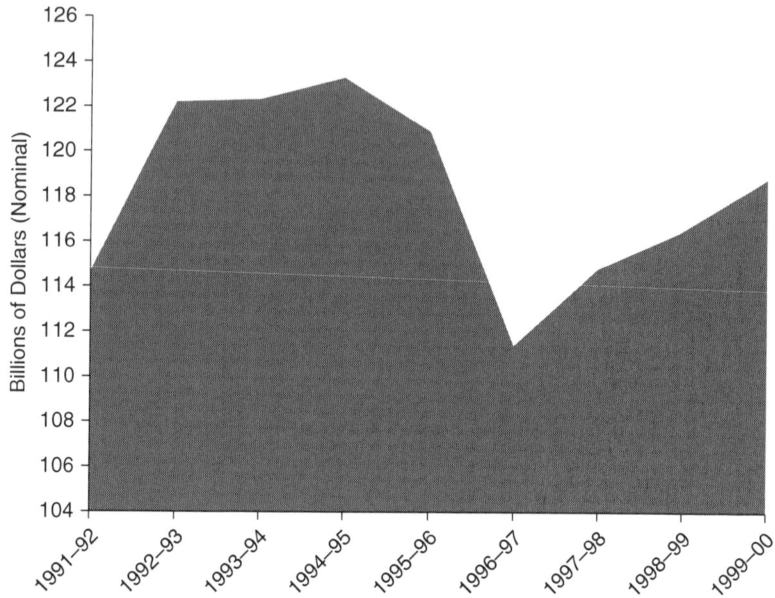

Figure 8.3 Canadian federal program spending (nominal dollars).

Source: Department of Finance, Canada (2012). Fiscal Reference Tables, Public Accounts. Ottawa: ON. Available at http://www.fn.gc.ca/frt-trf/2012/frt-trf-1201-eng.asp#tbl1.

expected rate of growth of spending. In other words, the amount of money spent in 1995–96, one year after the reductions began, was actually less than the amount spent in the previous year.

Another indicator of the genuine retrenchment of government during this period is that federal public sector employment declined by 14 percent in full-time equivalents during the period of reform.

One aspect of the federal reforms worth noting is the framework for program expenditure review introduced in 1994 and implemented in the 1995 budget. Every ministry and department was required to assess current spending and propose reductions based on a set of criteria provided by the Cabinet. Those criteria included: serving the public interest; necessity of government involvement; appropriate federal role; scope for public sector–private sector partnerships; scope for increased efficiency; and affordability.

The framework for reviewing federal spending had a number of distinctly Hayekian tones imbedded in the process. The framework required ministries to justify that current spending programs were priorities, in the public interest, and that they required government involvement. Implicit in these initial criteria was the acknowledgment that simply because a program was deemed to provide for a public good, or that it was an agreed-upon priority, did not necessarily mean that government had to be involved.

The framework reestablished a clear process by which to determine whether a program was best delivered by, or should even involve, the federal government. This criterion facilitated a number of decentralization initiatives.

The spending review framework also stressed the need to look for innovative solutions to problems and improvements in programs after they met the first three criteria. A number of federal programs began incorporating public-private partnerships as well as introducing efficiency-enhancing measures.

The combination of these various criteria was a key aspect of the success of the federal government in not only reducing spending but improving the spending that survived. From a Hayekian perspective, the delineation of separate spheres between the federal, provincial, and individual was critical. It meant a number of programs were decentralized to the provinces and in some cases the federal government simply ceased to provide or undertake certain activities and left them to the individual.

Provincial Reforms

In aggregate, the provinces[13] reduced their spending less than did the federal government. Specifically, all-provincial government program spending fell from C$148.5 billion in 1995–96 to C$145.6 billion in 1996–97, a decrease of 2.0 percent.[14]

Several provinces, however, enacted much deeper spending cuts. For example, between 1992–93 and 1995–96, the Alberta government reduced program spending by 21.6 percent (Tables 8.1 and 8.2). Quebec and Saskatchewan also implemented marked reductions in program spending of nearly 9 percent during the early 1990s. Interestingly, while the reforms enacted in Ontario were considered among the most radical, the actual size of the reduction (3.8%) was comparatively small.

Government Becomes a Smaller Player in the Economy

A different way by which to gauge the importance of these changes is how they affected government spending as a share of the economy. Put simply, over a short period of time, Canadian governments

Table 8.2 Summary of Canadian government program spending changes (as a share of GDP)

	Peak Program Spending (%)	*Trough Program Spending (%)*	*Percentage Point Change*	*Start Year–End Year*
Federal Government	17.4	12.1	−5.3	1992–93 to 1999–00
Newfoundland and Labrador	31.1	29.2	−1.9	1992–93 to 1995–96
Prince Edward Island	29.5	24.5	−5	1992–93 to 1996–97
Nova Scotia	21.6	19.5	−2.1	1992–93 to 1996–97
New Brunswick	27.0	20.3	−6.7	1991–92 to 2000–01
Quebec	22.5	17.1	−5.4	1992–93 to 2000–01
Ontario	18.9	13.5	−5.4	1993–94 to 2000–01
Manitoba	20.1	17.3	−2.8	1992–93 to 1996–97
Saskatchewan	21.4	14.9	−6.5	1990–91 to 1996–97
Alberta	21.6	12.9	−8.7	1992–93 to 1997–98
British Columbia	20.2	16.9	−3.3	1991–92 to 1997–98

retrenched their spending within the broader economy. As summarized in Table 8.2, federal program spending fell from 17.4 percent of GDP in the years 1992–93 to 12.1 percent in 1999–2000, representing a 30.5 percent reduction in the size of government as a share of the economy.

With Alberta leading the way, the provinces also enacted reductions in program spending: from 21.6 percent of the economy in 1992–93 to 12.9 percent by 1999–2000 (table 8.2). This represented a 40.3 percent reduction in the size of the government as a share of GDP in Alberta.

Saskatchewan (−30.4%), Ontario (−28.6%), Quebec (−24.0%), New Brunswick (−24.8%), and several of the smaller provinces similarly enacted reductions that led to a meaningful decline in the share of the provincial economies consumed by government spending (Table 8.2).

Canada–United States Comparison

Perhaps the most telling metric of the changes in Canada is seen in Figure 8.4, which depicts total government spending as a share of the economy for both Canada and the United States. Two things clearly emerge from Figure 8.4. First, beginning in 1993, there was a marked decline in the share of the economy consumed by government spending in

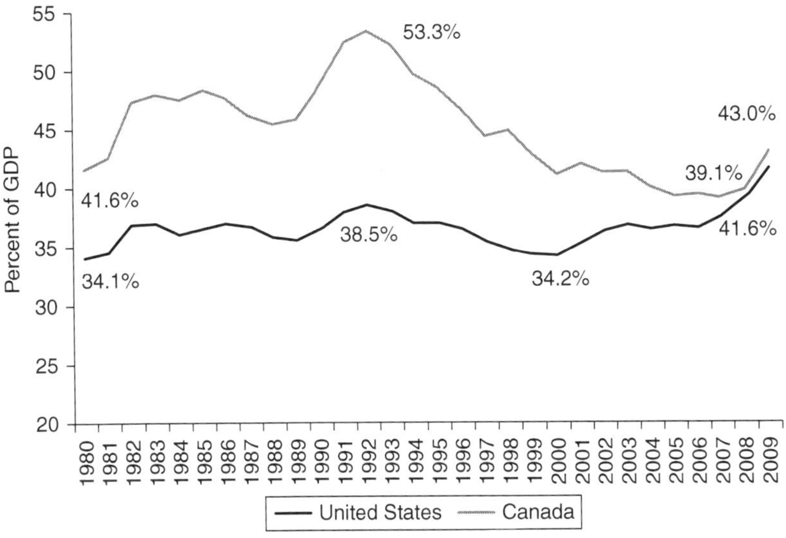

Figure 8.4 Canada–US all government spending as a share of GDP.
Source: OECD Economic Outlook, No. 86, November 2009 and No. 83, June 2008.

Canada. Specifically, all government spending as a share of the economy fell from its peak of 53.3 percent of GDP in 1992 to 39.1 percent in 2007. (It subsequently started to increase in 2008 as a result of the recession.)

Second, the gap between Canada and the United States with respect to spending was essentially eliminated over a 14-year period. At its peak, the gap between the two countries reached 14.8 percentage points. This translated into a government sector (as a share of the economy) in Canada that was 38.4 percent larger than the respective sector in the United States. By 2008, the gap in total government spending between the two countries as a share of the economy had declined to 0.7 percentage points.

The results of the retrenchment in government spending in Canada at both the federal and provincial levels were nothing short of stunning. Budgets were quickly balanced and debt began to decline as most governments in Canada operated in a structural surplus. This created a virtuous cycle wherein surpluses reduced debt, which reduced interest costs, freeing up yet more resources, resulting in surpluses.

Although not the aim of this chapter, it is useful to recognize the importance of the tax relief that was enabled by the balancing of budgets across the country. Sizeable reductions in many supply-side oriented taxes were introduced by the federal and provincial governments, starting in the late 1990s. These tax reductions included large-scale cuts in corporate income tax rates, the elimination of the corporate capital tax, sizeable reductions in capital gains taxes, and personal income tax relief, albeit limited.

The benefits of the fiscal retrenchment coupled with tax relief, particularly those cuts aimed at improving economic incentives, were not just limited to the balance and income statements of the governments. Canada entered a pronounced period of economic prosperity characterized by strong GDP growth, gains in individual income, strong employment growth, and low unemployment. Simply put, the short-term costs of fiscal retrenchment led to both short- and long-term gains for the Canadian economy and individual Canadians.[15]

This period of retrenchment, however, was not simply about smaller government. Indeed, one of the chief architects of the federal changes, former Finance Minister and later Prime Minister Paul Martin expressed it succinctly: "We are acting on a new vision of the role of government...smaller government...smarter government."[16] Governments not only enacted cuts in spending but, perhaps more importantly, changed and reformed the way in which they were spending.

Hayek and Welfare Reform in Canada

Prior to delving into the specifics of welfare reform, it is helpful to reexamine Hayek's acceptance of the idea that social welfare programs could be provided without necessarily jeopardizing individual liberty. Admittedly, Hayek was much more concerned with the traditional concept of socialism, which is the ownership of the means of production, rather than the advance of the welfare state that many former proponents of socialism had gravitated toward. Hayek himself states as much in *The Constitution of Liberty*:

> many of the old socialists have discovered that we have already drifted so far in the direction of a redistributive state that it now appears much easier to push further in that direction than to press for the somewhat discredited socialization of the means of production.[17]

Prior to the beginning of a marked expansion of the welfare state in the mid-1960s, Hayek repeatedly indicated his willing acceptance of a role for the state in social service provision.[18] One of the first statements along these lines appears in Hayek's *The Road to Serfdom*.

> There is no reason why in a society which has reached the general level of wealth which ours has attained the first kind of security should not be guaranteed to all without endangering general freedom... [T]here can be no doubt that some minimum of food, shelter, and clothing, sufficient to preserve health and the capacity to work, can be assured to everybody.[19]

Hayek further explicitly indicates a role for the state in such provision:

> Nor is there any reason why the state should not assist the individual in providing for those common hazards of life against which, because of their uncertainty, few individuals can make adequate provision.[20]

These passages from *The Road to Serfdom* are important for understanding Hayek's view that the state could provide for some minimum level of sustenance without jeopardizing individual liberty.[21] It is also worth noting that as the welfare state advanced markedly, starting in the 1960s through to the end of Hayek's life in the early 1990s—and continues to today—Hayek became more skeptical of the role of the state and welfare. This is particularly true with respect to the social justice aspect of the welfare state.[22]

Hayek's *The Constitution of Liberty*, published 16 years after *The Road to Serfdom*, expanded his discussion of the role of the state in providing for basic necessities. Several passages from Chapter 17: The Decline of Socialism and the Rise of the Welfare State are worth noting.[23]

> All modern governments have made provision for the indigent, unfortunate, and disabled and have concerned themselves with questions of health and the dissemination of knowledge. There is no reason why the volume of these pure service activities should not increase with the general growth of wealth. There are common needs that can be satisfied only by collective action and which can be thus provided for without restricting individual liberty.[24]
>
> It can hardly be denied that, as we grow richer, that minimum of sustenance which the community has always provided for those not able to look after themselves, and which can be provided outside the market, will gradually rise or that government

> may, usefully and without doing harm, assist or even lead in such endeavors. There is little reason why the government should not also play some role, or even take the initiative, in such areas as social insurance and education.[25]

Again, however, Hayek reiterates the efficacy of having such programs delivered by subnational levels of government.

> There are all kinds of public amenities which it may be in the interest of all members of the community to provide by common effort, such as parks and museums, theaters and facilities for sports—though there are strong reasons why they should be provided by local rather than national authorities.[26]

It seems fairly clear that prior to the massive expansion of the welfare state in the mid-to-late 1960s, Hayek was both consistent and clear that welfare-like programs could be delivered by the state without necessarily encumbering individual liberty.

Canadian Welfare Reform: Triumphs of Decentralized Experimentation and Innovation

As explained previously, the federal and provincial governments in Canada in the late 1980s and early 1990s were increasingly struggling with budget deficits and the question of how to constrain spending. [27] The combination of needing to restrain and reform spending coupled with the worrying rise in the number (and percentage) of Canadians receiving welfare (see Figure 8.5) set the stage for fairly dramatic reforms in the mid-1990s.

As illustrated in Figure 8.5, in 1990, some 1.9 million Canadians (including dependents) or 7.0 percent of the population[28] were receiving welfare benefits from the government.[29] Provincial and local spending on welfare reached C$8.6 billion in 1990–91 (inflation-adjusted 1996 dollars).[30] The combination of the 1991 recession and a general trend toward greater dependency resulted in the number of Canadians receiving welfare benefits reaching 3.1 million in 1994, an astonishing 10.7 percent of the population (see Figure 8.5).[31] Real spending on welfare by local and provincial governments hit C$14.3 billion in 1993–94.[32] The growth in dependency by the Canadian population,

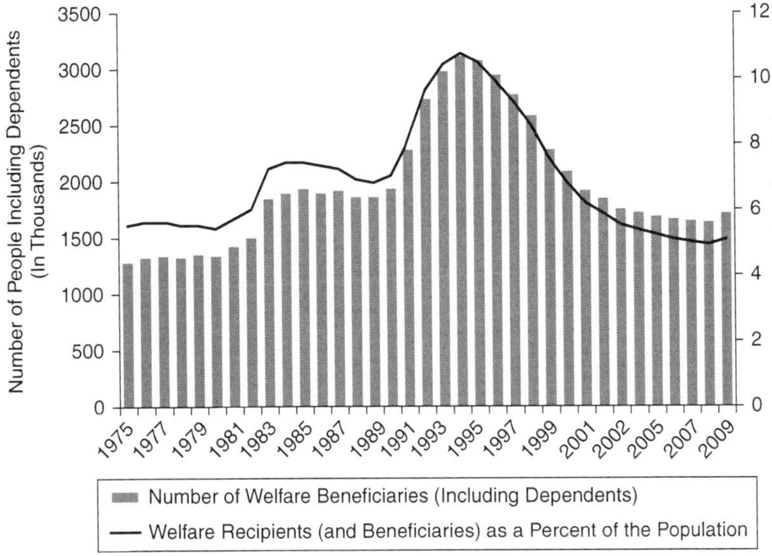

Figure 8.5 Number of welfare beneficiaries, including dependents (1979–2009).

Source: National Council of Welfare, 2006, Welfare Incomes 2005: Number of People on Welfare, 1995–2005, available at http://www.cnb-ncw.gc.ca/l.3bd.2t.1ils@-eng.jsp?lid=160; Institut de la Statistique Quebec, Interprovincial Comparisons, Table 5.7: Customer welfare, 2005–2009, available at http://www.stat.gouv.qc.ca/donstat/econm_finnc/conjn_econm/TSC/index_an.htm (updated on June 10,2011); Human Resources and Skills Development Canada, 2010, Social Assistance Statistical Report 2008, available at http://www.hrsdc.gc.ca/eng/publications_resources/social_policy/sasr_2008/sasr2008_eng.pdf; Statistics Canada, Estimates of Population, Canada, provinces and territories, CANSIM Table 051–0005.

coupled with the increasing pressure on governments to balance their fiscal affairs, set the stage for reform.

Federal Reforms: Changing the Incentives

A number of smaller reforms[33] had been implemented beginning in the late 1980s, but the real, fundamental reform of welfare began in 1995. In that year, the federal government implemented dramatic changes in the financing of social programs. The 1995 federal budget[34] replaced the Canada Assistance Plan (CAP)[35] and the Established Program Finance (EPF)[36] programs with the Canada Social Transfer (CST). The CST was renamed the Canada Health and Social Transfer (CHST) in 1996.[37]

The CHST is a single-block grant to the provinces that includes both cash payments and tax transfers to support provincial spending in post-secondary education, health care, and social assistance. The block transfer to the provinces reduced the amount of money transferred to the provinces by the federal government while providing more flexibility and autonomy to the provinces with respect to the delivery and design of these programs (excluding health care) by removing most federal restrictions and standards. The only condition attached to the funding for social assistance by the federal government was a prohibition against residency requirements for benefit eligibility. Critically, national standards prohibiting work requirements in exchange for welfare benefits were removed. Put differently, the federal government imposed greater financial responsibility on the provinces for the social assistance programs they delivered while also reducing the regulations and requirements imposed on the provinces. The result of the federal government's fiscally-driven reforms was an enormous incentive for the provincial governments to reform their social assistance programs to deal effectively with both increasing dependency and its underlying causes.

Contrast with the United States

Canada's approach to welfare reform was materially different from that of the United States. Unlike Canada, the United States chose to impose significant requirements on the states in their version of welfare reform.[38] For example, the federal government introduced a Maintenance of Effort (MOE) clause in their reforms, which required that states spend roughly the same amount of money on welfare and related programs post-reform as they did before.[39]

The Canadian approach was the opposite. The federal government provided a block grant with explicit terms that if provinces spent less they could reallocate the resources, but that any amount over the block grant would be financed entirely by the province.

Another example of a centrally-mandated provision in the US approach is the requirement for time limits for receipt of welfare benefits. The Canadian federal reforms imposed no such standardized provision requirement, although, interestingly, British Columbia introduced a time limit similar to that introduced in the United States.

The key difference to acknowledge from a Hayekian perspective was that Canada basically devolved all responsibility for the design, regulation, and provision of welfare to the provinces, coupled with a block grant. This contrasts with the US approach in which the federal government provided block grants to the States, similar to Canada, but retained partial control for both design and regulatory aspects of welfare. While both countries devolved responsibilities for welfare to the provinces and states, Canada did so to a much greater degree.

Provinces Reform Welfare

A number of common reforms were implemented by most, if not all of the provinces. One common feature of reform was a reduction in benefit levels, particularly for single employable people. While the narrative regarding the benefits was often about balancing the books on the backs of the poor, the changes were actually rooted in an increasing acknowledgment that incentives mattered for low-income work decisions.[40] Specifically, there was an increasing understanding that when welfare benefits surpass comparable income available from low-paid work, strong incentives are created to enter or remain on welfare.[41] Many of the reductions in benefit levels, particularly those for single employable people, were aimed at reestablishing a balance between welfare benefits and the income available to workers from low-paid employment.

Another fairly common reform was to integrate welfare and related services with employment programs provided by the provinces. For example, Saskatchewan,[42] Newfoundland, and the Northwest Territories all moved fairly quickly to integrate welfare delivery and government-provided employment services. In addition, a number of provinces including Alberta, Ontario, British Columbia, and Quebec undertook initiatives to improve the administration of welfare and related programs, including reducing fraudulent claims.

Not surprisingly given the altered incentives, many provinces also reformed their welfare systems to focus on better results, improved value-for-money in the services and support they offered people, and controlling expenditures. A brief overview of the reforms enacted is offered for some of the more reform-minded provinces. In particular, areas of reform that are somewhat unique to each of the provinces were highlighted in order to illustrate the plethora of approaches, experimentation, and innovations that were pursued by different provincial governments.

Alberta

Alberta was the first province to pursue genuine and broad welfare reform in Canada. In 1993, even before the federal transfer reforms, Alberta implemented an overhaul in the administration and ethos of the Alberta Family and Social Services Ministry. The cultural and administrative changes were focused on shifting from an emphasis on determining eligibility and mailing checks to preventing people from entering welfare before other possible avenues of support, including employment, were exhausted. The underlying premise of the change was the understanding that once people entered the welfare system, they had a much higher probability of using it again in the future. Thus, there were longer-term benefits to people in need if they could exhaust other avenues of support before entering the welfare bureaucracy. Additional administrative initiatives were also implemented to reduce fraud, such as adding investigators and review officers.

The combination of focusing on alternatives to welfare, and bringing benefit levels in line with low-paid employment opportunities, resulted in marked improvement. One study concluded that almost half of the 172,000 people who left the province's welfare rolls between 1993 and 1996 found full-time employment.[43] In other words, Alberta was able to reduce its welfare dependency in a way that promoted work and employment, which led to better results for its citizens, while reducing provincial spending.

British Columbia

British Columbia was one of the last provinces to enact reforms. The newly elected Liberal government moved quickly in 2001 to implement wholesale changes to the province's welfare system.[44] Most noticeable in its reform package was a rolling benefit time limit, which echoed one of the core US reforms. Specifically, each month a recipient received welfare benefits counted toward a 24-month limit within any five-year period. The program was announced in 2001 and became effective on April 1, 2002.[45] Reaching the limit for employable individuals would result in fairly stiff reductions in benefits, to zero in some cases, while more difficult cases like families with children would suffer much smaller reductions in their benefits. Put differently, the program was aimed at forcing employable individuals and couples with no children to think about welfare as an insurance program rather than simply as a potential source of income. The results were fairly dramatic. To a much greater extent than expected, single employable individuals basically stopped using welfare as a source of income and transitioned much more quickly back into the labor force. The result was a plunge in welfare dependency rates as well as a reduction in welfare-related spending.

Ontario

Ontario's welfare system had more than its share of problems.[46] Though it was the richest and most populous province, by 1994 it had the second highest rate of beneficiaries-to-population (12.3%) in the country, its spending was increasing at an unsustainable rate, and its benefit levels were encouraging ever higher rates of welfare use.[47] Ontario elected a new government in 1995 that immediately implemented a number of changes including reduced benefit rates, an increased focus on diversion to other nonwelfare alternatives, greater focus on employment, and administrative improvements such as reducing fraud and ensuring accuracy in determining eligibility.

The unique reform implemented by Ontario, though, did not arrive until 1998.[48] *Ontario Works* was introduced in 1998, making Ontario the only province with a formal and fairly broad "workfare" program. The goal of the program was to determine and secure the shortest route to paid employment for welfare recipients. Three options were available to recipients: employment support such as job-search assistance, community work through mandatory public-sector placements, and employment placement that relied at least partially on wage-subsidy programs.[49] The focus on employment was mandatory for all employable adults collecting welfare benefits. The result of the reforms, together with a much stronger economy, meant that Ontario's welfare rolls were reduced to a greater extent than observed nationally.[50]

Results of Welfare Reform

The introduction of the Canada Health and Social Transfer (CHST), which provided block grants to the provinces, also afforded them more flexibility and autonomy. This newfound responsibility and authority ushered in a period of innovation and experimentation across the provinces. There were a number of common welfare reform features, like bringing benefit levels back into line with comparable low-paid work opportunities and improved administration.

These reform features aside, the power of the decentralized delivery of government services is seen most tellingly in the varied and innovative approaches different provinces took to improve their welfare and related programs. Alberta, for example, introduced diversion programs to increase the likelihood that people would not enter the welfare system, Ontario focused on workfare programs, and British Columbia introduced a time limit for employable individuals that returned welfare to an insurance-based system of income support.

The results of these reforms were stark. By 2000, the number of welfare beneficiaries in Canada had declined to a little over two million (6.8% of the population) from a peak of 3.1 million (10.7% of the population) (Figure 8.5).[51] In addition, welfare-related spending had been curtailed, helping governments to move to a balanced budget position. Most importantly, however, the welfare programs that were being delivered seemed to be achieving better results by getting more employable individuals into the job market and dealing with some of the more pressing underlying problems that caused people to consider welfare.

K–12 Education: Two Markedly Different Approaches to Educating Our Children

Another difference between Canada and the United States that illustrates the Hayekian principles of decentralization, experimentation, and competition is the delivery of K–12 education.[52] An enduring difference between Canada and the United States is the relative balance between the federal government and respective subnational governments. A clear reading of the Constitutions of the two countries would lead one to believe the United States should have a smaller federal government, although it is worth noting that both countries were established with a view toward a limited central government.

There is perhaps no better illustration of the greater tendency toward centralization in the United States versus Canada than the two countries' approaches to K–12 education. Canada has no federal role, no federal ministry or department, and no federal cabinet position for K–12 education. It is under the exclusive control and authority of the provinces, and in many provinces the delivery responsibilities are further decentralized to local and regional boards of education.

Unlike Canada, the federal government in the United States is directly involved in K–12 education through both regulatory measures and direct spending. The United States has an entire federal department with over 4,200 employees and a cabinet-level secretary devoted to education.[53]

Given the premises of the Hayekian argument regarding decentralization, experimentation, and competition, it is important to explore the results (outcomes) and amount spent by both countries on K–12 education. According to the Organization for Economic Cooperation and Development (OECD), in 2008, the most recent year for which comparable information was available at the time of writing, the United States spent 4.1 percent of its economy (GDP) on K–12 education while Canada spent 3.5 percent of GDP.[54] Put differently, the United States spent a much larger share of its economy on K–12 education than did Canada.

A different way of looking at this data is to examine per student spending, adjusted for differences in national currencies. In 2008, the United States spent US$10,995 per student on K–12 education, including both public and private expenditures. Canada, on the other hand, spent C$8,388 on K–12 education.[55] The United States spent almost one-third (31%) more per student in 2008 for primary and secondary education. But while the United States spends more on K–12 education than Canada, on most international tests, Canada performs markedly better (or, in some isolated instances, the same) as the United States.[56]

The composition of educational spending is quite different in the two countries. Canada's federal government spends virtually nothing on K–12 education—the exception is Aboriginal education and some spending on the military—while the portion of revenues provided by the federal government for K–12 public education in the United States reached 9.6 percent in 2008–09.[57] This only includes direct spending by the federal government and therefore excludes the enormous regulatory impositions placed on state and local governments by the federal government.

The share of public education revenues provided by the US federal government has risen steadily since 1995–96, when it stood at 6.6 percent.[58] In fact, the proportion of public education resources provided by the federal government compared to what the states and localities contribute is approaching levels not seen since the Carter administration. And yet Americans continue to express their dissatisfaction with the K–12 education system and the more than US$593 billion spent annually among all levels of government.

There is widespread acknowledgment of the critically important role education, and in particular primary and secondary education, plays in economic development and prosperity. And yet, despite this acknowledgment and the enormous sums of money spent in the United States on education, the country's education system continues to struggle with an almost absolute view that more, rather than less, centralization is needed to solve the observed problems.[59]

The combination of large amounts of money spent on K–12 education and general parental concern with education has resulted in support for and interest in education reform in the United States across the political divide.[60] Illustrative of the tendency toward centralized solutions, President George W. Bush, a Republican from Texas, opted for an expanded role for the federal government in his 2001 education reform initiative dubbed *No Child Left Behind* (NCLB) rather than decentralizing and freeing up the states to innovate and compete.

The aim of the initiative was to have the federal government incentivize the states to improve their education performance. NCLB focused on testing and results, with stipulations that rewarded success and afforded choice to parents if schools continued to underperform. The reality of the program, quite unintended, has been an incentive for states to gerrymander and lower their standards in order to artificially achieve proficiency standards.[61] Put differently, states have naturally responded to the centralized incentives established under NCLB.

NCLB was meant to improve core education proficiency. At best, the domestic and international comparative results have been modest. At the same time, the United States has experienced tremendous growth in K–12 education spending. In nominal terms, President Bush's NCLB program has seen the federal government spending more than double on K–12 education, from US$22.6 billion in 2000 (the year before Bush took office) to an estimated US$68.1 billion in 2012.[62] The increased resources and direction from Washington, DC have generally not translated into improved scholastic performance but have furthered the involvement and power of the central government at the expense of state and local governments.

One-size-fits-all national approaches to policy are rarely as successful as more localized, decentralized approaches because different regions, states, counties, and even districts have different needs based on differing student populations.[63] The continued centralized approach to education, and indeed other policy areas, will continue to hinder real, meaningful, and effective reform of these programs for the foreseeable future. Indeed, current discussions in Washington, DC are focused on increasing the federal government's role in education.

Conclusion and Comments

The late 1980s and the entirety of the 1990s were a profound period of change and reform in Canada. Generally the reforms were toward smaller, smarter government with a focus on doing less but doing it better. This period of retrenchment coincided with an extraordinarily prosperous time in Canada with balanced budgets, declining debt, and tax relief coupled with a robust economy, strong job creation, and plentiful opportunities.

Many of the reforms enacted during this period contained a strong Hayekian character in terms of decentralizing authority and responsibility for service provision and not only allowing but facilitating experimentation at the subnational level. The results of these reforms, particularly when compared with changes in the United States, support the efficacy of Hayek's view of decentralization.

Notes

1. For an excellent summary of the reforms in Canada not written by the authors of this paper (three citations that include summaries of the reforms are listed in note 2), please see David R. Henderson, *Canada's Budget Triumph* (Arlington, VA: Mercatus Center at George Mason University, 2010). Available at http://mercatus.org/publication/canada-s-budget-triumph.
2. Much of the materials and discussion in this chapter rely on a combination of work contained in three publications that the authors have all, to varying degrees, been involved with: Brian Lee Crowley, Jason Clemens, and Niels Veldhuis, *The Canadian Century: Moving Out of America's Shadow* (Toronto: Key Porter Publishing, 2010), http://www.macdonaldlaurier.ca/mli-library/books/canadian-century/ (accessed May 2, 2013); Brian Lee Crowley, Robert P. Murphy, and Niels Veldhuis, *Northern Light: Lessons for America from Canada's Fiscal Fix* (Ottawa: Macdonald-Laurier Institute, 2012), http://www.macdonaldlaurier.ca/mli-library/books/northern-light-lessons-for-america-from-canadas-fiscal-fix/ (accessed May 2, 2013); and Niels Veldhuis, Jason Clemens, and Milagros Palacios, *Learning from the Past: How Canadian Fiscal Policies of the 1990s Can be Applied Today* (Vancouver, BC: The Fraser Institute, 2010). Available at http://www.fraserinstitute.org/uploadedFiles/fraser-ca/Content/research-news/research/publications/learning-from-the-past.pdf (accessed May 2, 2013). The authors would like to acknowledge the enormous contributions of Brian Lee Crowley to the *Canadian Century* and the *Northern Light* projects, which formed the foundation for this essay. We would also like to express our thanks to Milagros Palacios who provided invaluable assistance throughout the writing of not only this essay but also the three underlying books upon which it is based. Without her assistance and dedication it is unlikely any of these four papers could have been completed
3. Friedrich A. Hayek, *Law, Legislation and Liberty,* vol. 3, *The Political Order of a Free People* (London: Routledge, 1979), 146.
4. Hayek, *Political Order,* 146.
5. Friedrich A. Hayek, *The Constitution of Liberty* (Chicago, IL: University of Chicago Press, 1960), 263.
6. Friedrich A. Hayek, "The Use of Knowledge in Society," in *Individualism and Economic Order* (Chicago, IL: University of Chicago Press, 1948), 82.
7. Hayek, "The Use of Knowledge," 84.
8. For an accessible discussion of the risks of public debt, please see Carmen M. Reinhart and Kenneth S. Rogoff, *This Time is Different: Eight Centuries of Financial Folly* (Princeton, NJ: Princeton University Press, 2009). The controversy following the discovery of a spreadsheet computational error has challenged their core

statistical argument. Their general discussion of the risk of accumulating public debt is excellent and unaffected by the coding error. It is this general discussion to which we are referring.

9. Government of Canada, Department of Finance, "Table 54: G-7 General Government Net Financial Liabilities," *Fiscal Reference Tables* (Ottawa: Dept. of Finance, 2012). Available at http://www.fin.gc.ca/frt-trf/2012/frt-trf-1209-eng.asp#tbl54 (accessed on March 6, 2013).
10. For example, short-term interest rates—specifically the three-month treasury bill rate—started to increase markedly in February of 1994, rising from 3.85 percent in February 1994 to 5.4 percent in March 1994, and all the way to 8.2 percent in March 1995. Source: Bank of Canada, Selected historical interest rates, available at http://www.bankofcanada.ca/rates/interest-rates/selected-historical-interest-rates/; Scotia Capital Inc.
11. "Canada Bankrupt?" *Wall Street Journal* editorial, January 12, 1995. The editorial was attributed to John Fund. See Michael Walker, "Wall Street Journal Sounds Warning," *Fraser Forum*, February 1995, http://oldfraser.lexi.net/publications/forum/1995/december/FF-12–95.html (accessed May 2, 2013).
12. For a detailed summary of the departmental reductions in spending, see Veldhuis, Clemens, and Palacios, "Table 2," *Learning from the Past*, 32.
13. Aggregated provincial data also include the three territories in Canada.
14. Government of Canada, Department of Finance, "Table 31: All provinces and territories," *Fiscal Reference Tables*, http://www.fin.gc.ca/frt-trf/2012/frt-trf-12-eng.asp (accessed May 2, 2013).
15. For a discussion of the relationship between government spending and economic performance, please see Alberto Alesina, Silvia Ardagna, Roberto Perotti, and Fabio Schiantarelli,"Fiscal Policy, Profits, and Investment," *American Economic Review* 92, no. 3 (2002): 571–89; and Alberto Alesina and Roberto Perotti, "Fiscal Expansions and Fiscal Adjustment in OECD Countries," *Economic Policy* 10, no. 21 (October 1995): 207–48.
16. Paul Martin, *Budget Speech* (Ottawa: Government of Canada, Department of Finance, 1995), 6.
17. Hayek, *Constitution of Liberty*, 256–57.
18. For those sympathetic to Hayek's argument regarding state involvement in social services, we encourage a review of Professor David Beito's work on voluntary social service provision, and in particular David T. Beito, Peter Gordon, and Alexander Tabarrok, *The Voluntary City: Choice, Community, and Civil Society* (Oakland, CA: The Independent Institute, 2002); David T. Beito, *From Mutual Aid to the Welfare State: Fraternal Societies and Social Services, 1890–1967* (Chapel Hill: University of North Carolina Press, 2000); and Marvin Olasky, *The Tragedy of American Compassion* (Washington, DC: Regnery Publishing, 1992).
19. Friedrich A. Hayek, *The Road to Serfdom* (Chicago, IL: University of Chicago Press, 1944), 133.
20. Hayek, *Road to Serfdom*, 133.

21. For an interesting although admittedly debatable assessment of F. A. Hayek's views on collectively provided services by the state, please see Nicholas Wapshott, "Hayek on Health Care, Social Safety Nets and Public Housing," available on his website at https://sites.google.com/site/wapshottkeyneshayek/hayek-on-health-care-social-safety-nets-and-public-housing. Another interesting essay on this topic is Kevin Vallier, "Hayek on Serfdom and Welfare States," *Bleeding Heart Libertarians* (website) (2012), available at http://bleedingheartlibertarians.com/2012/05/hayek-on-serfdom-and-welfare-states/.
22. For example, the entire second volume of *Law, Legislation and Liberty* is devoted to the topic of social justice and its manifold problems.
23. Hayek, *Constitution of Liberty*, 263.
24. Ibid., 257.
25. Ibid., 257–58.
26. Ibid., 258.
27. This section relies heavily on materials and discussion from Crowley, Clemens, and Veldhuis, *The Canadian Century*; Crowley, Murphy, and Veldhuis, *Northern Light*; Veldhuis, Clemens, and Palacios, *Learning from the Past*; and Chris Schafer, Joel Emes, and Jason Clemens, *Surveying U.S. and Canadian Welfare Reform* (Vancouver: The Fraser Institute, 2001).
28. Please use caution when comparing Canadian welfare rates with the United States'. There are two groups of recipients included in Canadian welfare statistics that are not included in the United States': single employable individuals and individuals with disabilities. The US welfare system does not cover single employable individuals, and people with disabilities are covered under other programs.
29. Schafer, Emes, and Clemens, *Surveying U.S. and Canadian Welfare Reform*.
30. Ken Battle, *Transformation: Canadian Social Policy, 1985–2001* (Victoria, BC: The North American Institute, 1998).
31. Schafer, Emes, and Clemens, *Surveying U.S. and Canadian Welfare Reform*.
32. Battle, *Transformation*.
33. For example, the 1990 federal budget imposed a "cap on CAP." It limited the annual increase in federal cost-sharing under CAP to 5 percent for the three "have" provinces: Ontario, Alberta, and British Columbia for the years 1990 to 1991 through 1994 to 1995.
34. The details of the 1995 budget are available at http://www.fin.gc.ca/toc/1995/buddoclist95-eng.asp (accessed May 2, 2013).
35. The Canada Assistance Plan (CAP) was passed in 1966 and was designed to facilitate federal government cost-sharing with the provinces for social assistance programs. CAP basically consolidated four federal programs: Old Age Assistance, Blind Persons Allowance, Disabled Persons Allowance, and Unemployment Assistance. For more information on CAP, please see http://www.canadiansocialresearch.net/cap.htm (accessed May 2, 2013).
36. The Established Program Finance (EPF) consisted of transfers to the provinces for health care and post-secondary education.

37. It has since been split into two separate transfers: the Canada Social Transfer; and the Canada Health Transfer.
38. For an excellent overview of the US welfare both before and after the reforms see R. Kent Weaver, *Ending Welfare as We Know It* (Washington, DC: Brookings Institution, 2000).
39. One of the more prominent criticisms of US welfare reform from a market perspective was offered by Michael Tanner, *The End of Welfare* (Washington, DC: The Cato Institute, 1996).
40. An important experiment with respect to take-home income and employment incentives was completed in Canada. The Self-Sufficiency Project (SSP) was launched in 1992 by the Human Resources Development Canada (HRDC). The project encouraged single-parent welfare recipients who had been on welfare for at least one year to find full-time employment by offering them up to three years of additional (top-up) income. The supplemental income essentially doubled the average participant's earning compared to a minimum-wage job or welfare benefits. There have been disagreements about the longer-term implications of the study. For further information please see Reuben Ford, David Gyarmati, Kelly Foley, and Doug Tattrie, *Can Work Incentives Pay for Themselves? Final Report on the Self-Sufficiency Project for Welfare Applicants* (Ottawa: Social Research and Demonstration Corporation, 2003); Charles Michalopoulos, Philip Robins, and David Card, *When Financial Incentives Pay for Themselves: Early Findings from the Self-Sufficiency Project's Applicant Study* (Ottawa: Social Research Demonstration Corporation, 1999); and Todd Gabel and Sylvia LeRoy, "The Self-Sufficiency Project: No Solution for Welfare Dependency," *Fraser Forum* (September 2003): 31–33.
41. For an empirical examination of this issue during the 1990s, please see Joel Emes and Andrei Kreptul, *The Adequacy of Welfare Benefits in Canada* (Vancouver: The Fraser Institute, 1999), http://oldfraser.lexi.net/publications/critical_issues/1999/welfare_benefits/ (accessed May 2, 2013).
42. For a critical analysis of Saskatchewan welfare reform, see Jason Clemens and Chris Schafer, *Welfare in Saskatchewan: A Critical Evaluation* (Vancouver, BC: The Fraser Institute, 2002), http://www.fraserinstitute.org/WorkArea/DownloadAsset.aspx?id=4340.
43. David Elton, *Where Are They Now? Assessing the Impact of Welfare Reform on Former Recipients, 1993–1996* (Calgary: Canada West Foundation, 1997). Also, the claim that a large portion of Alberta's welfare recipients simply moved to British Columbia, which was often cited as an explanation, was found to be empirically unproven. For information, see Kenneth J. Boessenkool, *Back to Work: Learning from the Alberta Welfare Experiment* (Toronto: C. D. Howe Institute, 1997).
44. For a summary and analysis of the reforms enacted in 2001, please see Jason Clemens and Chris Schafer, *Welfare Reform in British Columbia: A Report Card* (Vancouver, BC: The Fraser Institute, 2002), http://www.fraserinstitute.org/WorkArea/DownloadAsset.aspx?id=4341.
45. Please note that as the deadline for the first two-year period in the five-year window of benefit eligibility approached, the regulations regarding the penalties

and deferrals were extended, which basically nullified the penalties and any sense of a real time limit on receipt of benefits. Please see Todd Gabel, Jason Clemens, Sylvia LeRoy, and Niels Veldhuis, "Staying the Course on Welfare Time Limits," *Fraser Forum* (December 2003): 22–24.

46. For a detailed examination of Ontario's welfare system, see E. (Rico) Sabatini, *Welfare—No Fair: A Critical Analysis of Ontario's Welfare System (1985–1994)* (Vancouver, BC: The Fraser Institute, 1996).
47. Schafer, Emes, and Clemens, *Surveying U.S. and Canadian Welfare Reform.*
48. Even before Ontario's focus on employment in 1998, Manitoba introduced work-focused programs for welfare recipients in 1996. *Making Welfare Work* was designed to assist employable recipients to transition from welfare to work. A number of targeted pilot programs were launched in the province, which made it a less ambitious and narrower program than pursued in Ontario.
49. See Organization for Economic Cooperation and Development (OECD), *The Battle against Exclusion: Social Assistance in Canada and Switzerland* (Paris: OECD, 1999); and Schafer, Emes, and Clemens, *Surveying U.S. and Canadian Welfare Reform.*
50. Schafer, Emes, and Clemens, *Surveying U.S. and Canadian Welfare Reform.* The execution of the work-focused program was not, however, flawless. A number of problems were identified, including less than adequate work availability in the community portion of the program, insufficient funding for certain aspects of the program, and a number of ongoing administrative problems. See OECD, *The Battle against Exclusion.*
51. Schafer, Emes, and Clemens, *Surveying U.S. and Canadian Welfare Reform.*
52. This section is based on work completed for Crowley, Murphy, and Veldhuis, *Northern Light.*
53. Information from the White House as of July 2012. Available at www.whitehouse.gov/our-government/executive-branch (accessed May 2, 2013).
54. Data from OECD, Statistic Extracts Database (2011), http://stats.oecd.org/index.aspx, accessed on July 24, 2012. The specific measure is "primary, secondary, and post-secondary non-tertiary" education spending. Canada actually had higher private spending in this category: 0.4 percent of GDP compared to 0.3 percent in the United States. In contrast, public spending (government) on K–12 education in Canada was 3.1 percent of GDP while the United States spent 3.8 percent of GDP.
55. All figures are quoted in equivalent 2008 US dollars converted using Purchasing Power Parity (PPP) for GDP based on full-time equivalents. The specific measure is "primary, secondary, and post-secondary non-tertiary" education spending per student, including private and public spending. Data from OECD, Statistic Extracts Database (2011).
56. An important source of international testing is the Lynch School of Education at Boston College. They undertake and publish both the Trends in International Mathematics and Science Study (TIMSS) and the Progress in International Reading Literacy Study (PIRLS) (http://timss.bc.edu/). The most recent results available from the TIMSS and PIRLS tests illustrate Canada's comparative strength

compared to the United States, particularly when the disparity in the amount of money spent on K–12 education is considered. For example, the eighth-grade mathematics test for 2007 shows the United States with a score of 508 compared to scores in Quebec of 528, Ontario 517, and British Columbia 509. The results for the fourth-grade testing are more mixed (see Ina V. S. Mullis, Michael O. Martin, and Pierre Foy, "Exhibit 1.2," *TIMSS 2007 International Mathematics Report: Findings from IEA's Trends in International Mathematics and Science Study at the Fourth and Eighth Grades* (Chesnut Hill, MA: TIMSS & PIRLS International Study Center, Lynch School of Education, Boston College, 2008), 39, http://timss.bc .edu/TIMSS2007/PDF/TIMSS2007_InternationalMathematicsReport.pdf (accessed May 2, 2013)).Similarly, the results from the science testing, also in 2007, show better Canadian performance, particularly at the higher grade level. The United States scored 520 on the eighth-grade science test compared to Ontario and British Columbia, who scored 526, and Quebec (507). Again, the fourth-grade testing had more mixed results (see Martin, Mullis, and Foy, "Exhibit 1.1," *TIMSS 2007 International Science Report*, 35, http://timss.bc .edu/TIMSS2007/PDF/TIMSS2007_InternationalScienceReport.pdf (accessed May 2, 2013)).The PIRLS tests are the final international comparative testing published by the Lynch School of Education. The 2006 results show the United States with a fourth-grade reading score of 540. The United States only outperforms the Canadian province of Quebec (533). All other Canadian provinces achieved higher scores: Alberta (560), British Columbia (558), Ontario (555), and Nova Scotia (542) (see Ina V. S. Mullis, Michael O. Martin, Ann M. Kennedy, and Pierre Foy, "Exhibit 1.1," *PIRLS 2006 International Report: IEA's Progress in International Reading Literacy Study in Primary Schools in 40 Countries* (Chesnut Hill: TIMSS & PIRLS International Study Center, Lynch School of Education, Boston College, 2007), 37, http://timss.bc.edu/PDF/PIRLS2006 _international_report.pdf [accessed May 2, 2013]). Another important source of international comparative testing is the OECD through their Programme for International Student Assessment (PISA), http://www.pisa.oecd.org/pages/0,2 987,en_32252351_32235731_1_1_1_1_1,00.html (accessed May 2, 2013). For example, the 2006 PISA test for science gives the United States a score of 489 compared to Canada's 534 and an OECD average of 500 (See "Table A5.1," available at http://www.oecd.org/document/9/0,3343,en_2649_39263238_41 266761_1_1_1_1,00.html (accessed May 2, 2013).

57. US Department of Education, Institute of Education Sciences, National Center for Education Statistics, "Table 171," in *Digest of Education Statistics 2008* (2008), http://nces.ed.gov/programs/digest/d08/tables/dt08_171.asp (accessed May 2, 2013).
58. Ibid.
59. Results from international tests are a key statistic illustrating some of the problems experienced in the US system of K–12 education. For example, the TIMSS is an international set of tests administered and analyzed by the Lynch School of Education at Boston College (http://timss.bc.edu/). Both the mathematics and science tests cover fourth- and eighth-grade students. The United States ranked

eleventh out of the jurisdictions included in the 2007 report for fourth-grade mathematics testing with a score of 529. The rankings for the United States are slightly better for the eighth-grade testing: the United States ranked ninth out of the 49 jurisdictions tested (see Mullis, Martin, and Foy, "Exhibit 1.1," *TIMSS 2007 International Mathematics Report*, 34–35, http://timss.bc.edu/TIMSS2007/PDF/TIMSS2007_InternationalMathematicsReport.pdf [accessed May 2, 2013]). However, the overall score for the United States for eighth-grade testing (508) indicates a near average performance (Mullis, Martin, and Foy, "Exhibit 1.3," *TIMSS 2007 International Mathematics Report*, 44–49). The other aspect of the TIMSS program tests for science knowledge and understanding. The 2007 report ranked the United States eighth out of 36 jurisdictions participating in the fourth-grade testing with a score of 539. The results for the United States for the eighth-grade testing are slightly lower: eleventh out of 49 jurisdictions participating with a score of 520 (Martin, Mullis, Foy, "Exhibit 1.1," *TIMSS 2007 International Science Report*, 35–36, http://timss.bc.edu/TIMSS2007/PDF/TIMSS2007_InternationalScienceReport.pdf (accessed May 2, 2013). More worrying, however, is that there has been a slight reduction in performance for the fourth-grade testing since 1995 (score of 542) and a marked reduction in the performance for eighth-grade testing since 2003 (527) (Martin, Mullis, Foy, "Exhibit 1.3," *TIMSS 2007 International Science Report*, 44–48).PIRLS is another international test administered by the IMSS and PIRLS Group at Boston College. This program tests reading and related skills at the fourth grade level only. The 2006 report ranked the United States 18th out of the 45 jurisdictions assessed with a score of 540 (Mullis, Martin, Kennedy, and Foy, "Exhibit 1.1," *PIRLS 2006 International Report*, 37. The results for 2006 indicated a decline in performance for the United States, although the official report deemed them statistically insignificant. Specifically, the United States went from scoring 542 in 2001 to 540 in 2006 (Mullis, Martin, Kennedy, and Foy, "Exhibit 1.3," *PIRLS 2006 International Report*, 44). Another important series of international studies on comparative education is published by the OECD through their Education at a Glance series. The 2011 publication is available at http://www.oecd.org/dataoecd/61/2/48631582.pdf. The private sector consulting company McKinsey and Company in 2009 examined the performance gap in American education. (Available at http://www.mckinseyquarterly.com/The_economic_cost_of_the_US_education_gap_2388, accessed May 2, 2013). It warned that a "persistent gap in academic achievement between children in the United States and their counterparts in other countries deprived the US economy of as much as $2.3 trillion in economic output in 2008."

60. See, for example, the Education Next polling data on American attitudes toward education, available at http://www.educationnext.org/.
61. L. Uzzell warned about this incentive effect of NCLB early on in the process. Please see Lawrence A. Uzzell, *No Child Left Behind: The Dangers of Centralized Education Policy*. Policy Analysis No. 544. (Washington, DC: The Cato Institute, 2005), http://www.cato.org/pub_display.php?pub_id=3769 (accessed May 2, 2013). In addition, scholars Hickok and Ladner reexamined NCLB in

conjunction with its reauthorization and came to similar conclusions. Please see Eugene Hickok and Matthew Ladner, *Reauthorization of No Child Left Behind: Federal Management or Citizen Ownership of K–12 Education?* Backgrounder No. 2047 (Washington, DC: The Heritage Foundation, 2007).

62. http://www2.ed.gov/about/overview/budget/history/edhistory.pdf (accessed May 2, 2013).
63. Thankfully some states are innovating in order to achieve better education results. For further information on state-level reforms, please see The Friedman Foundation for Educational Choice, *The ABCs of School Choice: 2011 Edition* (2011), http://www.edchoice.org/Foundation-Services/Publications/ABCs-of-School-Choice.aspx (accessed May 2, 2013); and Vicki Murray and Matthew Ladner, *Demography Is Not Destiny: Reform Lessons from Florida on Overcoming Achievement Gaps* (San Francisco, CA: Pacific Research Institute, 2008).

CHAPTER NINE

The Conjoint Quest for a Liberal Positive Program: "Old Chicago," Freiburg, and Hayek

Ekkehard A. Köhler and Stefan Kolev

The latest financial and economic crisis has undoubtedly reawakened public and academic interest for the scholarly discourse on economics of the 1930s. Large think tanks foster a reenactment of John Maynard Keynes or Friedrich August von Hayek with various methods and intentions, while scholars invite their audience to rediscuss economic ideas of the Great Depression and its subsequent period. One of these scholars is James M. Buchanan, who has highlighted the importance of the "Old Chicago" School (and sharply contrasted it from the "New Chicago" School's tenets); another is Viktor Vanberg, who has highlighted the importance of the Freiburg School of Economics. The Chicago School and the Freiburg School have remarkably influenced the design of post-war economic orders as well as scholarly discourse in economics in the United States and Germany.

This chapter explores the naissance of these schools of thought by a comparison of their academic agendas in economic policy and argues that they were mainly set by their founders Henry Simons and Walter Eucken. We argue that Hayek is a bridging element between the "Old Chicago" School and the Freiburg School, whose research agendas are remarkably similar by the end of the 1940s. In our opinion, the hypothesis of a Simons–Eucken–Hayek triangle of academic interaction can be justified since their scientific work of the 1930s and 1940s reflects a parallel search for a positive liberal program. Their programs share a surprisingly large degree of similarities, not only with respect to the proposed institutions and policy recommendation but, moreover, with respect to their conjoint revealed preference for rules over discretion.[1] In addition, the programs are long-run proposals that counter the status-quo of the economics of this time. This long-run and rule-oriented liberal approach is focused on the importance of "rules of the game" to be set by the government and the "moves of the game" to be left to the private individuals. In the unanimous opinion of the three authors, this is not interventionism but is the rule of law that is enforced by the state that stresses the constitutional prerequisites for the proper functioning of a market economy. They do not assign to the government the task of intervening and correcting results, but of setting up the fundamentals of the economic order. In a way, the three liberals focus their search on the "visualization" of Adam Smith's invisible hand by stressing the importance of proper rules for economic policy.

To discuss this hypothesis, we explore the role of Simons in the intellectual naissance of the Chicago School first. In a next step, the striking similarities between Simons, Eucken, and Hayek in the 1930s and 1940s are depicted. This section briefly discusses publication of the three authors from these two decades as well as three papers that Eucken, Hayek, and Aaron Director (as a disciple and colleague of Simons) deliver at the founding meeting of the Mont Pèlerin Society in 1947. Finally, a conclusion suggests the relevance of a rule-based economic policy in today's post-crisis period.

Henry Simons and the "Old Chicago" School

Frank Knight (1885–1972) and Jacob Viner (1892–1970) are often considered as the main founders of the Chicago School's perspective on economics.[2] Both plead for "less abstraction and more realism in economics so that the discipline can serve as a better guide for policy," as Razeen Sally characterizes their conjoint aim toward a problem-oriented perspective on economics.[3] Simons's (1899–1946)[4] contributions to the emergence of the "Old Chicago" School, especially with regard to its applied and policy-problem-oriented perspective, have been widely neglected in the modern discussion. Although a doctoral student of Knight, it is remarkable that Buchanan appraises precisely Simons as "the most articulate expositor of the 'old' Chicago School."[5]

By the end of the 1940s, however, Simons's unique role was appreciated: "Through his writing and more especially through his teaching at the University of Chicago, he was slowly establishing himself as the head of a school," as Director put it already in 1947 while introducing the volume *Economic Policy for a Free Society*, which includes Simons's major writings of his later career in Chicago.[6]

One of the reasons why Simons's contributions have been somewhat neglected in the meantime can be explained by the reception of the "New Chicago" School whose leading figures Milton Friedman and George Stigler have an ambiguous intellectual relationship to Simons. A highly interesting discussion among the "New Chicagoans" in the early 1980s crystallizes to the remarkable opinion that Henry Simons and his ideas must be seen from their "New Chicago" perspective as "interventionist."[7] In this context, it is thus not a surprise why the 1987 edition of *The New Palgrave Dictionary of Economics* offers a harsh critique on Simons's contributions to the Chicago School:

> Simons' view had a distinctly populist flavour that is absent from those more recently associated with Chicago economics. For example, he favoured use of government power to reduce the size of large firms and labour unions. Where such policies would lead to unacceptable losses of efficiency, Simons favoured outright public ownership. In sharp contrast to more recent Chicago statements on the matter, Simons emphatically supported progressive income taxation to promote a more egalitarian distribution of income.[8]

Despite this partial dispossession of Simons from his contribution to the Chicagoan legacy, which can be undoubtedly attributed to the methodological and political divergences of the "New" and the "Old Chicago" School, we are of the opinion that his contributions need to be analyzed in their historicity, that is, as they were articulated in the times of the United States' largest and most intense economic crisis.

The Theoretical Approach of Simons and the Role of Government

This section describes Simons's theoretical approach, that is, the underlying principles that lead him to formulate the positive agenda toward a rule-based framework that constitutes the economic system. For delineating these principles, a reconstruction of the "cascade" of arguments (forming the central topos of Simons's reasoning) is necessary.

To begin with, Simons is a pronounced adherent of democracy as the ideal form of government. This is quite important for the role that he eventually attributes to government since he permanently elaborates on the issue whether specifically a democracy can cope with the various potential tasks that one might assign to government in an abstract sense. Early in the essay, defining his own political predispositions, he describes democracy as "government by discussion" and depicts consensus as the key prerequisite for the orderly functioning of the democratic process.[9] The question arises, of course, as to which potential issues one can conjointly agree upon in a democracy and which issues will probably remain controversial.

Simons draws two important conclusions. First, consent of citizens is attributed a central function to legitimize the evolving order: Simons argues that likelihood to attain consensus is higher, the lower the level of the federal structure is, that is, he ardently pleads for strong federalism where (in the sense of subsidiarity) all issues that are manageable at the lowest level of the federation are to be tackled there.[10] Second, and more importantly in the following analysis, he envisions "a genuine 'division of labor' between competitive and political controls,"[11] even stresses that precisely "Laissez faire, to repeat, implies a division of tasks between competitive and political controls."[12] Already from this quote one can infer the *positive* role that Simons attributes to government: Government is obviously not only not an evil (to be rolled back by *negative* policies) but an absolutely necessary complement to a system of free markets.

What precisely is to be done by this democratic, "positive program" government? The following quote summarizes Simons's notion of the ideally functioning government in his theory of order:

> The proper function of the state ... is largely not that of providing services but that of providing the framework within which business, local-public and private, may effectively be conducted.[13]

This does not mean that there is no service function of the state, as the term "largely" already indicates: Government can provide services, in the best case at the lowest level of its federal structure and strictly disciplined by the rule of law. But this is not the core of Simons's theory. Instead, his notion is centered around the *framework concept* that government has to provide for establishing a market economy.

Before detailing his framework concept, it is important to formulate the criterion according to which this framework-based government is to be optimally organized: It is the presence of *power* in the economy and the goal to destroy any power concentration that—if not tackled by a consequent *decentralization*—can become a lethal threat to the market relationships. Decentralization as the chief instrument to achieve this is to be used in a political sense (i.e., by strengthening federalism) and especially in a sense of *disempowering* the economy. Another goal to be tackled by the government is the fight against inequality, which is primarily to be addressed by taxation. For the time being, let us remain with the issues of power and the concept of the disempowering framework.

What underlies this stance is a vision of the economy as a *game*, a game that necessarily requires *rules* in order to function in a proper (i.e., disempowering and inequality-combating) manner. The instrument of rules seems essential for the viability of a democratic government:

> There is no means for protecting the common interest save in terms of rules of policy; and it is only in terms of general rules or principles that democracy, which is government by free, intelligent discussion, can function tolerably or endure.[14]

It is these specific characteristics that enable democracy to find a *consensus on rules*, thus saving it from the constant quarrel on individual, discretionary decisions. Simons talks on several occasions about the necessary qualities of his ideal type of rules: "more definite and adequate 'rules of the game,'"[15] "simple rule or principle," "rules of the game as to money are definite, intelligible, and inflexible,"[16] or "definite, mechanical set of rules of the economic game."[17] Thus, the rules are to be clear interpersonally (minimizing the need for bureaucratic interpretation and discretion) and intertemporally (stabilizing the expectations of the private actors). With this in mind, Simons focuses on the economic order in the sense of the order of rules.

Two final comments are necessary to better understand the role that Simons attributes to government in his theory of order.

First, he often underscores the interrelationships *between the different societal orders*, which is to say between the legal, political, and economic order. As already mentioned above, the constitutional principle of the legal order is to be extended to the economic order for the reason of disempowerment and for the intertemporal stability of economic rules. In addition, he perpetually shows the intimate relationship between the economic and the political order, in other words, that economic policy decisions (e.g., the admissibility of deflation) can severely impair the functioning of a democratic political order.

Second, *within* the decisions on the design of the *economic order*, Simons shows that the different fields of economic policy (competition, fiscal, money, and foreign trade policy) are intricately interwoven and that every decision on one field should be analyzed as to the impulses it generates in the other fields. A good example would be the relationship between competition policy and the necessity for monetary reform. Simons shows here that monetary reforms would be of little help if his competitive framework concept is not simultaneously implemented: If the latter is not the case, the rigidity of the monopolistic price system will make it impossible for the economy to handle adverse shocks, regardless of how intelligently its monetary system is devised. Policy measures are thus to be conceived in terms of their encompassing effects on the various fields of an economic order and not only according to the immediately visible consequences in specific policy fields.

Let us briefly summarize the core elements of Simons's theory of order:

- Government is to be thought of as a *democracy* and only democracy-compatible tasks are to be assigned to it.
- This democratic government is highly important (is in a division of labor with the private actors) and for this reason has to permanently pursue a number of *positive policies*, that is, is not to be rolled back by negative policies.
- These positive policies are not primarily aimed at providing specific services, but at *providing a general framework* within which the private individuals are free to transact.
- This framework is to be designed in a manner that maximally *destroys the power concentration* in the economy (in all fields of economic policy) and in government itself (by federalism, decentralization, and the rule of law).
- Democracy can only find a *consensus on rules*, not on discretionary measures. For this reason the framework is to consist of these consensual rules (*interpersonally clear and intertemporally stable*).
- The framework is the extension of the *constitutional approach* from politics on the field of the economy.
- Consisting of rules, the framework is aimed at establishing the *rules of the game*, not at interfering in the moves of the game, that is, not at interfering in the relative prices and wages in the economy.
- All societal orders (economic order, political order, legal order, etc.) are highly *interdependent*. Also, all measures of economic policy are to be analyzed interdependently, that is, as a consistent program in their impact on all societal orders and on all fields of economic policy.

Economic Policy Implications

Having thus reviewed the theoretical approach of Simons and its central topos—that coincides with a rule-based economic policy that is again intended to safeguard the order of rules—it is helpful to complement this abstract view with the proposed institutional framework and specific proposals in the field of economic policy.

For the sake of explanation, we concentrate on Simons's "sound liberal strategy," which offers a pointed summary of his positive program.[18] Simons defines three objectives that mirror "requirements" of such a "sound liberal strategy" and discloses three proposals of institutional reform:

1. Restoration of a maximum of competitiveness in industry (including the labor markets).
2. Transition to a less preposterous structure of private money contracts and
3. Ultimate establishment of a simple, mechanical rule of monetary policy.[19]

Power and its maximum limitation are the main goals of competition policy in Simons's oeuvre. The effects of the concentration of power are perceived as extremely dangerous not only to the economy itself but, in the sense of the previously mentioned interdependence of orders, to society as a whole. The following quote already hints to the wide range of the disempowerment program:

> A cardinal tenet of the libertarians is that no one may be trusted with much power—no leader, no faction, no party, no "class," no majority, no government, no church, no corporation, no trade association, no university, no large organization of any kind. They must forever repeat with Lord Acton: "Power always corrupts"—and not merely those who exercise it but those subject to it and the whole society. The only good power is that of law based on overwhelming voluntary consensus of free men and built and rebuilt by gradual experimentation, organized discussion, and tolerant compromise. They do not deny that concentrated power may occasionally serve human progress as a temporary or transitional expedient.[20]

When it comes to the second case, the one of natural monopolies, Simons takes a path remarkable for a libertarian, the one of socialization. The reason for this solution, which does not seem intuitive for a liberal, is his disappointment with the regulation of natural monopolies in reality. Private power, be it here or in the monetary sphere, is absolutely not admissible, and even regulated private natural monopolies would still possess power. Simons seems to be aware of the problems that this visionary solution raises, for example, in the capacity of the administration to run its own natural monopolies, and thus pleads for experimentation in the different locations to find the best solution.[21]

The Influence of the "Old Chicagoan" Simons on Hayek and Ordo-Liberalism

Similarities in Publications

Taking into consideration the impact of the Great Depression on the scholarly discourse in economics, it is not surprising that Simons, Eucken, and Hayek have focused on the problem of how the economy could be improved by rules and institutions to allow for a better economic process than under the pre-crisis economic order. This objective is mirrored in the publications of these three scholars between the 1930s and 1940s. This is why we argue that Simons, Eucken, and Hayek have conjointly shared a research program in this period.

To begin with, the strategic position of Simons, Eucken, and Hayek vis-à-vis their intellectual surrounding in that period is thoroughly comparable. The supporters of liberalism in the classical sense are in a defensive position, not to say in isolation in their respective countries. Simons, when writing his "Positive Program for Laissez-faire" in 1934, is confronted with the overwhelming support that Roosevelt received for the New Deal and the fight against the Great Depression that the public acknowledges. Only some years later, with the decisions of the Supreme Court and the widely received book by Walter Lippmann,[22] the nonconformists to the Roosevelt program reach some consolidation (although it is notable that Lippmann does not quote Simons in his book a single time). The same is true for Eucken and his friends and disciples in Germany. From 1933 on, the small group around him in Freiburg consolidates but remains in an acutely endangered position at the geographical periphery of the Reich. Opposing Martin Heidegger during the summer term of 1933 in the university council, Eucken becomes isolated like his close friend Edmund Husserl at the University of Freiburg. Not only on a regional scale but also the entire national university system is subject to a triumphant procession of "national socialist economics." Departed disciples of the younger historical School, like Werner Sombart, mistakenly believe that "their time" has come. The field of economics becomes a more and more "interventionist" discipline with a harsh rejection of classical liberalism. Many German economists adopt more or less willingly the Nazi agenda;[23] others, like Wilhelm Röpke and Alexander Rüstow, leave the country very soon after the Nazi accession to power. "Half-exiles"[24] like Eucken and his group start organizing intellectual resistance circles in Freiburg in the late 1930s. Eucken's standing as well as that of his colleagues becomes increasingly difficult after 1942 and finally culminates in interrogation and arrests after the assassination attempt on Hitler in July 1944. Hayek leaves Austria on time, but after a short period of being a young "star" in London, he is gradually abandoned by his most promising students who change sides and join Keynes's side of the field.[25] After opening the second round of the socialist calculation debates in 1935, Hayek becomes extremely alienated both vis-à-vis the protagonists of the "Keynesian avalanche"[26] and the market socialists, being thus thoroughly isolated when writing his fundamental essay "Freedom and the Economic System"[27] and even more so in the Cambridge years when finishing *The Road to Serfdom*.[28] Therefore, Simons, Eucken, and Hayek all share a somewhat comparable situation, which is characterized by a principal rejection of their research program by their surrounding academic communities and by a deep concern about individual liberty.

Simons, Eucken, and Hayek develop in the 1930s and 1940s a *plea against laissez-faire* as the guiding principle of liberal economic policy. As the title of Simons's most well-known essay of 1934 shows, laissez-faire is to be understood as a condition in which government does not do "nothing" but, instead, where it is developing and implementing positive economic policy. See the following quote:

> The representation of laissez faire as a merely do-nothing policy is unfortunate and misleading... The great errors of economic policy in the last century may be defined... in terms of disastrous neglect of the positive responsibilities of government under a free-enterprise system.[29]

The stance of Eucken and Hayek on this central point is almost identical to Simons's:

> What was the core of laissez-faire economic policy? The answer is most commonly: It was the age of a "government-free"

> economy... The economic policy of laissez-faire was founded on the conviction that suitable market forms, thus a well-functioning economic order, would evolve from the spontaneous forces of society, if only liberty and the rule of law are guaranteed.[30]

as well as:

> Probably nothing has done so much harm to the liberal cause as the wooden insistence of some liberals on certain rough rules of thumb, above all the principle of laissez faire... The question whether the state should or should not "act" or "interfere" poses an altogether false alternative, and the term "laissez faire" is a highly ambiguous and misleading description of the principles on which a liberal policy is based.[31]

Instead of pleading for this nineteenth century rule of thumb, equally passionately discarded by Walter Lippmann in the "manifesto" of this generation of new liberals,[32] the three protagonists of the current chapter plead for a role of government that is centered around the concept of a *framework*, or, in other words, of the "*rules of the game*" metaphor. Government is to establish and implement the rules, within which the private individuals are free to act and interact as they wish. Since this was already explained above with respect to Simons, the below quotations should suffice here to indicate the almost identical perception of this concept by Simons, Eucken, and Hayek:

> It is an obvious responsibility of the state under this policy to maintain the kind of legal and institutional framework within which competition can function effectively as an agency of control.[33]

This is, in effect, nothing less than the plea for an adaptation of the "*constitutional approach*" of economic and legal scholars to the sphere of the economy. Thus all three authors treat the rules of the legal framework as an "*economic constitution*." Economic problem sets are therefore subject to an integrated perspective of constitutional and economic issues. But what are "good," "fitting" rules, that is, what is the criterion for deciding whether a specific rule, for example, in the field of liability, is suitable for a liberal economic constitution? There is a very far-reaching similarity between Simons and Eucken here: It is the aspect of disempowering that comes into play here. This aspect is also present in Hayek of the 1930s and 1940s:

> To split or decentralize power is necessary to reduce the absolute amount of power, and the competitive system is the only system

> designed to minimize by decentralization the power exercised by man over man.[34]

We thus see that the type of solution for the problems of economic policy of the three authors is extremely homogeneous, if not almost identical. They discard laissez-faire as an operational maxim for liberalism and instead work out a new philosophy that can be called "*laissez-faire within rules.*" Individual economic agents are free to extend their liberty and welfare as far as they abide by the rules of the competitive order. Government is also restrained by these same rules, so the goal is to attain a societal entity (as a combination of economy, society, and government) where arbitrariness and power are brought to a minimum and, via rules, liberty to a (orderly, that is, nonchaotic) maximum.

As a last point, it seems noteworthy that this absolutely central role of *government as arbiter* is not the only function that the "new liberals" assign to their ideal government. In addition, they see also government as a provider of specific services that society, if left to itself, would insufficiently produce. This *service function* of government (if it comes to, for example, an inequality-reducing progressive taxation and thus financed "socialized consumption" in Simons, an inequality-reducing progressive taxation in Eucken, or a minimum income, sanitary measures, etc. in Hayek) distinguishes these liberal thinkers of the 1930s and 1940s from liberal contemporaries like Ludwig von Mises or, even more so, Ayn Rand. It has induced today's extreme libertarians like Hans-Hermann Hoppe to convict Hayek of being an interventionist, or, in Hoppe's own words, a "social democrat."[35] In our opinion, this judgment is unwarranted and commits precisely the same mistake as the futile "classical liberal" versus "interventionist" debate: The Simons-Eucken-Hayek type of liberalism underscores that the interaction of individuals on free markets has absolutely necessary prerequisites, which they try to depict by the combination of an arbiter function and a service function of government.

Mont Pèlerin Society's 1947 Meeting as the "Melting Pot" of Ideas

On June 19, 1946 Henry Simons, aged barely 47, dies suddenly. This is a true setback for Hayek's endeavors during his visit to the United States in 1946. In November he writes to Eucken:

> It will by the way be of interest to you that the main goal of my America trip was an attempt to arrange in Chicago a larger study

> about the question as to what changes are necessary in the "legal framework" in order to make the competitive economy effective. Unfortunately the man on whom my plans were mostly centered, Henry Simons, died suddenly and I do not know yet if the project can be continued despite that. The idea was a positive complement to my book.[36]

Thus Henry Simons cannot attend the founding meeting of the Mont Pèlerin Society in April 1947; instead his disciple and colleague[37] Aaron Director is invited to give an address to the session "'Free' Enterprise' and Competitive Order," which takes place on April 1. Simons is specially mentioned in Hayek's address as a person who should have attended "this conference" and who has contributed important work on the topic "with rare courage and lucidity."[38] In the rest of the section, the papers by Director, Eucken, and Hayek will be analyzed and compared as they can be seen as the condensed versions of these three "theories of order" (Chicago, Freiburg, and Hayek) and their parallel development in the 1930s and the early 1940s.

All three papers underscore that they are aimed at a long-term program and not so much at the immediate problems after the war. Director, Eucken, and Hayek talk about their visions that it is the long-term impact of ideas that interests them when formulating the theory of the competitive order, as seen in the three quotations below:

> We are perhaps witnessing a fundamental change in our basic beliefs. The virtues of individual freedom no longer command the support they once did.[39]
>
> The factual development moves against us, whereas in the realm of ideas one can make out a new flexibility in our sense.[40]
>
> It is from this long-run point of view that we must look at our task. It is the beliefs which must spread, if a free society is to be preserved, or restored, not what is practical at the moment, which must be our concern.[41]

The long-term program of the competitive order is at the center of the three papers. This can be seen as a program developed in a parallel manner and probably independently from each other (due to the far-reaching isolation of Germany between 1933 and 1945), in Chicago, Freiburg, and London. What is competitive order about, according to the three papers?

The first unanimous aim of the papers is to show that the implementation of a competitive order is by no means equal to a laissez-faire type of policy. Instead, it is about a positive type of policy with the goal of establishing "rules of the game." Eucken concludes his paper with the passage that government should be concerned about the order (i.e., the rules) and not about the process (i.e., the moves of the private individuals) which is to be left free.[42] Director stresses that the mistake of theoretical liberalism was to believe that government, by doing nothing, establishes competitive markets; the latter has to be achieved, in his opinion, by an extension of this liberal theory that explicitly aims at the competitive character.[43] Hayek also warns of meaningless and ambiguous terms like "free enterprise," "freedom of contract," or "private property" and underscores that it is the competitive order that is to be aimed at by economic policy and not the above terms that at first lack a precise content.[44]

And yes, the framework of the competitive order is again closely related to the issue of power. Even though not central to Hayek, he does not miss to discuss the issue of governmental power as connected to the private power of organized groups.[45] But to Director and Eucken, the power problem is truly fundamental. They both speak of monopoly power on the side of the enterprises,[46] but in the same instance sharply criticize the monopoly power on the side of the trade unions.[47] Uniformly, they see the only possible solution of the power problem in the competitive order, due to (as described above) the competition's seminal property of disempowering.

The positive program related to the competitive order is not only about competition in the narrow sense. It is about a complex, above all interdependent set of policies that are to be applied jointly for the competitive order to come into being and to persist. It is about competition on the commodity and labor market, but also about monetary stability (Director speaks explicitly of a "monetary framework").[48] Eucken touches upon the importance of monetary issues for the rest of the economic order.[49] In addition, Director and Hayek speak about the question of equality and security and to what extent it has to be answered in the competitive order.[50]

Immensely important is that, apart from the interdependency aspect of these different intricate fields of policy, the measures themselves are to be thought not as "ad-hoc interventions"[51] but as "encompassing economic policy" ("Gesamtwirtschaftspolitik" in the original).[52] Thus, one can say that the establishment of the competitive order is tied to several prerequisites that are to be found in various fields of economic policy (treatment of monopoly (general problem, treatment of cartels, of natural monopolies), trade unions, monetary policy, patent regulation, contract law, etc.) and has to be conceived as a coherent program. The lack of such a consistent general program or philosophy is, in Hayek's words, one of the main reasons for the decline of liberalism and the usurpation of the state by special interests.[53]

Thus, in the immediate post-war period the group of new liberals at the Mont Pèlerin Society meeting, to which the Chicago, Freiburg, and Hayekian strands of thought intimately belong, is already quite advanced in their joint effort to replace the (in their eyes) useless dogma of laissez-faire with an operational goal for liberal economic policy, the competitive order. The meeting in 1947 was probably the *climax* of this research program. A few years later, Eucken dies. Director, after editing the *Economic Policy for a Free Society* volume of Simons in 1947–48, successively leaves the agenda of "Old Chicago" and joins forces with the new paradigm prevalent both at the Law School and at the Economics Department, related to Friedman and Stigler.[54] Hayek, after losing Simons and Eucken, also abandons the competitive order as the goal of a free society and gradually has his evolutionist turn, especially after the completion of *The Constitution of Liberty*.[55]

Only decades later, Constitutional Political Economy (CPE) rediscovered the importance of the economic constitution and, together with the few remaining representatives of the Freiburg School, develops a new research program that can well be traced back to "Old Chicago" and Freiburg of the 1930s and 1940s. The relationship between Simons whom Buchanan calls "the most articulate expositor of the 'old' Chicago School,"[56] and Buchanan's own research program of CPE (he calls himself "a representative adherent" of "old" Chicago School)[57] becomes clear by this statement and Buchanan's thoughts on the necessary distinction between Chicago "old" and "new."

Conclusion: The Post-Crisis Window of Opportunity

Due to the early deaths of Simons and Eucken, this research program that culminated in the 1947 founding meeting of the Mont Pèlerin Society only lives on in the oeuvre of Hayek, and there it undergoes significant variations in the course of the next decades' intellectual evolution. But ideas seldom die out completely, and thus it seems to us that James Buchanan's CPE research program is a true successor to the Simons–Eucken–Hayek triangle. We will show in a next version of this project the similarities and differences of modern CPE and "Old Chicago," as prominently suggested by Buchanan. As we hope to show with this chapter, these three strands of thought are compatible with and complementary to each other—especially with regard to their prudential arguments put forward in favor of a competitive market system.

We see in the world of 2013, with its severe problems especially in the monetary field but also in other fields of the economic order, the necessity to rediscover the debate about rules and liberty in economics. The boom-bust cycle of the last decades clearly indicates that non-rule-based policies in the complex reality we live in are doomed to failure and unintended consequences that nobody can forecast in advance. Thus rules, as seen by the Simons–Eucken–Hayek generation but also by later CPE scholars like Buchanan and Vanberg, should in our opinion become the focal point in the economic policy debate of today. This has severe implications both for economics as a science and for the politicians who would be the addressees of the rules. If we want to reap the fruits of globalization for a long time to come, we urgently need a constitutional framework that simultaneously ensures prosperity and stability. For our "Great Recession" not to become a new "Great Depression," the neoliberal ideas from the last big crisis of capitalism seem a good point to start.

Notes

1. The three authors, however, differ with regard to which extent they treat individuals as sovereigns and ultimate addressees of their proposals for a free society. By the end of the 1940s, they nevertheless share, as "most economists," "basic long-run objectives" such as "political freedom, economic efficiency, and substantial equality of economic power"—and that "all three objectives can best be realized by relying, as far as possible, on a market mechanism within a 'competitive order,'" as stated by Friedman in a very early paper of his, presented in September 1947 to the Econometric Society, only a few months after Friedman's attending the first MPS meeting. It is noteworthy that here Friedman consistently uses the language of "Old Chicago" when it comes to the terms "economic power" and "competitive order," and refers to Simons's articles on different topics. Milton Friedman, "A Monetary and Fiscal Framework for Economic Stability," *The American Economic Review* 38, no. 3 (June 1948): 246.
2. Melvin W. Reder, "Chicago School," in *The New Palgrave: A Dictionary of Economics*, vol. 1, ed. John Eatwell, Murray Milgate, and Peter Newman (New York: Palgrave Macmillan, 1987), 413–18.

3. Razeen Sally, *Classical Liberalism and International Economic Order: Studies in Theory and Intellectual History* (London and New York: Routledge, 1998).
4. Henry C. Simons was born in Virden, Illinois in 1899. He graduated from the University of Michigan in 1920, and began teaching immediately after graduation at the University of Iowa. In 1927 he moved to the University of Chicago, where he remained for the rest of his life. He died at the early age of 47, in 1946. Simons was surrounded by an unusually brilliant set of colleagues—Jacob Viner (1882–1970), Frank Knight (1885–1972), Henry Schultz (1893–1938), and Paul Douglas (1892–1976). (See Mark Blaug, "Henry Simons," in *Pioneers in Economics: Frank Knight (1885–1972), Henry Simons (1899–1946), Joseph Schumpeter (1883–1950), vol. 37*, ed. Mark Blaug (Aldershot: Edward Elgar, 1992), xi.
5. James M. Buchanan, "Chicago School Thinking: Old and New" (lecture, University of Richmond, Richmond, VA, June 2010). http://jepson.richmond.edu/conferences/adam-smith/buchanan.html (accessed September 24, 2013).
6. Aaron Director, "Prefatory Note," in *Economic Policy for a Free Society*, Henry C. Simons (Chicago, IL: University of Chicago Press, 1948), v–vii.
7. For the original statements of Ronald Coase, Milton Friedman, and George Stigler, see Edmund W. Kitch, "The Fire of Truth: A Remembrance of Law and Economics at Chicago, 1932–1970," *Journal of Law and Economics* 26, no. 1 (April 1983): 178–79. See J. Bradford De Long, "In Defense of Henry Simons' Standing as a Classical Liberal," *Cato Journal* 9, no. 3 (Winter 1990): 601–18.
8. Reder, "Chicago School," 414.
9. Henry C. Simons, "Introduction: A Political Credo," in *Economic Policy for a Free Society*, Henry C. Simons (Chicago, IL: University of Chicago Press, [1945] 1948), 7–11.
10. Ibid., 12–14.
11. Henry C. Simons, "A Positive Program for Laissez Faire: Some Proposals for a Liberal Economic Policy," in *Economic Policy for a Free Society*, Henry C. Simons (Chicago, IL: University of Chicago Press, [1934] 1948), 41–42. See also Simons, "Rules versus Authorities in Monetary Policy," in *Economic Policy for a Free Society*, Henry C. Simons (1936; Chicago: University of Chicago Press, 1948), 160.
12. Simons, "Positive Program," 55.
13. Simons, "Political Credo," 18.
14. Henry C. Simons, "Some Reflections on Syndicalism," in *Economic Policy for a Free Society*, (Chicago, IL: University of Chicago, [1944] 1948), 123.
15. Simons, "Positive Program," 57.
16. Ibid, 63.
17. Simons, "Rules versus Authorities," 173.
18. Ibid., 170.
19. Ibid.
20. Simons, "Political Credo," 23.
21. Simons, "Positive Program," 61–62.
22. Walter Lippmann, *The Good Society*, 3rd ed. (London: Allen & Unwin, [1937] 1944).
23. For more details of the economists' Nazi involvement see Hauke Janssen, *Nationalökonomie und Nationalsozialismus. Die deutsche Volkswirtschaftslehre in den dreißiger Jahren des 20. Jahrhunderts*, 3rd ed. (Marburg: Metropolis, [1998] 2009).

24. Daniel Johnson, "Exiles and Half-Exiles: Wilhelm Röpke, Alexander Rüstow and Walter Eucken," *German Neo-Liberals and the Social Market Economy*, ed. Alan T. Peacock and Hans Willgerodt (New York: St. Martin's Press, 1989), 40.
25. John Richard Hicks, "The Hayek Story," in *Critical Essays in Monetary Theory*, (Oxford: Clarendon Press, 1967), 203–15.
26. Brian J. McCormick, *Hayek and the Keynesian Avalanche* (New York: St. Martin's Press, 1992).
27. Friedrich A. Hayek, "Freedom and the Economic System," in *Collected Works and Correspondence of F. A. Hayek*, ed. Bruce Caldwell, vol.10, *Socialism and War: Documents and Reviews* (Chicago, IL: University of Chicago Press, [1939] 1997), 189–212.
28. Friedrich A. Hayek, *The Road to Serfdom*, 50th anniversary ed. (Chicago, IL: University of Chicago Press, [1944] 1994).
29. Simons, "Positive Program," 42.
30. Walter Eucken, *Grundsätze der Wirtschaftspolitik*, 7th ed. (Tübingen: MohrSiebeck, [1952] 2004), 26–27.
31. Hayek, *Road to Serfdom*, 21, 89.
32. Lippmann, *Good Society*, 184–92.
33. Simons, "Positive Program," 42.
34. Hayek, *Road to Serfdom*, 160.
35. Hans-Hermann Hoppe, "F. A. Hayek on Government and Social Evolution: A Critique," *The Review of Austrian Economics* 7, no. 1 (1994): 67.
36. Friedrich A. Hayek, Letter to Walter Eucken from November 3rd 1946, in F. A. Hayek Archives, Box 18/Folder 40, Hoover Institution Archives, Stanford University
37. Let us again quote Director on his relationship to Simons: "I never took a course from him, but I was greatly influenced by him," in Kitch, "Fire of Truth," 179.
38. Friedrich A. Hayek, "'Free' Enterprise and Competitive Order," Address to the Mont Pèlerin Society founding meeting on April 1, 1947, in F. A. Hayek Archives, Box 81/Folder 3, Hoover Institution Archives, Stanford University; Friedrich A. Hayek, "'Free' Enterprise and Competitive Order" in *Individualism and Economic Order*, Friedrich A. Hayek (Chicago, IL: University of Chicago Press, [1947] 1948), 117. The pagination for Hayek's address is taken from the reprint in *Individualism and Economic Order* since this is widely available. In Director's and Eucken's addresses, the pagination is taken as in the archival documents.
39. Aaron Director, "'Free' Enterprise and Competitive Order," Address to the Mont Pèlerin Society founding meeting on April 1, 1947, 1–2 in F. A. Hayek Archives, Box 81/Folder 3, Hoover Institution Archives, Stanford University.
40. Walter Eucken, "'Free' Enterprise and Competitive Order," Address to the Mont Pèlerin Society founding meeting on April 1, 1947, 2 in F. A. Hayek Archives, Box 81/Folder 3, Hoover Institution Archives, Stanford University.
41. See Fn. 38, 108.
42. See Fn. 40, 4.
43. See Fn. 39, 3–4.
44. See Fn. 38, 111–13.

45. Ibid., 116–17.
46. Director, "'Free' Enterprise and Competitive Order," 5–6 and Eucken, "'Free' Enterprise and Competitive Order," 2–3.
47. Director, "'Free' Enterprise and Competitive Order," 7 and Eucken, "'Free' Enterprise and Competitive Order," 1.
48. Director, "'Free' Enterprise and Competitive Order," 8.
49. Eucken, "'Free' Enterprise and Competitive Order," 3.
50. Director, "'Free' Enterprise and Competitive Order," 9–11 and Hayek, "'Free' Enterprise and Competitive Order," 112.
51. Director, "'Free' Enterprise and Competitive Order," 9.
52. Eucken, "'Free' Enterprise and Competitive Order," 3. [trans. EK/SK]
53. Hayek, "'Free' Enterprise and Competitive Order," 107.
54. Rob Van Horn, "Reinventing Monopoly and the Role of Corporations: The Roots of Chicago Law and Economics," in *The Road from Mont Pèlerin: The Making of the Neoliberal Thought Collective*, ed. Philip Mirowski and Dieter Plehwe (Cambridge, MA: Harvard University Press, 2009), 204–237.
55. Stefan Kolev, "Hayek as an Ordo-Liberal," Hamburg Institute of International Economics/Wilhelm-Röpke-Institute Research Paper 5–11 (2010), Erfurt, http://www.hwwi.org/uploads/tx_wilpubdb/HWWI_Research_Paper_5-11.pdf (accessed May 10, 2013).
56. Buchanan, "Chicago School Thinking," 3.
57. Ibid., 5.

CHAPTER TEN

Hayek and My Life

VÁCLAV KLAUS

Many thanks for giving me a chance to address this distinguished audience. This is my first visit to the University of Richmond and, if I am not mistaken, my first stay in the state of Virginia as well.[1]

Some of you may know that I am enjoying the first days and weeks of my post-political life. A month ago, I completed my second term as the President of the Czech Republic and it means—with a very high degree of probability—an end to my political career, which started in the moment of the fall of communism in November 1989. I am slowly discovering a new life. For the first time in two decades, I am moving about in this country without being accompanied by the United States Secret Service.

I take it as a great honor to be asked to speak here today about a man I admire and have admired for decades. Today's conference is not my first opportunity to speak about this great man. I spoke about him more comprehensively in May 2009 in Germany[2] when I was awarded the Hayek Prize by the Hayek Foundation. It was in the city of Freiburg where he spent the last three decades of his long and extremely fruitful life. The last time I spoke about him was in September 2012 at a Hayek Colloquium in Obergurgl, Tyrol, which is another of his places. As a devoted mountaineer he spent most of his European holidays there and, as is well known, he wrote his *The Constitution of Liberty*[3] there.

You have had a chance to listen to several scholarly speeches today, focused on one or another aspect of Hayek's legacy. I do not intend to compete with these distinguished speakers. As an economist who behaves rationally—at least I would hope so—I always try to maximize my comparative advantages, and I am well aware of the fact that after 23 years in politics they are not in the scholarly and detailed analysis of Hayek's very diverse contributions to the economic theory and other fields of social sciences.

I will try to add a more personal note to today's conference and will speak about Hayek as I saw him, as I was influenced by him, and as I saw his role during half a century of my adult life—when I was an ordinary citizen of the communist Czechoslovakia, an academic economist, and lately a politician who got the challenging task to transform the country from communism, from this oppressive political system and this irrational and inefficient centrally planned economy into a free society, parliamentary democracy, and market economy along the Hayekian lines.[4]

We all have our heroes and Hayek was for me one of the greatest ones. It all started in the 1960s. My country, then Czechoslovakia, experienced at the beginning of the decade an unexpected and, for communist leaders, ideologically unexplainable and indefensible economic recession, the first that happened in a centrally planned communist country in peacetime. It was something unheard of, something unimaginable. Planning was supposed to guarantee a permanent and harmonious economic growth. This surprising and unpleasant experience led even the most dogmatic communist politicians to think about a relatively far-reaching economic reform and to start implementing it. As is well known now, they tried to accomplish "a mission impossible," to put into reality "a third way," this utopian dream of all socialists and progressives, based on the belief in the possibility of having a fuzzy combination of plan and market.

It led to the weakening of the planning system and to the increase of the independence of—mostly state-owned—firms. It was a movement in a desirable direction. The Soviet politicians, together with our own hard-liners, criticized the reform from the left. The Czech economists of my generation (I founded and even became president of the Club of Young Economists then) criticized the reform from the right, for its evident insufficiency and inconsistency.

At that moment, in the mid-1960s, we discovered the famous dispute about socialism, the so-called socialist calculation debate,[5] between Austrians Ludwig von Mises and Friedrich von Hayek on one side and American socialists Oskar Lange and Abba Lerner on the other, which occurred in the 1930s. This debate gave us many powerful arguments about the impossibility of economic calculation under socialism, and about the futility of the idea to play the market instead of introducing a real market. It enhanced the doubts we were obtaining from observing the evident inefficiency of our own economic system. It is a pity that this famous debate is not part of an obligatory reading list for contemporary students. The highly regulated and subsidized economies in Europe (and in this country as well) should be discussed using the old, already canonical Hayekian arguments.

The real revelation came when we came across Hayek's article "The Use of Knowledge in Society"[6] originally published in 1945. You may ask how it was possible to get access to such articles in a totalitarian communist regime. Yet, it was possible. We could not get into our hands the *Wall Street Journal*, *Newsweek*, or *Time* magazine, but in the libraries of academic institutions we could get the *American Economic Review* and similar journals. They were sufficiently scientific and, therefore, incomprehensible for the communist censors. Even now, I give this Hayek article to my students as the best introduction into rational economic thinking. To understand the impossibility of centralizing dispersed knowledge is one of the most important ideas in the economic science, comparable to the classic formulations of Adam Smith.

Our relatively far-reaching and for that time rather unique economic reforms led to significant changes in the political life as well. In this respect, we got a lot of inspiration from Hayek's *The Road to Serfdom*.[7]

This book was illegally and unofficially translated in my country in the 1960s. It was widely read, and—what is even more important—it was understood as a decisive and final rejection of all kinds of totalitarianisms, collectivisms, and interventionisms, and as an authoritative defense of liberty, at least for our generation, which saw its task differently from students in Western Europe and America at that time. We wanted to introduce capitalism, not to destroy it.

Our promising era did not last long. On the morning of August 21, 1968, the armies of the Soviet Union and other Warsaw Pact countries invaded Czechoslovakia and crushed the—so-called—Prague Spring. That was, paradoxically, the first and the only moment I saw Hayek. I happened to attend a conference in the beautiful Austrian ski resort of Alpbach, which was the Austrian, much smaller version of today's World Economic Forum in Davos. This is where I heard about the brutal occupation of my country and about the collapse of our plans and dreams to get rid of communism. A group of Czechoslovak participants stayed there for the following few days not knowing what to do. Some of us decided to return home, and some decided to emigrate. As an irony of history, the next day after the invasion, Hayek was scheduled to speak at the conference. This was in his *The Constitution of Liberty*[8] years, and his speech could be more understandable for sophisticated constitutional lawyers than for a young economist from communist Czechoslovakia. I sat down in the auditorium, saw Hayek, heard his voice, but was not able to concentrate on his complicated argumentation. My head was full of thoughts about my occupied country.

It took us 20 long years to finally get rid of communism and of our Soviet oppressors. When this happened, I was, accidentally, again in Austria. The day before the student demonstration in Prague in November 1989, which started our Velvet Revolution, I was giving a lecture at the University of Linz. During my meeting with the economic faculty professors in the afternoon, I asked them about the role of the Austrian School of Economics and of Hayek in the country where he was born and where he spent an important part of his life. Their answer was very depressing: "Hayek is dead in Austria now. He is not on our reading list anymore."

In the evening, the university organized a panel discussion about the then-ongoing reforms in Central and Eastern Europe. Several hundred students were in attendance. In answering one of the questions, I made an unprepared but proverbial statement: "If Hayek is dead in Austria, we will bring him to life in Prague very soon." Of course, I did not know what would happen in Prague the next evening.

Very rapidly—in the middle of December, when the first noncommunist government was formed—we started dismantling communism and its institutions. As a minister of finance in charge of the transformation of the Czechoslovak economic system, I was—at least I hope —truly Hayekian. My radical reform program was to liberalize, to deregulate, to privatize, and to desubsidize the economy.

We also understood that Hayek's concepts of spontaneous order, of dispersed knowledge, of human action versus human design, and the like, were relevant not only for the understanding of normal functioning of a free economic and social system, but also for the process of its transformation. It became evident that the transformation of a complex system cannot be organized from above. The long-prepared sophisticated reform blueprints became—practically overnight—irrelevant. Such a transformation process is inevitably a complicated mixture of spontaneity and constructivism, and it must follow the logic of Hayekian evolution rather than the dreams of the always-ready-to-be-involved constructivists.

I dare say that we more or less succeeded in our task—more rapidly and with lower costs than the other postcommunist countries. The country became a parliamentary democracy and market economy relatively very soon. At the same moment, Hayek published his last book *The Fatal Conceit*,[9] which—I have to admit—I have never found time to read. Communism was a fatal conceit, undoubtedly; but for me, and for many of us, it was already over. We were preoccupied with the task of building a different society, and we assumed—correctly or incorrectly—that we knew enough about "the errors of socialism" (which was the subtitle of his book).

I do not want to say that Hayek is not relevant now. I do believe that he is as important, and worth studying, as in the past. We are again in a world that is based on a new (perhaps only slightly new) conceit. Today's society in Europe, and I am afraid more and more in America as well, is based on a similar error as in the past. Hayek was right in his *The Road to Serfdom* that interventionism is a very unstable system, which inevitably evolves away from a free-market economy (and society) into a more and more controlled, regulated, and administrated system. This truth should never be forgotten. We should read Hayek again and again.

The economic system in Europe at the beginning of the twenty-first century is not a free-market economy, but a "social market economy" (*soziale Marktwirtschaft*) with a very heavy load of environmentalism in it. Such a system is not tenable—it cannot function in the long run at all, and it cannot function efficiently in the short run. European sluggish economic growth, currently even stagnation, high unemployment, and increasing indebtedness are the inevitable (and expected) outcomes. The tragic mistake—the attempt to monetarily unify Europe by introducing European common currency—made it only more visible and more rapidly moving toward the end.[10]

Hayek's ideas returned to the forefront of our attention also with the financial and economic crisis at the end of the last decade (which my country survived relatively well). It seems evident that Hayek proved to be more relevant than Keynes in the analysis of the causes of such a crisis. Hayek tells us that a crisis is usually the result of "easy money policy," of the irresponsible playing with interest rates, and of the dream that fiscal policy can substitute for the much needed restructuring of the economy. The currently popular "quantitative easing" would be no doubt considered a pseudomedicine by him. Those who do not know it should reread his *Prices and Production*[11] published 70 years ago.

Europe needs Hayek and his merciless analysis of the overregulated, controlled, centrally administered European economic system, and of the slippery road to serfdom that we have already set out on. I wish the

American students—here in Richmond and elsewhere—could get a chance to understand this new "fatal" conceit. In the current American intellectual, political, and ideological, politically correct climate, it is not easy. That is another reason for expressing my thanks to the organizers of this conference, which makes the free discussion of these issues possible.

Notes

1. What follows is the transcript of a keynote public address, the culmination of a conference on Hayek and Modern World at the University of Richmond, Virginia, USA, April 12, 2013, http://www.youtube.com/watch?v=XC1j1PGVH3U&feature=youtu.be (accessed May 2, 2013).
2. Václav Klaus, "Hayek, Freiburg und unsere Zeit" (speech, Hayek Foundation, Freiburg, Germany, May 10, 2009) (http://www.klaus.cz/clanky/1874).
3. Václav Klaus (speech, Hayek Colloquium 2012, Obergurgl, Austria, September 13, 2012). http://www.klaus.cz/clanky/3184.
4. As the best summary of Hayek's achievements, I still consider K. R. Leube's "A Bibliographical Introduction" to the book *The Essence of Hayek* (Stanford, CA: Hoover Institution Press, 1984), xvii–xxxvi.
5. Friedrich A. Hayek, ed., *Collectivist Economic Planning* (London: Routledge, 1935). Very good analysis of this debate was done in Abram Bergson's article "Socialist Economics," in *A Survey of Contemporary Economics*, ed. H. S. Ellis (Homewood, IL: Richard D. Irwin, 1948), 412–48.
6. Friedrich A. Hayek, "The Use of Knowledge in Society," *American Economic Review* 35, no. 4 (September 1945): 519–30.
7. Friedrich A. Hayek, *The Road to Serfdom* (London: Routledge, 1944).
8. Friedrich A. Hayek, *The Constitution of Liberty* (Chicago, IL: University of Chicago Press, 1960).
9. Friedrich A. Hayek, *The Fatal Conceit: The Errors of Socialism* (London: Routledge, 1988).
10. See Václav Klaus, "European debt crisis" (speech, CATO Institute, Washington, DC, March 11, 2013), http://www.klaus.cz/clanky/3319.
11. Friedrich A. Hayek, *Prices and Production* (London: Routledge and Kegan Paul, 1935).

Conclusion: The Hayek Difference

David M. Levy and Sandra J. Peart

Why would the Jepson School of Leadership Studies sponsor a conference to focus on the contribution of a Nobel prize–winning economist? Our friend and mentor, the late James M. Buchanan, provided the answer to this question more than a decade ago. Buchanan first came to know Friedrich A. Hayek from a distance. Then, beginning with Hayek's lecture series presented at the Thomas Jefferson Center for Studies in Political Economy that Buchanan founded at the University of Virginia in 1961 and continuing over the next three decades, the two became closely connected. The question Buchanan asked 40 years after this relationship began was: What was Hayek's most significant contribution to the twentieth century? What was the "Hayek difference"? Buchanan urged his readers to think about Hayek as a leader rather than as a great economist and political philosopher:

> The "Hayek difference" lies, instead, in his creating himself, whether or not willingly, as "the classical liberal," which, in turn, provided a personalized target for his socialist enemies everywhere, and a personalized flag-bearer for his ideological soulmates. Who could have filled this role other than Hayek? And how different indeed would the century have been without his presence in this respect?[1]

Buchanan continues to argue that one should think of Hayek as a "social philosopher" and the leader of classical liberals:

> In its broadest terms, my answer is that this contribution is to be found in Hayek in the role of classical liberal social philosopher

> rather than in any role as economic theorist. Further, even within the role as social philosopher, narrowly defined, Hayek's net contribution does not lie in a set of identifiable theorems or propositions. Hayek found his own niche or slot in the century's history as the classical liberal. In a very real sense, Hayek represented and epitomized the stylized classical liberal, whose work embodied so much that is common among all of those who fit the broader rubric.

Importantly, Buchanan appreciated that the "starting point for Hayek's vast body of work is not the atomistic individual that characterizes much of twentieth-century economic theorizing but instead, persons embedded in social and economic networks." Hayek shared this foundational feature, conceptualizing economic actors as purposive beings tied to others by bonds of sympathy and reciprocity, with Buchanan, and, before Buchanan, Adam Smith, John Stuart Mill, and Buchanan's teacher, Frank Knight.[2]

Thus, Hayek's classical liberalism and his reading of classical economics directly challenged the "economic man" that pervaded economic analysis at mid-century, a "calculating machine" who acts on the basis of supposedly costless optimization. At best, the classical economists he defended suppose agents who try to improve their lot on the basis of what they observe around them. And around them they observe and account for other agents. It was this conception of economic actors as essentially social beings that, as we have seen in chapter 2, caused Hayek to separate his work from the twentieth-century "individualists."

Buchanan rightly stressed the importance of Hayek's role in the establishment and success of the Mont Pèlerin Society. Even as the Second World War raged, Hayek emphasized the importance of returning a democratic constitutional order to Germany. He stressed the importance of indigenous Germans taking charge of their own destiny. Constitutions cannot, he thought, be imposed from outside. These conclusions implied that Germans who survived the Hitler era must be allowed to take charge. Hayek was consequently excited that the German economist Walter Eucken was able to travel to the organizational meeting in 1947 of what would become the Mont Pèlerin Society. Bent physically but morally upright, Eucken stood as testimony to the existence of German liberals of unquestionable integrity. One man could attest to the integrity of others. And so this might be the means to start German postwar reconstruction. In 2008, the former president of Earhart Foundation, Richard Ware, remembered

Eucken from the 1950 Mont Pèlerin Society meeting. Ware recalled how important it was for former soldiers who bore wounds from the war to realize how much in common they had with liberals on the other side.[3]

Hayek is of course most famous for his sequence of essays in which he develops the concept of the division of knowledge. Here, too, he reinvigorated the economics of Adam Smith and John Stuart Mill to provide an alternative to the economic analysis that had taken hold by the mid-twentieth century. Although it is both conventional and helpful to stress Hayek's Austrian roots, the line of thought he develops was first put forward by W. Stanley Jevons and Philip H. Wicksteed.[4] On their understanding, a perfect market requires perfect knowledge, "complete communication."[5] By dropping the perfect knowledge assumption and taking the first step toward an economic approach in which social outcomes are the result of people sharing their several bits of local knowledge, Hayek created a richer sort of economic theory than simple-minded neoclassical optimization, one that importantly involves irreversibility.

What does an emphasis on division of knowledge do for leadership? Most obviously, it means that one cannot expect the members of a group to agree on fine details. Their opinions and the experiences they bring to the process of belief formation will contain many idiosyncratic elements. They may, however, agree on some general principles and then agree to disagree on many fundamental matters. Hayek's *The Constitution of Liberty* quotes Oliver Cromwell as offering a central teaching of his version of liberalism: "I beseech you, in the bowels of Christ, think it possible you may be mistaken."[6] This acceptance of fallibility suggests that when the members of the group disagree, group members will listen. As we consider Hayek's influence on the modern economy and modern economic thought, we should appreciate that his actions were (first) inspired by the felt need to bring together a group of liberals of wide-ranging competence and (second), once the group was gathered, to vet his own actions and words by the opinions of the group.

Notes

1. James M. Buchanan, "The Hayek Difference," in *Why I, Too, Am Not a Conservative: The Normative Vision of Classical Liberalism* (Cheltenham, UK, and Northampton, MA: Edward Elgar, 2005), 86–91.
2. Experimental economists, notably Vernon Smith, also share this conception.

3. Richard Ware interview by Sandra J. Peart and David M. Levy, 2008.
4. Sandra J. Peart examines the similarities between Jevons and the Austrian economist, Carl Menger. See Peart, "Jevons and Menger Re-homogenized: Jaffé After 20 Years," *American Journal of Economics and Sociology* 57, no. 3 (July 1998): 307–25.
5. In fact, Wicksteed dropped Jevons's assumption of complete communication. See Philip H. Wicksteed, *The Common Sense of Political Economy* (London: Macmillan, 1910), I.6.13: "Suppose at the opening of the market that some of the sellers offer damsons at a lower price than others. The market will doubtless be 'imperfect' (that is to say, it will not establish complete communications between all the persons concerned), and therefore some purchasers will deal at the stalls which they usually patronize without being aware that they could get the fruit cheaper at another stall."
6. Friedrich A. Hayek, *The Collected Works of F. A. Hayek*, vol. 17, *The Constitution of Liberty: The Definitive Edition,* ed. Ronald Hamowy (Chicago, IL: University of Chicago Press, 2011), 528.

CONTRIBUTORS

Bruce Caldwell is a research professor of economics and the director of the Center for the History of Political Economy at Duke University. A historian of economic thought, Caldwell has written extensively on the intellectual contributions of F. A. Hayek, and is the general editor of the book series *The Collected Works of F. A. Hayek*. He is currently working with Hansjoerg Klausinger on a full biography of Hayek.

Jason Clemens is the executive vice president of the Fraser Institute and the president of the Fraser Institute Foundation (Canada). He has more than 15 years of experience in applied public policy research in both Canada and the United States with more than 70 major studies and 300 shorter titles to his credit.

Andrew Farrant is an assistant professor of economics at Dickinson College. He is editor of *Hayek, Mill, and the Liberal Tradition* (London: Routledge, 2011). His current research interests include Hayek, the Attlee Government (1945–51), and John Stuart Mill.

Gerald Gaus is the James E. Rogers Professor of Philosophy at the University of Arizona, where he directs the program in Philosophy, Politics, Economics & Law. Among his books are *The Order of Public Reason* (2011), *On Philosophy, Politics, and Economics* (2008), *Justificatory Liberalism* (1996), and *Value and Justification* (1990). He was a founding editor of *Politics, Philosophy and Economics.* He is currently writing a book, entitled *The Tyranny of the Ideal*, to be published by Princeton University Press.

Václav Klaus is the former president of the Czech Republic. He served as the first prime minister of the Czech Republic from 1993 to 1997, and as the second president of the country from 2003 to 2013. He was the principal cofounder of the Civic Democratic Party, the country's largest center–right political party. After completing his mandate as president of the Czech Republic in March 2013, he moved to the newly formed Václav Klaus Institute, a liberal-conservative think tank.

Stefan Kolev is a professor of economics at the Westsaxon University of Applied Sciences Zwickau and managing director of the Wilhelm-Röpke-Institute in Erfurt, Germany. His doctoral thesis was devoted to the History and Political Economy of Neoliberalism.

Ekkehard A. Köhler is an economist and a researcher at the Walter Eucken Institute in Freiburg, Germany. His doctoral thesis was devoted to Financial Markets, Monetary and Fiscal Policy, and Constitutional Economics.

David M. Levy is a professor of economics at George Mason University and a Distinguished Fellow of the History of Economics Society. His PhD in economics is from the University of Chicago, where he wrote his dissertation under George Stigler. Sandra Peart and he revived the doctrine of analytical egalitarianism from classical economics. They have codirected the Summer Institute for the Preservation of the History of Economics for 14 years.

Christopher S. Martin holds a PhD in economics from George Mason University and for two years was the John Marshall Visiting Research Fellow at the University of Richmond's Jepson School of Leadership Studies. He is presently an assistant professor of economics at the University of Science and Arts of Oklahoma.

Peter McNamara teaches political science at Utah State University. He specializes in early modern political thought, American political thought, and political economy. He is the author of *Political Economy and Statesmanship: Smith, Hamilton and the Foundation of the Commercial Republic* and the editor of *The Noblest Minds: Fame, Honor and the American Founding*, and (with Louis Hunt), *Liberalism, Conservatism and Hayek's Idea of Spontaneous Order.*

Kenneth Minogue (1930–2013) was emeritus professor of political science at the London School of Economics. His final book is *The Servile Mind: How Democracy Erodes the Moral Life*, published by Encounter Books in 2012. He was immediate past president of the Mont Pèlerin Society, which was established by Hayek in 1947. He passed away returning from his final meeting at the MPS.

Sandra J. Peart is the dean of the University of Richmond's Jepson School of Leadership Studies. She obtained her doctorate in economics from the University of Toronto in 1989. She is past president of the History of Economics Society and was a Fellow of the American Council on Education from 2005 to 2006. She is the editor of *Hayek on Mill: The Mill-Taylor Friendship and Related Papers*, volume 16 of *The Collected Works of F. A. Hayek*.

Emily Skarbek is a lecturer in political economy at King's College, London. She received her MA and PhD in economics from George Mason University. Before joining King's faculty, Emily was an assistant professor of economics at San Jose State University and a researcher at the Center for the History of Political Economy at Duke University. Her scholarly articles have appeared in the *American Journal of Economics and Sociology*, *Studies in Emergent Order*, *Journal of Private Enterprise*, and *Erasmus Journal of Philosophy and Economics*.

Nicola Tynan is an associate professor of economics at Dickinson College. She has research interests in nineteenth- and twentieth-century British economic history. Her primary research project focuses on the economic history of London's water supply.

Niels Veldhuis is the president of the Fraser Institute and has written six books, more than 50 comprehensive studies on a wide range of topics, and more than 200 shorter articles that have appeared in such newspapers as the *Wall Street Journal*, *The Economist*, and the *Globe & Mail*.

INDEX

Printed in the United States of America